PNEUMANAUT

EXPLORING THE HEAVENS:
THE JOURNEY OF THE KING'S SCRIBE

Joy,
Up, up & away!

Dr Dale A. Fife

DR. DALE A. FIFE

True Potential
REACH THE WORLD

PNEUMANAUT
Exploring the Heavens: The Journey of the King's Scribe

Cover and Interior Page Design by True Potential, Inc.
Cover artwork by James Nesbit, www.jamesnart.com. Used by permission.

ISBN: 978-1-953247-00-1 (paperback)
ISBN: 978-1-953247-01-8 (ebook)

Library of Congress Control Number: 2020915686

True Potential, Inc.
PO Box 904, Travelers Rest, SC 29690
www.truepotentialmedia.com

For itinerary and booking ministry, you may contact the author at:
drdaleafife@gmail.com
www.drdaleafife.com

Produced and Printed in the United States of America.

*This book is dedicated to all
the spiritual pioneers who are not satisfied
with the familiar
and are courageous enough
to journey into the unknown.*

Contents

Foreword

by Michele Gunn

Thank you **so much** for your faithfulness, Dr. Fife!

This scroll absolutely takes my breath away. More than anything else you've written, it carries the intensity of pure truth from the Throne. Throughout the entire reading, I felt I was experiencing your journey into the heavenlies right alongside you. I literally could hear, see, smell, taste and feel what you were describing, so much so that sometimes I knew what you were going to say before you said it. I have wept almost without ceasing for the last three days from the impact. This is living, breathing revelation. It reminds me of cinematic depictions I've seen where a character opens a massive tome and light explodes out of the pages onto their face.

There's a tremendous amount of detail here, which I love, but it drew me on with anticipation much like an epic film, rather than clogging or overwhelming. A progression of intensity and wonder escalates seamlessly from beginning to end, as though we're ascending a spiral staircase from earth up to the River of Life. At no time did I feel like you were randomly running from scene to scene. Each new experience is more intense, more astounding than the last, and preparatory for the next; I couldn't have experienced the Conservatory without visiting the Library first. You have faithfully opened the royal scroll and let its contents spill out. Please, God, help Your Church—help me!—to eat this scroll from Your hand and do as You have commanded in spite of the tangled underbrush of earth gripping our ankles! How foolish we are to stare at the dust under our feet when we have access to the immediate presence of every characteristic of our Father.

Michele Gunn
Fresh Oil Ministries International
Firebrand2@hotmail.com

Preface
by Jay Bennett

You're holding in your hands a treasure chest, a road map, and a sacred invitation birthed out of countless hours of watching, listening and engaging in His presence. This book was not birthed out of the rational or even the irrational mind of a man, but out of the very heart of God Himself!

First Corinthians 2:9 says, *"Eye has not seen nor ear heard, nor have entered into the heart of man the things which God has prepared for those who love Him."* This verse is explicit that we're to watch and listen in our relationship with Christ, just like Dr. Fife has done. We see this even further in Revelation 4:1 where John, in the spirit, had an encounter with God that was a combination of seeing and hearing. He saw a door standing open in heavenly realms and heard a voice saying, *"Come up here, and I will show you things which must take place after this."* In response, John engaged with what he saw and heard and was transported to the very Throne of God. It was through spiritually hearing and seeing that John was able to come into that place of exponential understanding and experiential knowledge of Christ.

So, Scripture clearly indicates that both of these senses are necessary to bring us into all that God has for us. Yet, for the most part, the Body of Christ has focused primarily on the *hearing* and has relegated the *seeing* exclusively to those whom we term *seers*, people naturally gifted to see beyond the visible realm and into the invisible sphere. However, this thinking doesn't line up with our makeup as spiritual beings. As such we have spiritual eyes and are equipped to see in the spirit and to engage in heavenly realms. Now, of course, the naturally gifted seers have a head start, but through training and discipline, all of us can develop our spiritual sight and enter heavenly realities.

In fact, we're in a time and season when Father has resolved to open our spiritual eyes, for this equipping is imperative to the revealing of the mature sons and to the expansion of His Kingdom on earth. Isn't it interesting that Jesus did only what He **saw** His Father doing? He did not release the kingdom apart from seeing. Will it be any different for us? So, in order to take new ground for the kingdom, we need to learn to see and engage with what we see. Therefore, by God's design and provision, prophets and mystics are now coming forth to teach and train the Body of Christ to do this very thing, and Dr. Fife is one of these honored and trusted vessels who's been raised for such a time as this.

I've known Dr. Fife for more than twenty years and can attest to his wholehearted devotion to Christ and his deft passion to equip the Body. He's a man who has logged umpteen miles with Christ and has learned to see, hear, and engage in ways that are busting the boundaries of what we thought was possible in a relationship with God. So, if your heart has been calling you beyond only that which you can see and hear in the natural realm and into the 'eye has not seen and ear has not heard' of the heavenly realms, I highly commend Dr. Fife as one to bring you there; he knows the path! So get ready to receive from the wealth of his communion and unwavering 'yes' to Christ! Let this unstoppable pioneer of heavenly realms and the heart of Yahweh exhort you, inspire you, and lead you into all that He has prepared for those who love Him in this day. And may I suggest you put on a seat belt…you're about to be propelled into heavenly orbits!

Jay Bennett
Youth With a Mission (YWAM) International Teacher and Intercessor
Founder of Global Strategy Corp

Introduction

My passion is God's presence. My desperation for intimacy with Him drove me into the *secret place*, and there is where I prayed a simple yet deeply profound prayer: "Lord, I want to be like Enoch. I want to walk with you and be your friend."

That passion and prayer led me on a journey like no other. Never in my wildest dreams did I think it would lead from the Well of His Presence to heavenly journeys and the adventures of a spiritual pneumanaut. My prayer closet became a doorway, a portal into the heavenly realms of God's Kingdom. When we are obedient to close the door and wait upon Him in the *secret place*, God opens another gateway into the spiritual dimension where heavenly beings and angels reside, where time exists but not as we know it here on earth, and where people, sentient beings, and places abound that exceed our earthly capability to perceive. In this dimension, revelation flows freely. Knowledge, Wisdom, Understanding, Counsel, Might, the Fear of the Lord, and the Spirit of the Lord mentor and disciple us as sons and daughters of the Most High.

We have often prayed, "Lord, come down here and manifest your presence among us."

God's response is, "Come up here. I have things you must see and hear for these end times."

This gives an entirely new meaning and significance to what the Lord taught us to pray: *"Your kingdom Come, You will be done, on earth as it is in heaven."* (Matthew 6:10)

Like Apostle John on the isle of Patmos, I heard His voice one day in the spirit saying, "Come up here!",[1] and I obeyed His invitation. Thus my journey into the realms of His heavenly Kingdom began.

Come along with me into the celestial realms. Peek over my shoulder and be astounded just as I was. View vistas and places that have no earthly comparison. Meet the angels I have encountered and the heavenly beings who are so awesome that chills will run down your spine. You will want to bow in their presence. Listen carefully to the words of Understanding and Knowledge as they teach us.

To be informed is to be prepared, so let me give you some necessary information. On this journey you must not pack your intellectual suitcase. You must unpack it and leave it at home. If you bring it along, it will not help you. The wisdom and philosophies of this world will not suffice. Apostle Paul, a fellow pneumanaut who also went on heavenly journeys, explained it this way:

However, we speak wisdom among those who are mature, yet not the wisdom of this age, nor of the rulers of this age, who are coming to nothing. But we speak the wisdom of God in a mystery, the hidden wisdom which God ordained before the ages for our glory which none of the rulers of this age knew, for had they known, they would not have crucified the Lord of Glory. But it is written, "Eye has not seen, nor ear hear, nor have entered into the heart of man the things which God has prepared for those who love Him." But God has revealed them to us through His Spirit. For the Spirit searches all things, yes the deep things of God. For what man knows the things of a man which is in him? Even so, no one knows the things of God except the Spirit of God. Now we have received not the spirit of the world, but the Spirit who is from God, that we might know the things that have been freely given to us by God. These things we also speak, not in words which man's wisdom teaches but which the Holy Spirit teaches, comparing spiritual things with spiritual.

But the natural man does not receive the things of the Spirit of God for they are foolishness to him, nor can he know them, because they are spiritually discerned. But he who is spiritual judges all things, yet he himself is rightly judged by no one. For who has known the mind of the Lord that we may instruct Him? But we have the mind of Christ. (I Corinthians 2:6–16)

Suspend your analytical tendencies. Separate yourself from your preconceived ideas and theological preferences. Instead, allow Holy Spirit to activate your spiritual discernment. He will use your God-given imagination to engage the cosmic scenes and reveal the nature and reality of the heavenly realms of God's eternal Kingdom. Your imagination will become the page that God writes on. But you may ask yourself, "Is this just my imagination, or am I really witnessing something so extra-terrestrial that this just may be a reality in the spiritual dimension I have yet to discover?" Don't fall into that trap! It's not *just* your imagination! Judge by the impact the proceeding chapters make on your spirit-man! God speaks Spirit to spirit. You must discern spiritually.

My prayer for you is what Apostle Paul prayed for the saints in his day: *"That your heart may be encouraged and that you will attain to all of the full assurance of understanding to the knowledge of the mystery of God, both of the Father and of Christ, in whom are hidden all the treasures of wisdom and knowledge…"* (Colossians 2:2–3)

My warning is that you must *"Beware lest anyone cheat you through philosophy, and empty deceit, according to the traditions of men, according to the basic principles of the world, and not according to Christ. For in Him, dwells all of the fullness of the*

Godhead bodily: and you are complete in Him, who is the head of all principality and power. " (Colossians 2:8–9)

Are you ready? Then join me on this journey into the heavenly realms to discover and learn. Let me lead you to places you never dreamed of. You will quickly realize that what you thought you understood was a mere scratch on the priceless surface of deeper revelation and spiritual truth.

This may be your first journey into the heavenly realms, but it will not be your last! God is inviting His saints to access the heavenly realms in these final days. Why is this so important? It is because our calling is much greater than we ever realized. Yes, we are commanded to go into all the world and make disciples of all nations. But He is also calling us to ascend into the heavenly realms of His Kingdom to bring heavenly strategies and structure back to earth. 'As in heaven so on earth' is our mission. We are His culture changers.

Will you be among those who respond to His summons?

Is it time for you to join the pneumanaut corps?

Read and decide!

CHAPTER 1

Every Ending is a Beginning

"I am the Alpha and the Omega, the First and the Last, the Beginning and the End." (Revelation 22:13)

How can eternal God have an ending? He doesn't! He is unending. But there are instances after He finishes a task or project when He steps back and says, *"It is good. It is very good."* He even took a day off to celebrate and teach us to rest. That was just the beginning, a Genesis moment.

When Jesus, God in the flesh, was born in Bethlehem, He knew that He had a mission to fulfill in coming to earth. He was resolute. Nothing could or would deter Him. When His assignment was complete, He said, *"It is finished!"* But that was just the beginning!

Like God, our endings are beginnings. We call them commencements or graduations. Completing our education doesn't mean we're done. It means we are ready to begin. And so it is with our journey through life. Each lesson learned and assignment fulfilled qualifies us for a new beginning. God turns every ending into a doorway, every conclusion into an opportunity. Everything past is groundwork for what lies ahead. The cycle never ends. We move from revelation to vision, then obedience and finally fulfillment. Lots of stuff happens in the process, but one thing is guaranteed: on the journey we are being conformed to His image. If you have lived long enough on this earth, you have learned that we barely have time to celebrate one completed assignment when God gives us a new one. And so it was for me!

It was August 30 and New Wilmington, Pennsylvania, was embarking on the inevitable journey toward seasonal transformation. What I didn't realize, though, so was I. Summer flashed by, disappearing into the autumn hues of brown and faded green. Golden fields of grain undulated in the winds like ocean waves, and proud corn stalks boastfully waved their tassels in the breeze. Amish farmers harvested their fields with horse-drawn, antiquated machinery, reaping the fruit of their hard labor. Fall and winter were not far behind. The leaves from the stalwart maple tree in our backyard were already drifting to earth and landing on our deck like airplanes on an aircraft carrier.

My focus for the entire summer was to complete the manuscript for my fifth book, *The Imagination Master.* Day after day, I would spend hours in my *secret place* transposing my handwritten journal into my computer. God's presence was so powerful that I often lost all track of time. Gratitude filled my heart as I cherished each moment. *A single day in His presence is like a thousand elsewhere,*[2] I thought, *and here I am enjoying an entire summer's worth.*

On that momentous conclusive day, I reached the last page, the final word, the closing punctuation mark of the manuscript. There is something so satisfying about finishing an assignment from the Lord, especially when you know the entire process is part of fulfilling your calling and destiny. I am a royal scribe, and I write what I see and hear in the King's presence.[3]

Any scribe worthy of his calling must have the finest of instruments and parchment to record the decrees of the King. It has always been my practice to record the prophetic revelations in my 8 ½ x11 hard-bound journal. I use a special pen and often make drawings and sketches in color to capture what I see in detail. Once the King has indicated the revelation for that scroll is complete, I transcribe my journal into my computer. Without exception, the very act of transcribing releases more revelation, insight and understanding. The vision is expanded.

"Now it's time for me to attend to the care and maintenance of my scribal tools, especially my computer," I said with a sigh of satisfaction and relief. "I've been working for months. I better check my programs."

We have no internet service in our summer home, so I resorted to my convenient hotspot, set up my cellphone, and logged into the internet. Sure enough, there were several important upgrades. The program informed me: "This will take one hour and thirty minutes." I clicked on the download button.

This is a perfect time to rest in the Lord's presence and soak in His love, I thought. I moved from my desk chair and sat down in my recliner (my prayer chair) to relax and wait for the computer upgrade to finish. What happened next came as a complete surprise. In an instant, my ending became the beginning of one of the most significant revelations and spiritual journeys of my life.

Time for an Upgrade

"This is my favorite chair," I said as I settled into the supple, light-blue leather cushion and rested my arms on the ample, smooth armrests. "It fits me perfectly. His peace and presence are here."

My recliner is like the prayer shawl that priests use to cover their heads.[4] It serves as my personal *secret place,* a reserved private enclosure that is sanctified and anointed by His presence. I reserve it for my intimate communion with God.[5] I had an immediate sense that God wanted to speak to me. I waited, cherishing His presence and feeling His overwhelming love and favor flow into my spirit, but He was silent. I heard nothing. Finally I broke the silence.

"Thank you, Father, for helping me to finish this manuscript. But I have a question, Abba. What will I do now that it is finished?"

He responded immediately, "Just as you are in the process of upgrading your computer right now, I am going to *upgrade* you."

His words penetrated into my spirit like the prodding goad of a good shepherd.[6] Whatever He meant by 'upgrade,' I knew immediately that I needed something I didn't have yet. My next assignment would require an improved ability.

He continued, "Your most productive days are ahead of you! Keep your focus on Me. I will direct you and unlock mysteries and secrets to you. There are golden pens waiting for you as you seek Me.

"You are on the track of time, and the speed is accelerating. Enjoy the ride! Don't see your assignments as work or tedious. My anointing will grace you with great joy and unleash your imagination and creativity. Haven't you discerned by now that I am the Imagination Master? It is true! Allow me to unleash your creativity."

"Thank you, Father," I replied. "Whatever you mean by *'upgrade,'* I welcome and embrace it. Please release Your creativity in me and use my imagination as the screen you write upon. You know my heart better than I do. My greatest joy is to serve You. I love You so much, Abba."

This was amazing. I realized that what I thought was merely a time to wait for my computer to download new programing, God was using to download new information into my spirit.

The Mysterious Monk

I felt so refreshed and renewed inside. "I am free to proceed to my next assignment as His scribe," I said, relishing a new adventure of exploration in God's service. I waited, meditating on the words Father spoke, when suddenly a picture flashed spontaneously onto the screen of my mind. This is always a clear indication to me that God is saying something. He often speaks to me through images and in pictures. That is why the prophets in the Old Testament were called 'seers'; they saw what He was saying.

The details of the vision were crisp and clear. I saw an older monk wearing a chocolate-brown wool robe fastened at the waist with a simple rope belt. He was ascending through the air at a slight incline. No path or surface was under him. The monk held a lantern outstretched in his right hand. I knew he was leading others, although I couldn't see them. He was creating a lighted pathway for them to follow. He gazed into the distance above and ahead of him with resolute focus. This monk was on a journey upward. I realized I was the monk in the vision, but what were the implications? I quickly sketched the picture in my journal.

"Lord, what does this mean?" I asked.

"You will soon understand. Be faithful to what I reveal to you, My son. This is a strategic journey that will prepare and equip you and My Church for the days and years to come."

The Vision

The Navigator

In the next few weeks, the Lord began to unravel the hidden meaning of the vision. Each clue brought further insight. First, I received an email from a trusted friend who spends half of each year in Ireland and the other half in New England. This was unlike any other message he has sent to me over the years. He wrote, "Dale, I thought you would appreciate this prayer by Saint Brendan."

I had never heard of Saint Brendan. As I read his prayer, chills ran down my spine. Holy Spirit made the words leap off the screen into my spirit:

> Help me to journey beyond the familiar and into the un-known.
> Give me the faith to leave old ways and break fresh ground with You.
> Christ of the mysteries, I trust You to be stronger than each storm within me.
> I will trust in the darkness and know that my times, even now, are in Your hand.
> Tune my spirit to the music of heaven, and somehow, make my obedience count for You. Amen.

I was astonished. "This is no coincidence," I gasped. "God, first You give me a vision of a monk on a journey and tell me I am the monk, and then a few days later I receive a message about a lone monk who apparently was on a journey into the unfamiliar. I have to find out who Saint Brendan is. That should help me decipher the puzzle."

Well, Saint Brendan is not your average monk! He was born into a Catholic family in AD 484 in the southwest of Ireland. At the age of 26, he was ordained a Catholic priest. He was a gifted spiritual father and mentor, and this became very evident as he proceeded to establish a number of monasteries. But Brendan was not a settler. He had an apostolic calling. He was on the move, making several voyages. First, he sailed to the Aran Islands where he founded a monastery, to Argyll, an island off Scotland where he met Saint Columba. His second journey took him to Wales and finally from there to Brittany on the northern coast of France. Between AD 512 and 530 he built monastic cells at Ardfert (originally Ard Fhearta, which means 'hill of miracles.' Brendan may have known this when he was seeking a place for the monastery), and *Seana Cill,* (the Old Church) at the foot of Mount Brandon. It was from this humble monastic outpost that the inquisitive and adventurous monk embarked on his famous voyage of seven years to search for Paradise (the Garden of Eden). This legendary journey to the Isle of the Blessed, as described in *The Voyage of Saint Brendan the Abbot,* ensured his place in history. Many believe that he discovered North America.

As the legend of the seven-years voyage spread, crowds of pilgrims and students flocked to Ardfert. Religious houses were formed at Gallerus, Kilmalkedar,

Brandon Hill, and the Blasket Islands to meet the wants of those who came for spiritual guidance from Saint Brendan.

He has become the patron saint of sailors and travelers. At the United States Naval Academy in Annapolis, Maryland, a large stained glass window commemorates Brendan's achievements. At Fenit Harbour in Tralee Bay, Ireland, a substantial bronze sculpture was erected to honor him.

Brendan is considered to be one of the 12 apostles of Ireland. In his lifetime he was a passionate follower of Jesus, a founder of many monasteries, a mentor and spiritual guide, and a visionary who sought the Garden of Eden. Pretty impressive! But perhaps most significant to me, Brendan is known as 'The Navigator.'

I was flabbergasted. "It's clear to me why You would send me this information, Lord, but I'm still confused. Is the monk in my vision me or is it Brendan?"

"Both!" He responded. "Brendan was as an explorer and navigator who led My people into new, uncharted places. He gathered them and mentored them on the journey. I have called and commissioned you for the same assignment. You must draw My sons and daughters out of the familiar into the unknown dimensions of My Kingdom. This journey will require faith and courage. Don't allow the storms of doubt and questioning to deter you. I am greater than all your questions and reasoning. *I am the Christ of mysteries!* I am about to release new revelation and unlock secrets. The seasons are changing in the spiritual dimension. It is time for My people to possess fresh ground. This is the crossing-over age."

"Lord, I know there are hidden mysteries in Your heart," I said. "I long to draw them out. Only You can light my pathway on this journey. I choose Saint Brendan's prayer as my own and for all those who will follow. I will trust You in the darkness. My times are in Your hands. Tune my ears to the music of heaven and make my obedience count for You."

A new sense of purpose filled my days as I waited for more direction from the Lord. I had been on spiritual journeys with the Lord before, but I sure didn't want to initiate something in my own eagerness or fleshly desires. I had to carefully follow the direction of Holy Spirit step by step.

A Kairos Encounter

The following week I attended a meeting of Antioch International Ministries at the home of my neighbor Apostle Jim Erb. A mutual, longtime YWAM friend was scheduled to speak. When I arrived, people were clustered in groups catching up with one another after a month since their last gathering. We entered into an anointed time of worship and prayer and then Jay began to share. I instantly realized something was different about him. It didn't take long to determine what it was. His computer flashed to life and a PowerPoint presentation scrolled across the wall. Pictures of angels and quotes from Scripture and his mentors revealed the story of his personal journey into the heavenly realms. He spoke with confidence and experiential knowledge. My spirit was ignited. I knew this was another clue, a piece of the puzzle that was unfolding in my understanding. It had to do with my new assignment.

When the meeting ended, I immediately approached Jay. "I'm so impacted by your story," I said. "Can we get together this week? I really need to talk with you about this whole matter. I've met and spoken to angels in the past and have traveled with them as an intercessor, but this is a whole different realm."

"Of course. I'd love to," Jay said with an eager smile. "How about tomorrow?"

"Great!" I said. "Can you come to my house in the morning around 11:00?"

"See you then," he affirmed.

"Awesome. Thanks, Jay."

I left the meeting fully aware that the Lord was directing my steps. "This was not just another meeting, Lord," I prayed. "This is a *kairos* moment. You sovereignly placed Your servant Jay in my path at this time to help me understand what is coming. I have so much to learn, Holy Spirit. I am hungry and thirsty for Your truth and wisdom. Teach me and lead me into the heavenly realms as Your servant and warrior, Lord."

The Ascension Dimension

The late morning sun shone into my *secret place* through the sliding glass doors that led to a deck suspended three stories above the back yard. It offered a commanding view of the valley and rolling hills beyond. The sound of horses' hooves pulling Amish wagons along Cowden Road down in the valley filled the air with echoes of nostalgia and a simpler life. My private lookout from the top of our hill always inspired me. God had set the scene for another revelatory moment. From my comfortable recliner, I looked across the room at Jay. His face glowed and his hands trembled with the anointing of the Lord.

"What's happened to you?" I asked. "There's such a change in your countenance and a greater depth of understanding and revelation. You're different."

His eyes glistened as he spoke. His words carried the weighty presence of the Lord. "I've been on a journey of discovery in the spirit. The Lord has connected me with several individuals who have opened my understanding and mentored me regarding accessing the realms of God's Kingdom in the heavens. I've met and spoken with angels in the process. As I travel throughout the world ministering and teaching on intercession, prayer has become an experiential reality instead of a conversation. I've been with entire groups of anywhere from 3 to 15 people where we have actually travelled in the spirit to pray for individuals and nations with powerful dynamic results. We have been participating, not just conversing, with God about the needs and situations He leads us to pray about. Through all of this, I have come to see and discover that the heavenly realms are open and accessible to us. We can go there now and return."

He paused to seek the Lord's direction and then continued. "Did you know that the seven spirits of God are not Holy Spirit? The Spirit of Knowledge, the Spirit of Counsel, the Spirit of Wisdom, the Spirit of the Lord, the Spirit of Understanding, the Spirit of Might, and the Spirit of the Fear of the Lord are our mentors. They are preparing us for the days ahead. This awareness alone has transformed my life. I desire to be mentored by the Spirit of Might. I think this training will be more important than ever when engaging the enemy in the future."

Jay's comments rocked my world. My thoughts were like scrambled eggs: *mentored by the seven spirits of God, accessing the heavenly realms, speaking regularly with angels, mentors who have experiential wisdom and knowledge, actually participating in intercession.* My human hard drive needed time to buffer this information.

"This is all new to me!" I exclaimed, stunned by my lack of knowledge.

In that instant, God gave me further explanation regarding His word to me. "Did I not say to you that I am going to *upgrade* you? In the days to come, you will discover new truth and receive prophetic revelation. Holy Spirit will unlock the Scriptures. You will see a new dimension and level of meaning that to this point has been hidden from your eyes of understanding.

"I am preparing you for your departure into the heavenly realms. Knowledge, Understanding and Wisdom will assist you on the journey that will soon begin. Even now I am upgrading you. You must let go of the old wineskins of concepts and beliefs. I am pouring the new wine of revelation into you. Proceed in My peace and joy. The greatest journey of your life lies ahead of you. The old has passed away. The new has come. This is the beginning season, the crossing-over time. You are about to enter the ascension dimension."

I couldn't speak. I grabbed my journal and hastily recorded the Lord's instructions. Jay watched with curiosity but remained silent. "You have no idea how significant this time together is," I said, laying my pen and journal aside. "God has given me my next assignment," I explained. "And now I understand what He is saying, at least in part anyway. I'm sure much more insight is to come, but 'upgrade' means more than understanding and revelation. He is preparing me to enter the heavenly realms. I must know who these individuals are who have mentored you. How can I connect with them?"

"Let me recommend someone who I believe is a forerunner in this regard," Jay said. "Something he said has really helped me. Did you know that if you have already received a prophetic vision, you can go back and revisit that same vision in the spirit? God will give you more insight and expand the vision."

A spiritual explosion went off inside me. "That's it! The Unfinished House! The Lord's guidance is so clear now," I blurted out, interrupting him. "Jay, you've read *Spirit Wind: The Ultimate Adventure,* haven't you?"[7]

"Yes," he said.

"Then you remember the vision of Frontier Town and the buildings on Main Street. There's one building in Frontier Town that I have tried to enter, and every time I go there in the spirit, the Lord will not let me go inside. It's the Unfinished House. That's the only building on Main Street that I have not been allowed to access. To this day it remains a mystery. I keep going there but never succeed. I have longed to discover its mysteries, but Spirit Wind keeps guard and I am forbidden to proceed.

"Whatever's inside the Unfinished House," I said, "I am now convinced, has to do with my new assignment. All I can do is hope I will be granted permission to enter it."

"Dale, I know some forerunners in this spiritual realm who have helped me greatly. Let me recommend a particular book that I think would be a perfect starting place for you."[8]

The first thing I did after Jay left that afternoon was to order the book. I have been mentored by many individuals whom I have never met in person, but their books and messages have been impacting, formative resources and have shaped my thinking and spiritual life. I knew this book would be a spiritual milestone for me. I eagerly awaited its arrival. But I couldn't stop thinking about the Unfinished House and what lay beyond the front door. God told me at the very beginning of the vision of Main Street that things aren't what they seem to be in Frontier Town. What was behind the door of the Unfinished House? I was determined to find out.

A Pneumanaut in Training

A few days later, we left New Wilmington and returned to our home in Florida. Every day I eagerly greeted the mailman, hoping the book had arrived. It was like Christmas morning when it finally did. I prepared myself for a spiritual banquet, planning to savor its contents. Even the chapter headings intrigued me. I knew I was in for a real feast, but I soon realized this was not a buffet. It was an expertly prepared gourmet meal of spiritual insight. I had to read each chapter slowly and then reread it. My effort paid off. I grasped so much more the second time. I underlined and highlighted the text and then took notes. Then I read the entire book again to comprehend the depths of his understanding and teaching. I wanted to glean every nugget of wisdom and understanding I could.

The author's principles were so helpful, like reading a pilot's instruction manual. *I'm a spiritual apprentice in training,* I determined. *Just as astronauts need to prepare for flight into space, I am in training to become a pneumanaut, a spiritual navigator.*[9] *Who better to mentor me than a seasoned pneumanaut?*

You would think most Christians would know that heavenly journeys are valid, but that is far from the truth. The majority of the Church believes "we are landlocked, earthbound creatures, who occasionally may see an angel. But going into the heavenlies ourselves? Get real! That's for a select chosen few and only in the past. We are stuck here until the rapture." I thought the same way until I realized this way of thinking is nonsense! We need to expose this belief as false, with no biblical basis. Entering the realm of the Kingdom of Heaven **is** real! It is for this age, and even more vital, it is of utmost importance as we approach the end of days. If angels are His air force, then we are His heir force.

We need a new paradigm, a pneumanaut mindset. We must expand the limitations of our thinking with revelation, not repackaged knowledge. How do we do this? We begin by posturing ourselves for this experience. In other words, we intentionally become a candidate available for the King's service in His pneumanaut corps. Our desire must be to serve God's will and purposes. Be aware this is not some weird tourist trip into a spiritual fantasyland called heaven for our personal pleasure and enjoyment. It has eternal consequences and strategic purposes. It is wonderful and exciting, but it can be dangerous.

With revelation comes responsibility. Fear and trembling are a good place to start. We are about to access the divine, holy realm of God's Kingdom of Heaven. Humility is required. Set yourself to be God's servant. Speak words of faith and belief. Ask the Lord to cleanse your imagination in the blood of Jesus.[10] Align your thinking and beliefs with His eternal Word and find some godly mentors and teachers.

I urge you to submit to the Lord's training regimen. In earth's realm, not everyone who trains to be an astronaut ends up going into space, only those who are chosen. That doesn't minimize their training or give them cause to slack off. But God's ways are not our ways. You are a spirit being who has a soul and lives in a body. You are one of God's chosen people, and the Lord Jesus loves and cherishes you. You are a royal priest, a citizen of God's holy nation, a peculiar person.[11] You are not limited by earth's gravity. In the spirit you can fly.[12]

CHAPTER 2

From Revelation to Visitation

An important, dynamic process is involved when engaging the heavenly realms. It is called progressive revelation. Revelation is a vital part of our walk and life as Christians. We are spiritual beings who are led by Holy Spirit. We thrive on prophetic revelation. Without it, we are like a ship without a rudder. We just drift on the sea of life, blown about by every wind that comes along. We have no destination and do not know how to navigate our course. We wander aimlessly through life. The Bible provides the reason for this indomitable spiritual fog. *"Where there is no prophetic vision, the people cast off restraint."* (Proverbs 29:18)

A friend of mine defines vision or revelation as an inspired look at reality. I agree! Revelation is life giving and vision enabling. It is the unique process whereby God shows us something we could not see by ourselves or tells us something we could not know by our own intellectual capability. We can liken it to a window in heaven that has a curtain covering it. Only God has the authority to open the curtain. As we wait in His presence, He chooses to open the veil and allow us to see what's inside. What we see and hear are revelation. In that instant, we are energized and enlightened with supernatural knowledge and information. Then God closes the curtain. A single moment of divine revelation can be sufficient for an entire lifetime. We are Holy Spirit enlightened and directed.[13]

This is the process I experience in my *secret place* as I wait in His presence and fellowship with Him. He opens the curtain and reveals things to me in visions and then speaks by His Spirit to explain what they mean. All the books I have written are a result of this process. I record the revelation in my journals as His scribe and sketch what I see and hear in His presence. I call my journals, *The Golden Scrolls from the Well of His Presence.* They chronicle my journey as His scribe and are a record of the ongoing flow of revelation from Him.

A single revelation has many layers of truth. I have discovered that when I receive a vision from the Lord, I am able to return to that vision in the spirit and revisit it whenever I desire to do so. I am always astounded by the result. I inevitably discern more truth and garner more information. The vision increases. It sometimes becomes book length, revealing so much more than I first perceived. I journal the vision, review it, sow prayer into it and then I go back and revisit it for more insight. Journal your time in God's presence and meditate on the revelation or vision. Focus and recall your last experience. Then go back and revisit it.

Moving From Revelation to Visitation

Apostle Paul writes, *"Be not conformed to this world, but be transformed by the renewing of your mind, that you may prove what is that good and acceptable and perfect will of God."* (Romans 12:2) Our minds must be transformed, so we think and perceive like God, instead of like the world. How does this happen?

God gives us *information* and then by His Spirit, He *reveals* what that information really means from His perspective. The purpose of this *revelation* knowledge is *transformation.* He gives us revelation in order to change us, not just to make us feel super spiritual. We are no longer the world's clones, thinking and living as the culture does. We know that what is impossible in worldly terms is possible with God. We now walk by faith in the supernatural realm, empowered as God's sons and daughters. We are enlightened servants of the King.

Apostle Paul stresses that the end result of being transformed is the ability to *prove* something. Transformation must result in *application.* We must become living witnesses of God's Kingdom. We are God's proof. We *prove* (manifest or demonstrate) by our lives that obeying His will is the perfect way of living. Revelation is meant to transform us, so we can *engage* in the spiritual realm and manifest God's will and fulfill His strategies on earth. Our supernatural mission is to be change agents, manifesting heaven on earth.

The mental conversion process moves from information to revelation to transformation and then application. Application is the key! We are meant to *engage* the supernatural realm, not simply know about it. The Church is full of people who have information and revelation about the spiritual dimension but are not interacting with the unseen realm of the spirit.

Countdown: a Voice, a Vision, a Visitation

Revelation has to do with receiving supernatural *information* and truth. Visitation is another dimension wherein we actually enter into and become a *participant* in the spiritual activity. Apostle John on the isle of Patmos is a prime example. He heard a voice, saw a vision, and entered into that vision. He visited heaven! This is his testimony:

Pneumanaut John

> *I, John, your brother and partner in the tribulation and the kingdom and the patient endurance that are in Jesus, was on the island called Patmos on account of the word of God and the testimony of Jesus.* **I was in the Spirit** *on the Lord's day, and I heard behind me a loud voice like a trumpet saying, "Write what you see in a book and send it to the seven churches, to Ephesus and to Smyrna and to Pergamum and to Thyatira and to Sardis and to Philadelphia and to Laodicea."* **Then I turned to see the voice that was speaking to me,** *and on turning I saw seven golden lampstands, and in the midst of the lampstands one like a son of man, clothed with a long robe and with a golden sash around his chest. The hairs of his head were white, like white wool, like snow. His eyes were like a flame of fire, his feet were like burnished bronze, refined in a furnace, and his voice was like the roar of many waters. In his right hand he held seven stars, from his mouth came a sharp two-edged sword, and his face was like the sun shining in full strength. When I saw him, I fell at his feet as though dead. But he laid his right hand on me, saying, "Fear not, I am the first and the last, and the living one. I died, and behold I am alive forevermore, and I have the keys of Death and Hades. Write therefore the things that you have seen, those that are and those that are to take place after this. As for the mystery of the seven stars that you saw in my right hand, and the seven golden lampstands, the seven stars are the angels of the seven churches, and the seven lampstands are the seven churches.* (Revelation 1:9–20, ESV) (Emphasis mine)

> *After this* **I looked, and behold, a door standing open in heaven!** *And the first voice, which I had heard speaking to me like a trumpet, said,* **"Come up here, and I will show you what must take place after this."** *At once I* **was in the Spirit,** *and behold, a throne stood in heaven, with one seated on the throne. And he who sat there had the appearance of jasper and carnelian, and around the throne was a rainbow that had the appearance of an emerald. Around the throne were twenty-four thrones, and seated on the thrones were twenty-four elders, clothed in white garments, with golden crowns on their heads. From the throne came flashes of lightning, and rumblings and peals of*

thunder, and before the throne were burning seven torches of fire, which are **the seven spirits of God,** *and before the throne there was as it were a sea of glass, like crystal. And around the throne, on each side of the throne, are four living creatures, full of eyes in front and behind: the first living creature like a lion, the second living creature like an ox, the third living creature with the face of a man, and the fourth living creature like an eagle in flight. And the four living creatures, each of them with six wings, are full of eyes all around and within, and day and night they never cease to say, "Holy, holy, holy, is the Lord God Almighty, who was and is and is to come!" And whenever the living creatures give glory and honor and thanks to him who is seated on the throne, who lives forever and ever, the twenty-four elders fall down before him who is seated on the throne and worship him who lives forever and ever. They cast their crowns before the throne, saying, "Worthy are you, our Lord and God, to receive glory and honor and power, for you created all things, and by your will they existed and were created."* (Revelation 4:1–11, ESV) (Emphasis mine)

Pneumanaut Jacob

John also discovered a basic principle of engaging the unseen realm. He saw the entrance or doorway to access it and responded to the invitation. He wasn't the only one who had this kind of experience. Consider Jacob:

> *Now Jacob went out from Beersheba and went toward Haran. So he came to a certain place and stayed there all night, because the sun had set. And he took one of the stones of that place and put it at his head, and he lay down in that place to sleep. Then* **he dreamed, and behold, a ladder was set up on the earth, and its top reached to heaven; and there the angels of God were ascending and descending on it.** *(Genesis 28:10–12, ESV) (Emphasis mine)*

> *And he arose that night and took his two wives, his two female servants, and his eleven sons, and crossed over the ford of Jabbok. He took them, sent them over the brook, and sent over what he had. Then Jacob was left alone; and* **a Man wrestled with him** *until the breaking of day. Now when He saw that He did not prevail against him, He touched the socket of his hip; and the socket of Jacob's hip was out of joint as He wrestled with him. And He said, "Let Me go, for the day breaks."*

> *But he said, "I will not let You go unless You bless me!" So He said to him, "What is your name?"*

He said, "Jacob."

*And He said, "Your name shall no longer be called Jacob, but Israel; **for you have struggled with God and with men, and have prevailed."***

Then Jacob asked, saying, "Tell me Your name, I pray."

And He said, "Why is it that you ask about My name?" And He blessed him there.

*So Jacob called the name of the place Peniel: "For **I have seen God face to face,** and my life is preserved." Just as he crossed over Penuel the sun rose on him, and he limped on his hip. Therefore to this day the children of Israel do not eat the muscle that shrank, which is on the hip socket, because He touched the socket of Jacob's hip in the muscle that shrank.* (Genesis 32:22–32, NKJV) (Emphasis mine)

Jacob engaged the spiritual realm. He spoke with angels. He saw and entered a spiritual portal between heaven and earth. Afterward, he used his stone pillow to erect an altar to keep the portal open. He wrestled with God and came away with a lifelong limp and a new name and identity to prove it. Jacob's experience was not exclusive.

Pneumanaut Paul

Apostle Paul speaks of a pneumanaut that he knew personally who entered into heaven. This person couldn't tell if his journey was in his fleshly body or by his spirit being. He returned with such powerful revelation and knowledge that he couldn't find words to describe what he experienced. I believe that person was actually Paul himself who was describing his own experiences in the wilderness in God's presence.[14]

*I must go on boasting. Though there is nothing to be gained by it, I will go on to visions and revelations of the Lord. I know a man in Christ who fourteen years ago was **caught up to the third heaven**—whether in the body or out of the body I do not know, God knows. And I know that this man was caught up into paradise—whether in the body or out of the body I do not know, God knows—and he heard things that cannot be told, which man may not utter. On behalf of this man I will boast, but on my own behalf I will not boast, except of my weaknesses—though if I should wish to boast, I would not be a fool, for I would be speaking the truth; but I refrain from it, so that no one* *may think more of me than he sees in me or hears from me. So to keep me from becoming conceited because of the surpassing greatness of the revelations, a thorn was given me in the flesh, a messenger of Satan to harass me, to keep me from becoming conceited. Three times I pleaded with the Lord about this, that it should leave me. But he said to me, "My grace is sufficient for you, for my power is made perfect in weakness." Therefore I will boast all the more gladly of my weaknesses, so that the power of Christ may rest upon me. For the sake of Christ, then, I am content with weaknesses, insults, hardships, persecutions, and calamities. For when I am weak, then I am strong.* (II Corinthians 12:1–10, ESV) (Emphasis mine)*

Paul went into the desert, which is traditionally considered as a *secret place* in the history of the Church's desert fathers and mystics. In this isolation, apart from society and the context of religious constraints or human influence, Paul met with Jesus in the *secret place*.[15] His experience must have been like Enoch's. He walked with God and was instructed in God's theological school. He visited heaven and no doubt spoke with angels and stood before the Throne of God.

Pneumanaut Enoch

Speaking of Enoch, he was the ultimate example of a human pneumanaut. Enoch was seven generations removed from Adam. *"All the days of Enoch were three hundred and sixty-five years. Enoch walked with God, and He was not because God took him… By faith Enoch was taken so that he did not see death, and was not found, because God had taken him; for before he was taken he had this testimony, that he pleased God."* (Genesis 5:21–24; Hebrews 11:5, NKJV)

The Bible tells us that Enoch was God's friend and he walked with Him. The Bible provides little information about this mysterious man, but there are other ancient writings that are biblically endorsed. These extra-biblical texts are recognized and referred to by the Scriptures as legitimate historical documents. They flesh out the biblical narrative, providing more insight to Enoch's lifestyle. Israel knew and often referred to or quoted these sources. "Jasher and Enoch are two of thirteen ancient history books that are recommended reading by the Bible"[16] Although not considered cannon, Enoch and Jasher enrich our understanding. Jasher writes:

And the spirit of God was upon Enoch, and he taught all his men the wisdom of God and His ways, and the sons of men served the Lord all the days of Enoch, and they came to hear his wisdom. And all of the kings of the sons of men, both first and last, together with their princes and judges, came to Enoch when they heard of his wisdom, and they bowed down to him, and they also required of Enoch to reign over them, to which he consented...

Enoch resolved to separate himself from the sons of men and **to secret himself** as at first to serve the Lord... he kept away from the sons of men three days and then went to them one day... he did this for many years and afterward concealed himself for six days and appeared to his people one day in seven, and after that once a month, and then once a year until all of the kings and princes, and sons of men sought for him, and desired again to see the face of Enoch, and to hear his word; but they could not, as all of the sons of men feared to approach him on account of the God-like awe that was seated upon his countenance; therefore no man could look at him, fearing he might be punished and die.

And when Enoch was teaching them the ways of God, behold an angel of the Lord then called to Enoch from heaven, and wished to bring him up to heaven to make him reign over the sons of God as he had reigned over the sons of men upon earth...

When Enoch at that time heard this he went and assembled all of the inhabitants of earth....and he said to them, "I have been required to ascend into heaven, I therefore do not know the day of my going and therefore I will give you instruction before I leave you, how to act upon earth whereby you may live;" and he did so. And he taught them wisdom and knowledge, and gave them instruction, and he reproved them, and he placed before them the statutes and judgments to do upon earth, and he made peace amongst them, and he taught them everlasting life, and he dwelt with them some time teaching them all of these things...And it was upon the seventh day that Enoch ascended into heaven in a whirl-wind with horses and chariots of fire.[17]

Enoch lived in the *secret place* of intimacy with God. It was his lifestyle. He didn't just practice God's presence; he lived in God's presence. He knew the angels by name. He measured the Garden of Eden and served as the fallen angels' attorney to plead their case before God to no avail. He walked with God and traveled into the heavenlies on a regular basis. Enoch was not an angel; he was flesh and blood just like you and me. He even received prophetic revelation regarding the end times that is recorded in the Bible in the Book of Jude:

Now Enoch, the seventh from Adam, prophesied about these men also say-ing, "Behold the Lord comes with ten thousands of His saints, to execute judgement upon all, to convict all who are ungodly among them of all their ungodly deeds which they have committed in an ungodly way, and of all the harsh things which ungodly sinners have spoken against Him." (Jude 1:14–15, NKJV)

One common thread runs through all these testimonies: John, Jacob, Paul and Enoch all discovered a gateway, doorway or portal (I use these words interchangeably) that provided access into the spiritual dimension. They passed through these doorways into the spiritual realm and accessed heaven in the Spirit. John heard a voice and saw a door open in heaven. He entered by the Spirit.[18] The result was the Book of Revelation. Jacob not only saw the portal between heaven and earth, but also he may have climbed it because he saw God standing at the top. Then he had a real wrestling match with God himself, a physical encounter with the Almighty. Equally fascinating is that the angels were also using the portal to travel back and forth from heaven to earth. Paul and Enoch spent hours, days, years— and for Enoch an entire lifetime—in the *secret place* of intimacy with God. It was a portal into His presence.

Portals: Spiritual Launchpads

This establishes a biblical principle. There are access points into the heavens that were available to these spiritual pneumanauts. The same principle operates today. Portals are also available to us. This is not science fiction. It is fact. The Bible clearly describes them. These passageways connect the earthly realm and the heavenly realm. "Portals are points where heaven and earth converge. At portals, believers experience the phenomenon of heaven released into the earth."[19] Sometimes they appear like a whirlwind, transporting God's servants and prophets into heaven. They can also be stationary like Jacob's ladder. But the questions that beg answers are where are they today, and how can we access them now?

Portals have two types of entry points. First, portals can be *physical* places on the map. One portal actually existed in the basement sanctuary of Francis Metcalf's home in Idyllwild, California.[20] Altars or mountain tops are often portals that God as well as people use. Consider Abraham and Moses on Mount Sanai, and Jesus on Mount Hermon where He was transfigured.[21] Portals existed between heaven and earth in all of these actual places.[22] Study the history of Mount Hermon, now known as the Golan Heights, which is the highest mountain in Syria at 9,232 feet above sea level. The rebellious watcher angels opened a satanic doorway on this mountain in what was then known as the region and kingdom of Bashan where Baal was worshipped as god, and the Nephilim giants terrorized the region. This area was the northernmost part of the Promised Land. The tribe of Dan dwelt on the border and built the city of Dan in the pagan evil territory of Bashan. To this day, Mount Hermon is considered the gateway to hell.[23]

Portals also have all kinds of traffic. Humans, angels and demons use them to travel between the spiritual and physical dimensions of heaven and earth. Those who establish and open the portals govern them and determine the spiritual atmosphere and domination of the region where they exist.[24] This is why God instructed Israel to tear down the altars and destroy the high places of the pagan gods when they entered into Canaan. These cities were dedicated to destruction, and every living thing in them—animals and people—was to be killed.[25] God demanded that Israel destroy the pagan altars, close all the demonic portals and annihilate the people who opened them.

Doorways also exist in the spiritual realm and are not limited to a physical location. If you own a Bible, then you possess a spiritual doorway. The Word of God is a safe passageway into the realm of heaven. It is a gateway into the spiritual realm. The Word is our barometer, and plumb line to all that is spiritual. It authenticates and legitimizes subjective spiritual experiences. It is not only profitable as a source of wisdom and understanding, it is life giving, revelation releasing, vision enabling and faith producing. Scripture is a launchpad into the spiritual dimension. It is inspired by Holy Spirit who invites us to enter into the text and become a part of the narrative.[26] No other book in the entire world is like it. Through the Word of God, we can access the spiritual and heavenly realms.

You may have heard or used the phrase 'There is an open heaven in this place.' This occurs as a direct result of the saints entering into worship or intercessory prayer. It is common for intercessors to experience travel in the spirit to other locations on the earth.[27] Our activity opens the heavens to permit angelic and heavenly visitations and sometimes the manifestation of God's presence. This is becoming a regular occurrence in these days. Worship and prayer can open portals and enable us to be transported to other places.

Revelation and vision are key doorways that provide stepping stones into the realm of visitation. Visions, dreams and prophecy all serve as gateways into the spiritual dimension by which we can enter into the heavenly realm and engage the revelation and interact with it. We enter the gateway by faith. Our imagination becomes the viewing screen that God uses.[28] We go through the doorway of revelation in the spirit. It is an entry point into heaven. Once this portal is opened, we can go back and revisit the vision and pass through the doorway whenever we choose.

The *Secret Place*

The most significant doorway or portal in my personal spiritual life is the *secret place*. During His teaching on the mountainside, Jesus said:

When you pray, you shall not be like the hypocrites. For they love to pray standing in the synagogues and on the corners of the streets, that they may be seen by men. Assuredly, I say unto you, they have their reward. But you, when you pray, go into your room and when you have shut your door **pray to the Father who is in the secret place;** *and your* **Father who sees in secret** *will reward you openly.* (Matthew 6:5–6, NKJV) (Emphasis mine)

It is no coincidence that immediately following Jesus' command to go into the *secret place,* He instructs us *what* to pray once we are there. Our first request should be, *"Our Father in heaven, Hallowed be Your name, Your kingdom come, Your will be done on earth as it is in heaven."* (Matthew 6:9–10, NKJV)

The connection between the *secret place* and accessing heaven is obvious. The *secret place* is a portal into the heavenlies. When we close the physical door to the world and seek the presence of God, the intimacy we share with God opens the portal into the heavenlies. Jesus guarantees it! There is a portal inside the *secret place.* This intimate, private encounter with the living God enables us to access heaven.

Pneumanaut Boldness

Scripture says, *"Therefore, brethren, having* **boldness** *to enter the Holiest by the blood of Jesus, by a new and living way which He consecrated for us,* **through the veil, that is His flesh,** *and having a High Priest over the house of God,* **let us draw near** *with a true heart in full assurance of faith, having our hearts sprinkled from an evil conscience and our bodies washed with pure water."* (Hebrews 10:19–22, NKJV) (Emphasis mine)

Jesus made it possible. He is the gateway. How else can we activate God's will unless we can access heaven to see, hear and discern His strategies, designs and ways, and bring them back to earth? As in heaven, so on earth! That's what Jesus did for us at the crucifixion. He opened the portal into God's presence. In these last days, we need to avail ourselves to things that only exist in the heavenly realms. If we go there, we can bring them back with us. We need to be UPGRADED!

Created to be a Pneumanaut

"But wait a minute," you say, "this sounds too mystical and other worldly to me. Shouldn't we just be winning souls to Christ? Let's not get distracted from the primary mission."

My answer is, "Yes and no!"

The Samaritan women at the well in John chapter four had no message to give until she *first* spent intimate time with Jesus. Then she had something to say to the entire town that followed her back to meet Him. *Evangelism follows intimacy with*

God. It does not precede it. If we don't spend time with Jesus, we have no message to deliver.

This is our indictment. We need to overcome 'group think' that tells us that we are earth bound until the rapture or resurrection of the Church. We have believed a lie that engaging the heavens was for a select few and is not for modern-day saints. We have been held hostage by the general acceptance of non-spiritual Christianity. We have succumbed to brain freeze because we have sucked on the Icey Freeze of a lifeless doctrine and religious rubrics. It took a Martin Luther to explode us from it in the past. What will it take today?

Dr. Michael Heiser, in his revolutionary book *The Unseen Realm,* accurately describes our problem. "We've been trained to think that the history of Christianity is the true context of the Bible... There is a pervasive tendency in the believing Church to filter the Bible through creeds, confessions, and denominational preferences. We've been desensitized to the vitality and theological importance of the unseen world... We assume that a lot of things in the Bible are too odd or peripheral to matter."[29]

We are guilty of trying to sow new clothe onto old garments. We have been drinking the old wine for so long that the wineskin has gotten brittle. It cannot contain new revelation. Our clothing symbolizes our identity, and the wineskin represents our worldview or paradigm. Who are we? We are not just people who profess to be followers of Christ; we are spiritual pneumanauts. We must embrace a new identity. We are made to engage the heavens! Furthermore, our old concepts of the Church must be put away. We need a new wineskin—one that embraces the fact we are spiritual beings who have a soul and live in a body. We are designed for the spiritual realm. We are in this world but not of it. "The reality of the Kingdom of Heaven is what the Church is missing, and it's what I have been missing."[30]

You may read your Bible and cherish every word. You may know and experience the presence of God through prayer and worship. The power, gifts and fruits of Holy Spirit are manifested in your life. Prophecies, visions and dreams have encouraged and guided you. You may have even experienced the reality of angels, demons and heavenly beings. But you may be unaware that these experiences are the entranceways into the spiritual realm. These occurrences and encounters are doorways that open up possibilities. They are portals into the spiritual and heavenly realms. God wants you and me to know that heaven is accessible now.

God had to change my belief system and theology before I could begin my journey into the heavenly realms. It took twenty years, countless *kairos* encounters and required spirit-filled and anointed mentors who could teach me the basics. During the process, I obtained a new identity and a whole new worldview.

Now the time had finally arrived, and my conversation with Jay confirmed it. I had unfinished business that demanded my return in the spirit to the vision of Frontier Town. I wasn't sure what would happen when I got there. I just knew that when I did, I was going to be UPGRADED! I intentionally set aside the entire next day to revisit my vision and prepare myself in the spirit to return to Frontier Town and enter the Unfinished House.

CHAPTER 3

Revisiting the Vision

Returning to Frontier Town

The moment had arrived. I trembled with anticipation as I entered my *secret place* to keep my appointment with the Lord. I knew that in order to possess my future, I had to revisit my past. The way forward was backward.

The sacred silence of the room enfolded me like angel's wings. I sensed His presence and divine protection. I sat down in my prayer chair and opened my old journal to the recorded vision I had scribed twenty years ago. The green, hardbound volume was sacred to me. It was more than a journal; it was my spiritual biography. The secrets and spiritual lessons it revealed had supernaturally transformed my life. The anticipation of what lay ahead gripped me. I knew the next few hours in His presence would be extremely important.

"This is a divine appointment, Lord," I prayed. "Open my spiritual eyes again to the reality and significance of this prophetic vision. I have come in obedience to Your prompting to revisit Frontier Town. I ask that You grant me permission this time to enter the Unfinished House."

The Setting

The sequestered location where the vision of Frontier Town occurred was quaint. I was staying at a rustic unpainted clapboard cabin in the Connecticut woods. Only the basic necessities were provided. Even the drinking water had to be carried in. It was owned by some dear friends who had dedicated it to be used for prayer retreats. They called it the *Postinia,* which is a Russian word for 'house of prayer.' A large deck overlooked the blazing multicolored fall foliage reflecting in the placid lake below it. Just the memory of the smells, sights and sounds drew me back into the past, or was it the future? I was about to find out.[31]

Join me now on this journey back to a day in the distant past when God revealed to me a supernatural place called Frontier Town. The vision was preceded by the spontaneous arrival of a flock of Canada geese, obviously sent by the Lord. It had all happened so unexpectedly.

Journal date: 08/30/2000

"Lord, it's so good to be here alone in Your ..." Before I could finish the sentence, a muted, honking sound skipped across the water, shattering the silence. I scanned the distant shore of the lake trying to locate the disturbance. It grew steadily louder until finally a flock of Canada geese came into view, soaring over the lake in V-formation like a squadron of bombers looking for a place to land. I watched in delight as they made several investigatory circles over the lake in front of the cabin as though they were waiting for permission to land from the control tower.

The formation banked toward me, flew overhead, and then circled back toward the opposite shoreline. They came in low, legs outstretched like landing gear, feathers set at full flaps, honking like the stall warning horn on a Cessna. Splashdown was awkward, noisy and beautiful. It made me think of what my flight instructor once told me after an unusually bad landing: "Any landing you walk away from is a good one."

The geese honked back and forth at one another like they were taking roll call, and then a calming silence returned to the woods.

"Lord," I prayed, "that's just how I feel. I've been so busy. Our arrival here at the Postinia was just like these geese. Splashdown was awkward, but I can already feel Your peace settling into my spirit. I dedicate these next few days to You, Jesus. I am here to walk with You like Enoch did. Open my spiritual eyes and ears. Speak to me, Lord. I'm listening."

In an instant, the vision of a western town appeared. I grabbed my journal and began to record the images as fast as I could draw and write. In a few minutes, I had filled several pages with drawings and notes.

"What is this place, Lord?" I asked.

"This is Frontier Town," He said. "In the coming days, I am going to bring you here in the spirit. There are many things I want to teach you. You will discover them in this supernatural place. This is where I train my spiritual pioneers to become end-time warriors."

"Just the thought of such a place makes me wonder if I am up to the challenge, Lord," I replied.

And so my training in the school for end-time warriors began in earnest. It would prove to be one of the most incredible spiritual adventures of my life. In the short period of three weeks, I recorded more than two hundred and fifty pages of revelation in my journal as Holy Spirit unfolded the mystery of Frontier Town.

Welcome to the West

The next day I returned to the cabin deck. In an instant, I was immersed in the Well of His Presence and the vision returned spontaneously.[32]

I found myself standing on an arid, open plain in the American West. In the distance I could see the rugged frontier town's main street. A raised wood-plank sidewalk stretched the entire length of the street in front of the typical stores, businesses and houses you would expect to find in such a place. What really confused me, though, was that the town was *brand new* and *freshly painted*. It, and I, seemed out of place chronologically. The scene strangely resembled a theatrical set specifically designed and constructed for a cowboy movie.

"I know I am in the twenty-first century, Lord," I said, intrigued by the enigma, "but Your choice of a frontier town is no coincidence. This is a place of exploration and challenge that pushes the limits of spiritual experience. I'm eager to learn the lessons of this newly built frontier town in the old west. I feel like a spiritual green beret."

The Stage is Set

The aroma of freshly cut pine filled the atmosphere like a lumberjack's cologne. *Must be a saw mill nearby,* I thought. Each house or shop on the single thoroughfare directly ahead was newly constructed, and most were made of clapboard.

The buildings on Main Street were joined together in a continuous progression by a wide, elevated boardwalk that stretched the length of the town. This walkway provided easy access to each structure. Wooden stairways of varying sizes led from the dirt street onto the decking in front of every doorway.

To my dismay, unlike yesterday, Main Street was now deserted. There were no identifying signs of life. No placards, advertising or billboards hung on the buildings. No rocking chairs or merchandise were positioned on the boardwalk. Horse tracks dotted the street, but not a single tether was provided. But the most surrealistic feature of Frontier Town piqued my curiosity: only one side of Main Street had buildings on it. The whole scene gave the impression that the town was a stage set for a drama whose scenes were yet to be acted out. The plot was just beginning.

"This is exactly how God speaks," I reasoned. Vision is the prophet's language, and story is the teacher's venue. A single street in the middle of a nowhere wilderness called Frontier Town—I couldn't wait to see what really took place here on Main Street.

A Close Up of Main Street

"You told me that You designed Frontier Town to train and equip your servants, Lord. Where are the people I saw yesterday?"

"I will introduce you to them at the appropriate time, son," He replied. "But first you must learn about Main Street. I have designed every structure here with a specific goal in mind. In the days to come, you will learn the purpose and function of each building. In the process you will meet your instructors and those who are in town for training."

We walked together up the deserted street in silence. Jesus paused momentarily in front of each of the buildings but offered no explanation for their purpose. I carefully noted the size and shape of each structure, sometimes venturing a guess at its intended use. Since there were no addresses, I assigned a number to each one for my convenience.

The Bunk House

The first building was small, one story with a flat roof sloping from front to back. A single door with two paned windows a few feet from either side of the entrance highlighted the otherwise non-descript front wall. A fresh coat of navy-like, grayish-blue paint gave the small wooden structure a crisp well-tended freshness. The white accent trim around the door, windows and corners of the structure added a homey touch.

The Saloon

The second structure was quite large—the tallest building on the street. It shared a common wall on its right with the first building but extended several stories above it. Its bright, soft-yellow paint gave a happy glow to Main Street. Shutter-like swinging doors hung in the otherwise open entrance. On either side of the doorway facing the boardwalk were two very large glass windows. White curtains covered them, hanging in large masculine pleats tied back on the sides with simple matching cord sashes. Someone had traced letters on the upper part of the windows in preparation to paint a sign on them permanently, but I could not determine what they spelled.

A large balcony jutted out above the boardwalk, providing a porch roof along the front. This balcony encircled the entire length and breadth of the second story. Several doors led from this walkway into private rooms. The third story was accented by paned windows on the front and side walls. The roof was similar to the first building, sloping from front to back and covered with black tar paper.

The Storage Shed

The third building was a real puzzlement. "I've never seen anything quite like this," I said to myself, wondering what its purpose was. "It's extremely low, not even one single story high, and it's constructed with tongue and groove planking. Looks to me like porch decking placed vertically. Sure would be hard to break into. The absence of windows really looks suspicious too. I wonder if some sort of secret activities take place inside."

The short access door was built like the walls and reached to within inches of the flat roof. It was fastened to a sturdy frame with strong triangular-shaped hinges and secured with a cylindrical combination lock that had three dials on it. The dials contained symbols instead of numbers, but the Lord moved on before I could examine them more closely.

Every time I glanced away and then looked back at this structure, its width and length appeared to increase slightly. It had a life-like, amorphous quality about it. *Could this be some sort of supernatural shed?* I thought. *You have to stoop just to get in the door, and you couldn't possibly stand up straight once inside. And why does its size change? It keeps morphing.*

The Silo

Mannor—one of the three angels accompanying us—intentionally brushed my arm as we approached the next building. He looked like he was going to explode if he didn't speak but restrained himself, not daring to divulge the purpose of the structure.

I wonder what that's all about. There must be something special about this particular building, I thought, stopping to study the mysterious circular edifice entirely covered with wooden shakes. *This is really quite exceptional. It seems peculiarly out of place. It looks like a silo.*

When I first saw this building from a good distance away, it appeared to be joined to the rest of Main Street, but now I could see that it stood separate and distinct from the other structures, except for a low passageway. A rectangular, windowless tunnel connected the vertical cylinder at its base to the rear of the previous shack, about thirty-five feet away. The only way into the silo was through the mysterious shed and the passageway connecting them.

A familiar longing unexpectedly coursed through my spirit. I sensed an overwhelming desire to get to the *secret place*. The Lord smiled and placed His hand on my shoulder. "Do you feel it, son?" He asked, confirming what I was sensing and pointing toward the silo.

The unusual building had a powerful allure. In the spirit I discerned it had windows, but I just couldn't see them. *I wonder if the windows are visible from inside the building but hidden to those who casually walk by*, I thought. *Like one-way glass—if you're inside, you can see out, but anyone outside can't see in.*

I had no sooner thought of the hidden windows, than the walls of the silo became transparent. I stared in astonishment. A stone well stood in the middle of the circular room. A lantern hung above it on the crossbeam, emitting a holy glow into its depths. A cloud of mist filled the room, and angelic beings stood guard around the well.

The revelation exploded within me. "The Well of His Presence!" I shouted. "It's the Well of His Presence!" That's why my spirit leapt within me. The well has an opening here in Frontier Town. That explains why Mannor brushed my arm; he knew about this.

Now it makes sense why this building is detached from the wooden sidewalk and separated from the other houses. There's no stairway from the street in front of it on the boardwalk either. Only those individuals who feel its pull and discern its significance will take time to investigate it. But if they do, they will discover its secret and gain access to the well.

I didn't want to go any further. "This building and the Well of His Presence can take me to a million undiscovered places in the spirit," I said, looking over at Mannor. "This is how I got here in the first place."

"But there is still a lot more to see on Main Street," Mannor encouraged. "We must move on."

The General Store

The next building had the look and feel of a typical western general store. Round wooden posts supported a porch roof that extended over the boardwalk. The stark-white building was accented with kelly-green latticed shutters. Through the front window, I could see shelves lining the walls that were well-stocked with provisions of every kind. A large piece of furniture stood in the center of the room, about the size of a china closet. It had small wooden openings on both sides.

"Post office boxes," I said, "apparently for distributing mail to the inhabitants of Frontier Town. But who are they? Sure would like to see the names on those compartments."

The Schoolhouse

Gillar, Mannor and Malchior, my angel companions, were eager to proceed. By now I was thoroughly immersed in the fascination of Frontier Town. A delightful white clapboard one- room schoolhouse sat adjacent to the store, set back from the wooden sidewalk and separated from the buildings on either side by a vibrant green lawn. The sight evoked visions of children at recess flying kites in a stiff western breeze off the prairie or romping to-and-fro in playful pursuit with their shirts hanging out and poplin dresses swirling about. But the schoolyard was empty now—no sounds of play anywhere.

The stalwart steeple towered overhead, its school bell glistening in the midday sun. Multicolored shafts of light reflected from the surface of the silver object with the brilliance of a faceted diamond. Squinting up into the light beams, I could tell the bell was inscribed with etched words, but I couldn't read them from this distance.

Black shutters hung permanently open at each window and were secured to the exterior walls of the schoolhouse. I peered into the screenless openings. "There's a refreshing clarity inside!" I exclaimed. "The interior of this school really has an atmosphere conducive to learning."

The Unfinished House

A typical two-story frame house, like you might find in any city, sat next to the schoolhouse. It had no porch and connected directly to the boardwalk. A center front door and lots of windows provided light for each room. It was rather plain and indistinct. I hadn't a clue to its purpose and function. It was partially painted a pilgrim kind of New England blue-gray to a height just above the first story. The abrupt jagged paint line circumnavigating the structure gave the impression that the builder ran out of paint in the middle of the job. Bare wooden walls were exposed the rest of the way up to the two-sided roof that sloped to a peak.

I was puzzled by its unfinished exterior, but I knew how wisely and carefully the Lord builds. Nothing is by accident or without purpose and function here in Frontier Town. "Time will reveal its enigmatic place in the scheme of things," I said.

The Koinonia Café

Turning to explore the next building on Main Street, I suddenly realized that my three angel companions, Gillar, Mannor and Malchior, were gone. The only trace left of their angelic presence was the outline of footprints in the dusty street. I figured they must have another important assignment to attend to.

"Just a few more buildings to see," Jesus said, redirecting my attention but offering no explanation to the whereabouts of our departed companions.

A cerulean-blue one-story rectangular building appeared next. Its full length stretched along the boardwalk. I immediately recognized it as a restaurant. White lace curtains hung from rods in the two generous windows on either side of the doorway. Through the spotless windowpanes, I could see a number of round tables inside covered with red and white checkered table clothes. Captain's chairs with red padded seat cushions encircled the tables. A counter ran the length of the back wall with tall stools randomly spaced along it for groups of customers. A bubbling five-gallon coffee urn sang a barely audible perking song in the far left corner.

I detected the smell of fresh bread baking. Apparently, the scintillating aroma came from the kitchen just beyond the back wall of the establishment. "That smells great," I said, sniffing the delightful scent and salivating with sudden hunger. Wisps of steamy white smoke puffed intermittently out of the partially open kitchen door just beyond the counter.

The Potter's Shop

We were now approaching the far end of Main Street. Only two more buildings remained. Just past the restaurant, an unpainted pine-board structure with a well-weathered look sat quite a ways back from the boardwalk. Smoke steadily rose skyward from a single stone chimney jutting at least eight feet above the roof's surface.

This must be the blacksmith's shop, I thought at first sight.

In a few more paces, I could see through the large, open barn-style doors. A white-hot oven glowed with super-heated brilliance. Huge leather bellows sat next to the fiery furnace.

"This isn't a blacksmith's shop; it's a pottery business!" I declared, as the shelves lining the right wall came into view. All kinds of pottery in various sizes, shapes, colors and phases of completion were stacked in random order along the dusty, bare, wood shelving.

Curious, I pondered. *Why would there be a pottery shop here in Frontier Town? I didn't see that many people yesterday. There doesn't seem to be enough inhabitants to warrant such a business?*

The Log Cabin

We finally arrived at the last building on Main Street at the far end of the boardwalk.

"This place has a distinct pioneering atmosphere to it," I said, glancing over at the Lord. "It's far more rustic than all the others."

"Look carefully," He replied, nodding in agreement.

Built of pine logs, the one story cabin perfectly exemplified the natural frontier look. The white barkless tree trunks with their knot blemishes glistened under a fresh coat of maple-syrup-colored lacquer that ran down into the caulking between the spans like drops of sticky honey.

To my fascination, the only readable words on the entire street were placarded on the cabin. They were printed at the top of a small wooden sign hung with a shoelace-size strip of leather on a single nail next to the door. There's no way I could have noticed the sign from a distance. Its color and leather cord blended right into the cabin wall. The sign read: "Arriving & Departing." The words appeared directly above their respective columns. The lower part of the sign was designed to accommodate removable letters and numbers that could be changed when necessary.

This must be a schedule of some kind, like a marquis or bulletin board, I thought. *Maybe this is a stagecoach stop. It's obviously some sort of staging area for the town.*

A Construction Site

The planked sidewalk ended abruptly at the end of the log cabin. Steps led down to a vacant lot where a pile of lumber lay on the ground in disarray like giant pick-up sticks dangling in different directions. Surveyor stakes were driven into the dry soil. A single line of string was stretched between the stakes.

"They must be getting ready to build," I said with delight. "Construction isn't finished here. New things are happening in Frontier Town. Soon the walls of a new structure will rise. I wonder what it will be."

Your Life Will Be Changed

"Now you have seen Main Street in its entirety," Jesus said. "In the days to come, you will visit each of these buildings. In the process your life will be changed! It is critical that you recognize this is no ordinary town. It is a supernatural place of preparation and equipping for everyone whom I've chosen and called to be an end-time warrior.

"Each building represents a unique encounter with My kingdom purposes. Only the committed and courageous can survive here. Some of those who have come did not stay. They retreated back into their complacency and chose to settle in a place of spiritual comfort and convenience. Do not follow their example. I will abundantly reward those who overcome.

"This place is as old as time itself but always new to those who arrive in each generation. Its function is clear: here is where I train and commission My warriors to possess their spiritual destiny. I will take back all that the enemy has stolen; all of creation is My possession. Ultimate victory is ensured. I have come 'to conquer, to love, and to redeem.' This is the battle cry of my servants. 'My kingdom will come! My will shall be accomplished on earth just as it is in heaven.'"

I pondered His words carefully: Every generation trained and commissioned... conquering warriors taking back what the devil has stolen... ultimate victory...

What will tomorrow bring? I wondered.

CHAPTER 4

The Pneumanaut's Guide

My second day in Frontier Town began at sunrise. I watched in worshipful silence as the beauty of God's creation unfolded above me. The western sky spread over the roofs of Main Street like a watercolor canvas under the masterful hand of the Almighty. The intensifying pastel brilliance poured through the dispersing clouds in a waterfall of orange and violet light heralding a new day of adventure in this supernatural training ground.

"Sunrise in Frontier Town sure does arrive with majestic grandeur," I said, starring at the thin wispy clouds slowly dissipating into translucent vapor like a curtain rising on a celestial stage. "What does God have in store today?" I wondered. I quickly realized the answer was on its way!

A Welcome Surprise
Toward the rising sun, beyond the street and houses in the far distance, just barely visible on the horizon, a small cloud of dust rose from the plain. It formed a narrow line tinting the distant skyscape brown.

"A stampede of horses or buffalo might raise such a cloud," I reasoned.

Closer and closer it came, like a wind-driven sandstorm, until finally a single horse became visible beneath the cloud. The regal white stallion galloped toward me with energized grace and authoritative freedom. His mane rippled in the air like roiling waves crashing onto the seashore. He breathed in a deep, long cadence. Heat from his nostrils produced intermittent puffs of condensation in the morning air. Saddled, but riderless, he came steadily on with determined vigor.

I was completely caught off guard. I stared at the approaching horse like someone who unsuspectingly walked into a room to discover a surprise birthday party. Sudden realization exploded within me. "This is the same white stallion that I saw in the *secret place* months ago on one of my first prophetic journeys,"[33] I said, realizing the significance of his arrival.

I remembered every detail of that experience with great delight. On that first encounter, we were galloping along an ocean beach in the brilliant sunshine. I will never forget the power and excitement I felt as the water sprayed around us in every direction. There was no saddle or reigns because Jesus was teaching me an important lesson. I needed to overcome my fear of not being in control. At the very beginning of my prophetic training in the Well of His Presence, He was teaching me the vital necessity of trusting Holy Spirit unquestioningly.

"This white horse represents My Spirit," Jesus told me then. His instructions alleviated my trepidation and gave me great assurance. "You must trust My Spirit to carry you where I want to take you. I desire to move you into deeper places and introduce you to My hidden secrets. Each day will bring a new environment and a new dimension of revelation. Let My Holy Spirit teach you. Allow him to lead you. He will move only by My permission. I will give him specific instructions concerning you."

The Wind of the Spirit

The tempo of hooves gradually slowed to a trot as the stallion approached. Whinnying in the dusty air, he sauntered up to my side and lowered his head, nudging my shoulder with an affectionate shove.

"Welcome," I said, respectfully stroking the side of his neck in one sweeping motion. "You run like the wind!"

Just touching his glistening white coat sent an overwhelming burst of awe and inspiration through me. "Who is this, Lord?" I asked.

His response came deep inside of me. "This is Spirit Wind! I have sent him to guide you through Frontier Town."

"Spirit Wind…" I paused. "Then that's what I'll call you," I said with heartfelt respect. "Lead the way, Spirit Wind!"

The aroma of genuine leather emanated from the new saddle. An intricately patterned border was masterfully carved into its outer edges. But what really caught my attention was the saddle horn. Made of rich, smooth, deep-brown leather, its hand-polished finish sparkled like the surface of a mirror. Its seams were stitched with silver thread.

I reached up to grab the horn with my left hand. Placing my left foot into the stirrup, I paused to affirm Spirit Wind's approval and then thrust my full weight onto his muscular frame. "It fits perfectly," I said, inching slightly toward the back of the saddle. With no more than the slightest pressure from my knees, Spirit Wind turned in a predetermined direction and headed toward Frontier Town.

Spirit-Led Vision

I had absolute confidence in the ability and wisdom of Spirit Wind. No longer detached beings, we became one entity moving gracefully ahead with unrestrained power and freedom. But if I tried to steer by gently tugging to either side of the horn, he would huff in a tone of resistance and continue on in the direction he was heading. *I shouldn't be surprised,* I thought. *He's obeying another Master.*

It still felt awkward without reigns, but I reminded myself, "I'm better off without them." I leaned forward, held onto the saddle horn with my left hand and reached my right arm toward Spirit Wind's muscular neck. I could feel the uncommon strength coursing through his veins. With the slightest pressure of my fingertips, his head bent slightly to the right as if he were saying, "Thank you, my friend." I realized in that instant that communication between us did not require words.

Expect the Unexpected

When we arrived at Main Street, I fully expected Spirit Wind to stop in front of the one-story first building at the head of the street. "Whoa…!" I shouted to no avail, as he galloped right past it without even hesitating. Everything within me wanted to stop him, but I remembered the Lord's words: "Trust My Spirit and do not try to control or guide him."

We charged up Main Street, leaving a cloud of yellow dust behind us. I could tell that Spirit Wind was enjoying this display of unbridled energy. We passed every building and only slowed to a trot when we came to the last structure on the street. Jesus stood in the road just beyond the boardwalk waiting for us. A brand new tethering post, which did not exist yesterday, stood firmly in place at the edge of the street. The single pole had an exquisite carving on top. It was a perfect replica of Spirit Wind.

The royal steed slowed to a walk and stopped in front of the tethering post. Jesus stroked his side and then whispered something in his ear. Spirit Wind stood perfectly still. *He will never move from this spot without a command from the Lord,* I thought.

When I dismounted onto the street, I was shocked to see that Jesus was wearing blue jeans.[34] He spoke in a hardworking tone like the foreman on a work site. It was immediately clear that He had planned our agenda for the day. He was all business.

There's much to learn and experience ahead, I thought. *I need to pay close attention.*

The End is the Beginning

Before I could ask, Jesus began to explain why we were positioned at *what I thought was the end* of Main Street. "Good Morning, son," He said. "We are starting at this construction site because this town is like no other you have ever seen. What seems like the beginning is really the end, and what appears to be the end is really the beginning. This is true in all of life. My ways are not your ways, and My thoughts are not your thoughts. Didn't I say that 'the last shall be first, and the first shall be last'? That's how it is here in Frontier Town. What appears obvious to human reasoning is not necessarily so in the spiritual realm."

Jesus' words penetrated my spirit. A scene from the Bible flashed into my thoughts. I could see the prophet Samuel standing in a field, talking with Jesse. Each of Jesse's sons was brought before the prophet to be considered as the one chosen by God to become Israel's king. From the eldest to the youngest, Samuel carefully sought God's will, his horn of anointing oil in readiness. None of Jesse's sons passed the test.

Finally, Samuel, unsettled in his spirit, asked if there were any sons remaining. Jesse replied, "Only David, *my youngest,* but surely he cannot be the one."

"Call him here!" Samuel retorted.

God chose David, the most unlikely son, to be king. Samuel poured the oil of anointing upon the young shepherd's head. This was the first of three times David would be identified by God's anointing as the chosen one.[35]

"The last shall be first," I affirmed.

Jesus' words brought me back to the moment. "You must be careful how you see things here in Frontier Town. I call women and men whom the world and the Church think are the least likely or qualified to be My spiritual pioneers. This is contradictory to the logic of men, but those who have prophetic discernment like Samuel, my prophet, understand that I do things differently.

Never Assume

"Your second lesson here in Frontier Town is *never assume you understand something.* Don't rely on your human knowledge, logic or the familiar, recognizable nature of things. My army of end-time warriors will not be chosen for their human abilities, status or past spiritual accomplishments. Those I am drawing by

My Spirit to Frontier Town will have a different set of qualifications. Promotion comes from Me. I raise up one and set down another. I choose whom I will. My training contradicts the world's standards. You will soon learn what I mean by this. Always remember, *things are not what they seem to be in Frontier town!"*

I'll catch up with you later

For the next three weeks, I hurried to my *secret place,* knowing I would continue the exploration in Frontier Town with Spirit Wind as my guide. Every day, God would reveal the significance and contents of each building. I was always surprised by what I discovered along the way. One of my greatest blessings occurred one day when I entered the Koinonia Café. A young man invited me to sit with him. Timothy, a fellow spiritual pioneer, introduced himself by saying he had been waiting for me. I was shocked to hear it. We shared precious conversation as we enjoyed our steaming hot mugs of coffee. From that moment on, Timothy and I became fast friends and were inseparable for the rest of our time in Frontier Town. We were traveling pioneers. I couldn't help but compare our relationship to that of Paul and Timothy. On what I didn't realize was my last day in Frontier Town, the two of us were busy forming an evangelistic posse among the many frequent visitors who were always coming to the Koinonia Café to enjoy the fellowship and share their experiences.

"Go, in Jesus' Name!" I said. "The harvest is waiting."

Groups of two or three banded together in agreement and left the Koinonia Café headed down the street toward the saloon.

"Come on, Tim," I said, "let's join the laborers."

We strolled out the door and turned toward the saloon at the far end of Main Street when I heard a familiar neighing. I spun around in delight; there stood Spirit Wind calmly waiting by the hitching post at the opposite end of the street. Gillar, Mannor and Malchior stood at ease beside him.

"Go ahead, Timothy," I encouraged. "I'll catch up with you later! If somehow we get separated, meet me tonight at the Bunk House."

"All right, partner," he said and sauntered off alone down the wood sidewalk whistling a happy tune of praise. My last view of Timothy was when he stopped abruptly on the deck in front of the half-painted Unfinished House next to the café. He suddenly turned, approached the door and vanished into the unknown interior. I was stricken with such disappointment that I ached inside. I so wanted to join him and enter the unfinished building. But it was not to be.

My departure time from Frontier Town had come. I was overwhelmed with gratitude, but a major disappointment remained. Why was I denied the opportunity to enter the Unfinished House along with Timothy? Would I ever know what undisclosed truth it concealed?

The rest of the page was empty.

***

I closed my journal and laid it on the lamp stand next to my chair. The long-lasting ache in the pit of my soul flickered to life again. "That was two decades ago, but it's more than just a memory, Lord. It's a reality," I said.

Reading my journal had provoked determination in my spirit. "There is more to be revealed, and it has to do with what lies hidden inside the Unfinished House," I affirmed. "It's the only building I haven't entered, even though I've tried. What does Timothy know that I don't? Could this be my appointed time? Will Holy Spirit grant me access? Frontier Town still exists twenty years later, and I am longing to complete my journey. I must enter the Unfinished House now, today. This time I hope I will not be denied."

Photo courtesy of Mandy Adendorff. Used with permission.

CHAPTER 5

Entering the Portal

"It is time!" I announced with an impulsive, sudden boldness. It was a declaration not a question. Something had shifted in my spirit. My pronouncement activated something in the unseen realm.

Returning to the Unfinished House

The transition was instantaneous. In the spirit, I found myself standing in Frontier Town in front of the Unfinished House.

"Every ending is a new beginning," I reminded myself. "And here in Frontier Town, every doorway is a new opportunity, a new dimension or revelation. Each doorway is a gateway into a different realm, each one a total surprise."

My hands trembled with eager anticipation. One major barrier stood before me: Spirit Wind. He stood at attention, diligently guarding the access to the half-finished house. Every fiber and muscle of his being was ready to spring into action. My heart sank. "Oh, no. Not again," I whispered, shivering with anxiety. He had always blocked my entrance in the past.

"Greetings, Spirit Wind." I said, mustering all the courage I could. "May I proceed?" I asked, searching his dark, mysterious eyes for any hint of approval.

I broke the determined conviction of his rigid stillness. Spirit Wind was faced with uncertainty. He looked at me and then turned to gaze into the distance, no doubt searching for direction from the Lord. He needed God's approval to allow me to enter the house. No immediate answer came. The process continued for several anxious minutes, and still Spirit Wind could not determine what to do. His uncertainty led me to a point of decision.

Qualifications

Suddenly, I was struck with a bold idea. "It's up to me!" I said. "It's up to me, Spirit Wind! I have to make the choice to enter. This door is unlike all of the others here in Frontier Town. It can be entered only by personal decision."

I spoke with confidence. "I choose to enter the door into the Unfinished House!"

The Lord spoke so powerfully that I heard His instructions. "It's okay now, Spirit Wind. He has met the qualifications required to enter this dimension of revelation."

"Lord," I asked. "What qualifications? Is that why I couldn't enter before? I wasn't qualified?"

"Yes. You were not prepared," He answered. "Don't you understand? You *are* the Unfinished House. You are a work in progress. If you had entered this stage of revelation to complete your journey prematurely, it could lead to confusion, deception and fear.

"There are four major qualifications. Each step is necessary. First, you must acknowledge that you are a work in progress and that you have not arrived at full maturity. Your life is an unfinished house! Second, you must desire and choose to enter into the heavenly realm. Then you must enter at the appointed time! You must come into the heavenlies on assignment with My approval and by My invitation. The final essential requirement is faith.

"I have tested you to discern if you are ready now. You are prepared. You have chosen to enter, and it is the appointed time for you to proceed. You have met all of these requirements. As with every step of your journey, you must proceed by faith. Only those who believe can enter into this dimension.

"It took ten years for you to complete the assignments I gave you as My scribe and to comprehend and understand the revelations you needed for this new mission. You have learned much in these ten years and have served me faithfully."

"But I still have so much more to learn, Lord," I admitted.

"And so you will. All that you have experienced and learned on your spiritual journey is a precursor to this moment. Every scroll you have written is preparatory revelation. It is written in the volumes of the scrolls and upon your heart, my son.

"It is your time to move beyond revelation to visitation. You have experienced this in the past in a limited way by angelic invitation and direction. When you proceed through the doorway of the Unfinished House, visitation will become your new normal. The Unfinished house is an entry point. You must prepare for the unexpected. But there is one more thing you will need."

"Lord, I humble myself before You," I prayed. "I feel like Isaiah.[36] I am mere flesh, a man of unclean lips. Without Your mercy and grace, I can do nothing. I say yes to Your assignment. Here I am; send me. I am sure I don't fully understand what You mean when You say visitation will become normal, but I know that understanding usually follows obedience. I trust you, Jesus, and I love You. Guide me and protect me on this new journey."

Silence wrapped Main Street like a blanket of new fallen snow. Nothing moved. My eyes were fixed on the beautiful white stallion keeping watch over me. We were the only two beings in town. Spirit Wind nodded his approval. I turned from the dusty street of Frontier Town and stepped up to the entrance of the Unfinished House. When I reached for the door, I hesitated. "Things are not what they seem to be in Frontier Town," I said to remind myself. "I must never assume anything here in the supernatural realm!"

Supercharged

"At long last, I am going to experience the unexpected just as He prophesied to me," I whispered.

My fingers encircled the gleaming brass doorknob. I shrieked instantly in distress. It was as hot as a blacksmith's poker. My entire body convulsed. The sudden scorching heat was unlike anything I ever experienced.

"I refuse to let go. No one could pry my hand from this door!" I groaned, gripping the knob more tightly. The heat slowly ascended up my arm and poured into my entire body. I felt like a vessel being filled with hot oil as the Spirit of God flooded into me. Heat radiated from the pores of my skin. My feet were on fire. The door appeared to be shimmering like a mirage in the desert heat. I held on, knowing that if I let go, I would fall backward onto the wooden deck and not be able to get up. Several moments passed before the heat began to dissipate.

"I'm so energized," I mumbled in shock. I wasn't recovering as much as I was soaking in a new awareness of His presence and power. "This must be what Jesus said I still lacked. I didn't realize how badly I needed to be refilled by Holy Spirit.[37]

All my senses are reinvigorated. My spiritual discernment is crystal clear. Now I'm truly ready to enter the Unfinished House."

The Unfinished House

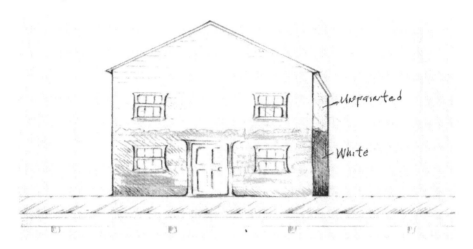

Into the Darkness

"Faith is essential," I remarked, as I cautiously pulled the door open and gazed inside. I was instantly dumbfounded by the total absence of light. I stared blindly into the fathomless blackness. "I can't see a thing," I confessed. "Why is this mysterious cloak of obscurity here?" My eyes struggled to adjust to the impenetrable darkness. It took several minutes before I could see a few inches inside the entrance.

"Wait a minute!" I said. "There's something down here just inside the door." I knelt to touch the surface, groping in the darkness like a blind man relying on touch and sound. What I thought was the floor, began to move slightly under my pressure, mimicking the motion of my hands. I traced the plank to its edge and discovered that heavy ropes supported the moveable floor. I stood and traced the hemp moorings back to the doorway. They were securely anchored to the inside walls on each side of the entry door. "Aha!" I uttered. "Mystery solved. This must be a suspension bridge leading into the abyss."

"Okay, now I feel like Indiana Jones," I said with a surge of adventure. "This looks dangerous. I've traversed bridges like this before that crossed over huge gorges and cascading rivers in the Mexican mountains, but I wouldn't dare attempt to traverse them in the dark. God knows how high this bridge is and where it leads." I said, dreading the thought. Then I realized, "That's right. He does know and He has always required me to trust Him. Why should I be fearful now? Besides, I don't have a choice; there's no other way in."

I mustered my courage. "We walk by faith and not by sight," I confessed, as I stepped onto the wooden planks and cautiously tested their strength. Confident they would hold me, I closed the door and the darkness immediately engulfed me like a smothering black vapor. I gripped the ropes on either side to steady myself and waited to gain my equilibrium.

"I must move forward. I can't allow the darkness to defeat me. It's one step at a time," I said.

The moment I began to walk forward, the bridge began to sway back and forth. With each proceeding step, the wooden planks creaked and bowed under the pressure of my weight. I descended deeper into the darkness with barely enough perception for me to see a few feet ahead of me. "What have I gotten myself into," I whispered.

"What was that?" I shouted in alarm, as shivers ran up and down my spine. Several spiritual beings flashed by on each side of the bridge, like bioluminescent deep-sea creatures. One had a ghostly filmy-white appearance. It was quite old and had such a mean expression that it reminded me of the Ghost of Christmas past in Dickens' *Christmas Carol*. It wore a dark green robe and scowled with such despicable nastiness. My discernment was quickened. Now I could sense other spiritual beings moving in the darkness, and even see those that were close to the bridge. Some seemed peaceful and friendly while others had a wandering-homeless painfulness about them.

It took me several minutes to arrive at the lowest point of the bridge where the swaying was most pronounced. I was beginning to feel seasick. I fought the vertigo and stared down at my feet to steady myself. The scratchy hemp rope handrails felt like rough sandpaper as I tightened my grip and began to ascend toward the other side of whatever I was passing through or over.

Finally, a pinpoint of light appeared in the distance. "Thank you, Lord. Now I have two points of reference:" I gasped in relief, "the closed door behind me and the mysterious light ahead. I must keep my focus centered on the light."

The Hall of Pillars

I lost all sense of time as I continued my resolute journey through the darkness. At last I approached the far end of the bridge. The light shone brighter now, and I could see that it was illuminating an unusually shaped column rising up out of the darkness. The end of the suspension bridge was anchored to it. The pillar was about twelve feet in diameter and the top was perfectly flat and smooth. This mysterious platform was so pure it looked like polished milk-white marble. I couldn't see a single blemish. It was not a perfect circle. The circumference of the column looked like the folds of a sculpted theater curtain. The formed pillar was made from some sort of metallic gray ore or stone that I had never seen before. It looked like super-heated lava was extruded from the darkness below to form curtain folds running along its entire length.

An unusual light illuminated the top of the column like a subdued streetlamp operating at a reduced voltage. I stepped onto the top surface of the pillar. "I'm glad to be off the bridge," I said in relief. "But now what am I going to do? I'm on the top of a pillar in this ether of darkness. Let me get my bearings."

Suddenly I realized there were other columns ahead of me in every direction. They were all the same height but were different distances apart from one another. There was no obvious pattern to their location, but I knew they must have been purposely placed at each position.

"This is a Hall of Pillars," I gasped, gazing out into the velvet black distance. This is like staring into the desert night sky at the stars," I recalled, thinking about the night sky at Wadi Rum in Jordan. It was so beautiful. Each pillar sparkled like a homing beacon.

The Pneumanaut Dimension

"But it's far beyond my natural ability to explore them. It's impossible to reach these pillars," I confessed in total frustration. "Why would you do this to me, Lord? You know I'm an explorer at heart. Even the closest pillar is way too far to jump to, and the last thing I want to do is fall into the darkness below. That's not an option."

Then I realized this was a test. "There's no way forward to the next pillar and the next one after that, except to fly in the spirit. God wants me to transition into the pneumanaut dimension."

My rational mind refused this option. I had to ignore its warning.

"Here goes!" I said, in faith, but mostly wondering if this would work. "This is how Peter must have felt when he stepped out of the boat to come to Jesus, walking on the water."[38] I stepped off the platform with my right foot, desperately searching for a place to put it down in empty space. It was an eye-opening, sense-defying, illogical moment. I didn't sink. I put both feet into the nothingness. I was suspended in midair. "This is like swimming in the Dead Sea," I reflected, recalling my attempts to submerge in the mineral rich water. No matter how hard you try, you can't swim underwater. You just learn to float and steer with your hands. I had just taken my first baby step into the dimension of traveling in the spirit. I left the surface of the pillar, stepped off the platform by faith, and began to walk on air.

Once I started, I immediately realized I could easily travel in the spirit to each pillar. It was effortless and delightful, more spirit than body. I felt at home in this supernatural environment. In fact, I realized I was created with this ability and had finally discovered that God made me this way. "I am not a body having a spiritual experience. I am a spirit being, with a soul, having a bodily experience. My spirit-man is longing to be free to function at its fullest potential."

I chose the nearest pillar and headed toward it. All I had to do was look in the direction I wanted to go and lean that way. The farther I leaned, the faster I traveled. When I approached the platform on the top of the pillar, an angel was waiting for my arrival.

The moment I came to rest on the surface, I was instantly enshrouded in a supernatural light from above. I was standing in a spotlight shining down directly over my head. It glowed all around me and infused me. It was not blinding but rather purifying and comforting.

I spoke humbly to the angel, "Please help me. What is your name?"

"My name is Matradus," he replied.

"Where am I and why are you here?"

"I am assigned to guard this pillar," he responded. "You are in the Hall of Pillars that leads into the heavenly realms. Each pillar is an entry point into the realms of the kingdom. Some are doorways; others are gateways. When you stand on the pillars, light enshrouds you. You travel in the light that encompasses you. The pillars are ladders, gateways or portals into the heavenly domain. The columns are made of a rare and priceless heavenly metal, like platinum, slate-gray in color and perfectly flat on top. When this metal is polished, it has a pure, shiny white marble appearance.

"You must intentionally choose to enter the doorway and cross the bridge between the rational world and the spiritual dimension to reach the launching pillar into the Hall of Pillars. To reach the rest of the pillars, you must learn to travel in the spirit. It is truly a leap of faith.

"Pneumanauts as well as angels travel in the spirit through air and space to access the pillars. Then we travel at light speed through the beam that floods the passageways. The pillars are doorways, or departure and arrival points like Jacob's ladder, that enable angels and people to ascend and descend into the third heaven. Remember, Jacob's ladder had a stone base. These pillars are solidly established on stone foundations. This is how you enter into the realms of the kingdom."

Angel Sentries

"Matradus, are there angels assigned to each pillar?"

"Yes," he replied. "Each pillar leads into a different part of the heavenly realm. Once you become aware of these spirit-ways and travel through them, you will become familiar with many pillar-gateways and can choose the one you need to take you to where you must go on your assignments or explorations.

"Many experienced saints access the heavenlies, and more are coming each day. We are so excited and often discuss among our councils what the meaning of this is and consider the season we are in. The heavenlies are full of activity more so than ever before. Great warfare may be coming."

"How are the angels selected for this duty?" I asked.

"This is a sacred assignment and very important. We are stationed at the pillars to keep the passageways open and to protect and instruct those who come to us.

"We must be on guard at all times. The enemy's hosts will do anything to disrupt travel in the spirit realm. Even now we are being watched. But they fear the light. We are safe in the light and as we travel in it. Only when we are drawn away from the pathways of light does the enemy have access to us and can torment and confuse us."

The Hall of Pillars

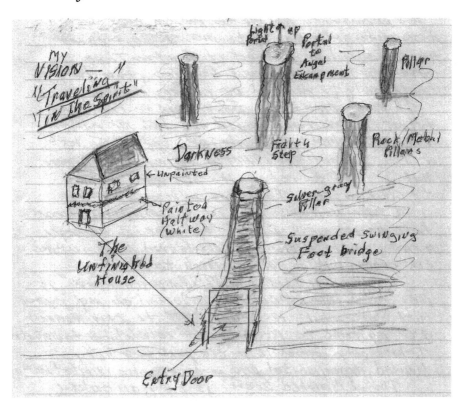

The Golden Scroll of a King's Scribe

"What is your name, warrior?" Matradus asked.

"My name is Dale."

"You are mighty and discerning. What you carry is a golden scroll. You must be a scribe in the King's service."

I was shocked by his observation. I stared in amazement at the gold cylinder in my right hand. When I entered the Unfinished House, I wasn't carrying anything. Now, somehow, unexplainably, I was carrying a royal object so priceless and beautiful that it took my breath away.

"This *is* a golden scroll," I gasped in surprise. "It's unlike anything I have ever seen before. It's so smooth. Look, Matradus. It contains silver streaks flowing along the entire length of its glistening body. They look like currents of energy. The swooshes are flowing in beautiful patterns. I think it must be able to communicate in a heavenly language. It's sonic silver and gold. I can hear it humming! It's singing. It must be some sort of a musical composition. I think I'm causing it to sing," I whispered.

Each end of the scroll was adorned with pure gold-braided rope encircling the openings. I moved the scroll back and forth and, unexpectedly, light emanated from each end of the cylinder. Depending on how I moved it, the light changed from royal blue to flaming red.

"I have seen other sacred scrolls but none like this. Whatever your assignment is, it must be of great importance," Matradus responded, staring in wonder at the object.

I trembled at his words. "Matradus, this is the fourth golden scroll from the Well of His Presence. The King told me in a dream four scrolls would be given to me. Each was an assignment that would release prophetic revelation to His people.

"I am a prophetic scribe in the service of my Lord Jesus Christ! I love His presence. I love Him with all my heart and soul and mind and strength. But I feel so inadequate. All I can do is humble myself before Him. I think I know now what this fourth assignment is. I am to record the way into the heavenly realms of His Kingdom for others to follow."

"The King chooses only those who make themselves available," Matradus said with reassuring confidence. "You are a surrendered one. Wherever your assignment takes you, write what you see and hear. The journey of the fourth scroll began the moment you stepped through the doorway into the Unfinished House. This royal scroll is the journal of your journey into the heavenly realms. It is a guide for others who have the faith, passion and courage to follow."

I knew this was a supernatural pen just like the other scrolls I had received from the angels to record my journeys into the *secret place,* the Hidden Kingdom and Frontier Town. When I write with it, the words are recorded supernaturally on the inside surface. I could see just inside the top end that something was already recorded on the royal scroll.

The scroll grew dim and the scene faded away. My time in the *secret place* was concluded for now. I was disappointed. Everything in me wanted to continue, but I knew I really needed some time to process this amazing journey.

The Royal Golden Scroll

CHAPTER 6

The Chariot Corps

Power Surges

My life is filled with excitement and a constant flow of revelation, I thought. *From now on, every day when I enter the **secret place**, I will be transported in the spirit into the Hall of Pillars. I am moving between earth and heaven in the spirit.*

The days flashed by with new adventures and explorations. But what was occurring in the spiritual realm was having a direct impact on my physical body. Something was transpiring deep within me with increasing intensity, and it was affecting me physically. I couldn't control the involuntary jerking that made my entire body convulse like I was having a severe dose of hiccups. One night in bed, I kept jerking and grunting. The entire bed was vibrating. I had to find out what was going on.

"Lord, why is this happening to me?" I asked.

He answered, "These are power surges. You are plugged directly into Me, and the power of My Spirit is surging inside you. If I allowed My full power to completely flow in and through you, your physical body wouldn't be able to handle it.

"Remember how I hid Moses in the cleft of a rock and covered his eyes and face so he wouldn't die?[39] Exposure to My full glory and the Spirit of Might (and power) is more than the flesh can contain all at once. Remember what you observed in the Holy Place of My tabernacle when the ministering priest touched the Lampstand?[40] That was my power surging through his body."

"Now I understand, Abba." I said. "I have the distinct sense that when Your power is manifesting in me that if I laid hands on others, they would be healed. I want Your power to flow through me to bless others in healing and impartation. Teach me how to receive and release Your power. I am willing to be Your servant in the dimension of power ministry. I want Your glory to shine and cover the earth, Lord Jesus. I surrender to You. Accomplish this in and through me."

"Son, do you realize that My power is accompanied by cleansing and sanctifying holy fire? It is a burning and branding consuming fire. It is the fire of My passion and love for you and all mankind.

"My fire is a fire of love—white-hot consuming love. Those who draw near to My love will embrace and encounter My holy fire! Do not fear! Know that your soul and body will experience the fire of My love as I embrace you Spirit to spirit.

"I love you, My son!"

"Abba, the fire of Your love is cleansing me. My body bears witness to Your passion for me. Now I understand why I am physically affected. May my love for You always be white-hot and passionate."

My question was answered. Just like an electrical system can experience power surges during certain times, our bodies also experience power surges that are an indication of an increase in the anointing of His presence. Our bodies may respond involuntarily in numerous ways. We cannot control them.

I want to grow in spiritual ability so that I have no resistance to Holy Spirit coming from my flesh or my soul (mind, will and emotion). I desire to be a pipeline that allows the Spirit of Might (and power) to move through me unhindered. I pray also that I will not let my love for Him grow cold.

My prayer for you, as you read this, is that you will passionately pursue His presence, stay white hot and let His Spirit of Might (power and love) flow through you.

God Speed
The anointing of the Lord was so strong that each day brought an increasing sense of anticipation of further revelation. I would enter my *secret place* and eagerly open my journal and pray: "Lord, I'm here to continue my journey into the heavenly realms. Lead me, Holy Spirit."

Each time, I would put into practice the principle of revisiting the vision: I retraced each phase of my pathway in the spirit. I re-engaged the vision, passing through the doorway of the Unfinished House, across the suspension bridge into the Hall of Pillars, taking my first step of faith, learning how to travel in the spirit, and arriving at the portal into the heavenly realm.

This particular day, just as I expected, Matradus was still on duty. It was time for me to proceed farther into the realm of the heavenly Kingdom.

"Matradus, where does the passageway from this pillar lead?" I asked. "I would like to go there if I may."

"I am here to guard this entrance from those who might come seeking to do evil and harm, but you are a sent one. You have been called, and you have chosen to risk all and enter the heavenly realms. You have arrived at this specific pillar first because the Lord has ordained it. This is His plan and purpose for your assignment. He has chosen this portal first."

Matradus stood to his full height, stretching upward into the light above us. The light increased in intensity.

"Go!" he said with angelic authority. "This passageway leads to one of the encampments of the angel armies. On future journeys, you may access this pillar if you like, but I suspect that the King will have other plans for you.

"God speed!" he said. And those were the last words I heard.

You may be wondering, 'What is it like to travel at light speed?' It is instantaneous. You are here one moment and there the next. I felt no sensation of speed, acceleration or slowing down. It's faster than the blink of an eye. It was very different than flying in the spirit when I left the first pillar at the end of the bridge and stepped into empty space. Then, I had to exercise my will and command my spirit to proceed. Not so in the passageways of light. I guess 'time-warp' is best to describe what I experienced. All I know is that one second I was with Matradus, and the next I was standing before a massive military encampment of legions of angels.

The Chariot Corps

As far as I could see in every direction, there were angelic beings—thousands upon thousands. Perfection characterized their encampment. Military order pervaded the atmosphere. Beautiful, gracefully waving flags were visible above each section of the camp identifying every distinct military unit.

I moved forward, instantly aware of an unusual texture beneath me. "What is this?" I said. "I'm walking on some sort of invisible surface, but I am not sure what it is; it's not earthy, more like congealed air but firm."

A rustling sound drew my attention away from the surface. The angels were standing to acknowledge my presence. Their focus was on the golden scroll in my hand. They talked among themselves as I passed by. A few sped off, racing ahead of me in the direction I was heading.

In a few moments, an angel approached directly toward me from a distance. He stopped about seven feet in front of me. I was overwhelmed, frozen in my tracks and surrounded by angelic warriors. I couldn't breathe.

He spoke with great authority. "Welcome to the King's chariot corps, Warrior. We have been waiting many days, as you number them on earth, for your arrival.

"The scroll you carry identifies you here in the heavenly realm. You must keep it visible everywhere that you go. It will give you passage to the most secret hidden places in the kingdom realms. It is not only your authentic key of entry, but also it is an instrument of worship and a powerful weapon to be used in the second heaven when necessary."

"I... I am honor... honored to be he...here in... in ah... your en...campment, sir," I replied, stuttering with nervous apprehension.

"No, we are the ones who are honored. You serve our Master, Jesus, in ways that we cannot. What is your name, Scribe?" he asked with a tone of respect.

"I am Dale, one who walks with the Lord. I am Jesus' friend."

"So it is for certain, Dale. You carry His mark of approval. I am the archangel..." Then he went silent. He would not give me his name.

"Follow me, Warrior, and write what you see and hear," the commanding general ordered.

He turned to his left and led me with a measured step into the ranks of angels. As we passed the sons of God, they stood at attention. I could see their hearts beating as if their bodies were transparent. Their spirit was aflame with devotion to the King. Their absolute love for God was palpable.

They definitely love God beyond my understanding, I thought, *but in a different way than I do. It's obvious they honor their commanding general. The expressions of affection and love on their faces at the sight of the commanding general are obvious. Their service is motivated by supernatural love and it pervades their being. Strength and love exude from them. I suppose that even in the heat of battle, with absolute anger at evil, their motivation remains their love for God, man, and one another.*

This amazing assembly of God's angelic army was comprised of the most awesome loving beings whose fierce warrior instincts and training were molded by the Creator out of His heart of love. They clearly reflected His passion for life and hatred of evil. Their love is truly supernatural.

The Hanger

"Where are we going, General?" I asked with child-like excitement.

"I want to show you the hanger first," he replied. "We're almost there."

Several buildings appeared ahead of us. The one on the left was massive. No exterior markings identified it. It had no windows and to my puzzlement I could not see any doors. The building was suspended in air. Its sides were hinged at the top, much like a garage door, except that the entire side was hinged along its length enabling the whole side to open. Numerous angels were circling the building or standing on guard nearby.

"What are the angels doing," I asked.

"They are on sentry duty, Warrior. We must guard this facility at all times. Our enemies would love to get their hands on what's inside."

As we approached the building, I searched for an entry door, but there was none. Suddenly, the entire terminal area burst into life. The facility blazed with brilliant powerful lights. It was lit up like an airport. Runway lights led from the facility in multiple directions.

"What is this place?" I asked in amazement.

"This is the chariot terminal," the commanding general replied. As he spoke, a partition began to open in the wall. Apparently, the entire wall was constructed in sections that could be opened individually, or in combinations, but the entire side of the building could be raised at once if needed. I was stunned by what I was seeing. I stared in incredulity. Rows of gleaming chariots were perfectly positioned with military exactitude in parallel rows. The first thing I noticed was the many different types of chariots. I always thought 'a chariot is a chariot' with one single purpose and design.

"This is incredible," I said in awe.

"Yes, it is. I know what you thought about chariots. All who come here have the same misconception. Notice the different types," the commanding general commented.

Kingdom Express

"The chariots are designed for different categories of service. Some are shuttles used for pick up and transfer. Elijah rode in number 80," he pointed to a specific one. "I drove that one on the day I was assigned to pick him up and transport him to the heavenly realm.

"Over here," he pointed as we walked through the hanger, "are chariots designed for long distances between galaxies and into the outer reaches."

Outer reaches? I pondered. *I wonder what he means by that?*

We walked through the massive supernatural hanger as the commanding general continued to explain the purpose of each type of vehicle. "This section houses chariots designed just for transferring things from heaven's storehouses to earth. Requisitions are received in the Throne room and recorded by the scribes. Then they are sent here when necessary to be filled and delivered to earth." He pointed to the back of the section. "Those chariots are able to carry enormous loads, but notice the smaller ones with less capacity. These are used for smaller items when requested."

As he spoke, the words of Apostle Paul scrolled though my mind. *"Rejoice in the Lord always: and again, I say, Rejoice. Let your moderation be known unto all men. The Lord is at hand. Be careful for nothing; but in everything by prayer and supplication with thanksgiving let your requests be made known unto God. And the peace of God, which passes all understanding, shall keep your hearts and minds through Christ Jesus."* (Philippians 4:4–6) (Emphasis mine)

It is true that our heavenly Father knows our needs and hears our prayers. This place certainly validates Paul's instructions. God honors our prayers and fills our petitions when we send the requisition form to the Throne room.

Battle Chariots

Proceeding toward the far end of the hanger, we stepped across a line on the floor. It divided the next section from the rest of the chariots behind us. "This is where we keep the battle chariots," the commanding general explained. "From this point to the far end of the facility, you will find the vehicles that are designed for warfare. Their appearance strikes fear into the hearts of the enemy."

I was struck by the sheer number of chariots—beyond imagination. This must be how Elisha's servant felt when the prophet prayed: *"Open his eyes, Lord, that he may see." Then the Lord opened the servant's eyes, and he looked and saw the hills full of horses and chariots of fire all around Elisha.*[41]

"May I look more closely at this one, sir?" I asked.

"Yes," he said, "and be sure to record what you see."

The overall appearance of the supernatural vehicle was like a royal chariot fit for a king's army. The carriage glistened like polished silver, reflecting the ambient light in all directions, but on closer examination the metal was white. Its composition was unknown to me. Precious gemstones of all kinds and sizes were embedded into the surface. Some were smooth and polished while others were multifaceted. A pattern of particularly large gems appeared to be positioned intentionally to serve as location identifiers, much like the wing and tail lights of our aircraft on earth. Other supersized gemstones protruded from the surface like antennas. I presumed they were for navigational purposes.

The commanding general observed my fascination. "We can track each chariot," he explained. "We know exactly where each one is and can coordinate attacks and strategies from command central."

I ran my hand across the bejeweled, polished metal surface of the chariot, admiring its character. To my complete surprise, sparks flew off the surface behind my hand motion. The entire chassis was energized and charged with power. I felt like I was painting the chariot with sparks. My hand acted like a brush on canvas, and the paint was sparkling gold.

Wheels Within the Wheel

My curiosity was rampant. I could wait no longer. I just had to examine the chariot wheel. I knelt beside the left wheel. "Oh, my goodness!" I exclaimed in utter admiration. I began to write as fast as I could with the supernatural pen.

"Just look at it, but don't touch it!" the commanding general warned. "Absorb its construction and design into your spirit."

I examined the wheel carefully. This was no ordinary wheel. It was symbolic in every detail. All of its many components were powerful dynamos of supernatural power.

"Now that you have seen it up close, let me explain how it functions. Come here!" he ordered.

A nearby angel attending the commanding general handed him a large coiled document. He unfastened the clasp and unrolled it to its full length, about four feet long and three feet wide. The document was not made of paper. Some type of electronic surface or screen covered its interior surface. The wheel was depicted in detail on the page. The commanding general waved his hand over the drawing and suddenly a full hologram of the object appeared, floating above it. This was not simply an engineer's rendering of the chariot wheel on a flat piece of paper. The screen could project the drawing as a four-dimensional image.

The commanding general reached out and touched the multicolored image floating in the air. To my surprise, he could manipulate it and move it in tact through the air. He lifted the wheel from above the scroll and turned to me, holding it in his hands. "Let me explain how this wheel functions," he said.

I lifted my pen, so I could capture every word as he explained how this incredible device worked. I quickly sketched the wheel with its component parts, carefully recording the nomenclature. I scribed his words as he spoke.

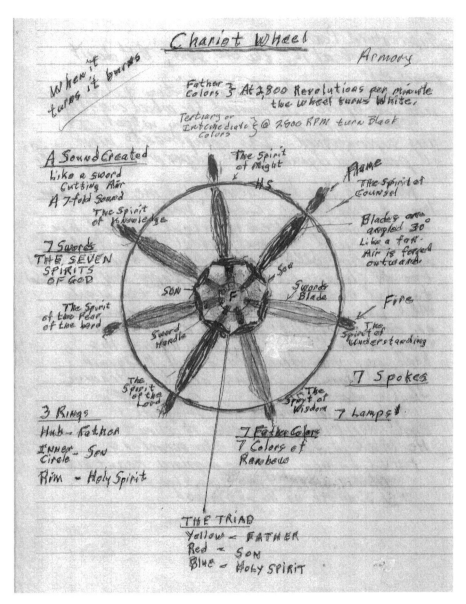

"Do you see this?" he asked as he pointed to the inner rim of the wheel at the junction where the blades joined the handle. His finger traced the handle from that juncture to the hub. "While it appears there is a separation between the hub and the inner rim, it is all one integral piece. In fact, the entire wheel is one solid piece, not separate pieces joined together to form a whole. It is like the Lampstand in the Tabernacle. It is not made of separate parts; it is a seamless whole that is formed, not constructed. It conveys singularity and oneness.

"This entire wheel is forged in the fire of exploding stars," he explained with admiration. "These are the celestial furnaces and forges of the creation processes. It is shaped in intense heat and the malleable metal is aligned supernaturally. It is indestructible!

"Notice the nomenclature on this whole-o-gram."

"Well, *whole-o-gram* is a term I never heard before," I frowned. "But it certainly is appropriate. I'll add it to my vocabulary of new words. It would be inappropriate to say 'parts' because the wheel is a whole. There are no parts."

"That's correct," the commanding general continued. He pointed to each location, explaining its symbolism and function. "The center or hub is the preeminence of Father from which all other aspects radiate. The inner circle is the Son, Jesus. The outer rim is Holy Spirit. Notice the seven swords that join the rims to the hub. These swords radiate like spokes from the hub in seven directions. The heavens are not defined or identified by coordinates like those used on earth. You are only familiar with four directions of navigation, but in the heavenly realms there are seven directions. The navigational-heptad will be revealed to you at a future time.

"The seven swords are the seven spirits of God. Each blade is different and has a specific and unique character and purpose. The swords are living spirits. They are revealed as the seven lamps on the Lampstand. Each sword tip is a holy fire, a burning torch of intense flame.

"Notice that each sword is a different color. They represent the color palette, or Father-Colors, derived from the Trinity-Colors. These Trinity-Colors blend to produce all the other colors. When the wheel turns, the number of colors produced is infinitesimal. Some have been seen only in the heavenly realm, but these colors will be released in the final battle. Each color has an ability to create certain atmospheres and release energy into the environment.

"When the wheel turns, it burns!" the commanding general warned, flinching slightly. "Fire comes forth from the tips of the blades on the outer rim. This is the seven-fold fire that cannot be extinguished. The rotating sword blades cut through the air in both directions. The sound they produce is like rumbling, vibrating thunder. They slice the atmosphere with such ferocity that the sound causes terror in the hearts of the enemy."

The commanding general paused and then looked me straight in the eyes: "Now you understand why I cannot allow you to touch these wheels. They are sacred and sanctified by the Master Designer. They are holy and must be treated with the utmost respect. They are the supernatural source of the chariots' power. They are a dynamo of holy energy that mirrors and releases the power of God. You wouldn't dare touch the Ark of the Covenant lest you die. Neither do you touch the chariot wheels."

The commanding general placed his hands on opposite sides of the circumference of the outer rim, 180 degrees apart. With the wheel between his outstretched arms, he pressed his hands toward each other, squeezing the whole-o-gram. The image yielded to the pressure and diminished in size until his hands touched. The image shrunk and disappeared into thin air and was gone.

"Now that you have had a tour of the hanger and examined the chariots closely, we need to press on. You have much more to see here in our encampment," the commanding general said with a determined tone.

Obviously, he has orders for my time here in the encampment and is following the agenda carefully, I thought.

CHAPTER 7

The Horses of Heaven

"Where are we going next, commanding general?" I said, eagerly.

"We will proceed to the stable," he directed. "These majestic creatures are regarded highly among heaven's mighty warriors."

My heart leapt. "Of course!" I replied. "Where there are chariots there must be horses nearby."

I followed closely behind the commanding general as we exited the terminal at the back corner of the war chariot section on the opposite end from which we had entered. I was absolutely delighted. It was snowing!

A narrow roadway provided a path to our left. It led downhill, and we started walking toward a bend to the right at the bottom of the gentle slope. The surface of the road was constructed of ancient cobblestones and made me think of the many roads in Pittsburgh that I loved to drive on as a teenager. The rumbling sound they produced when the tires traversed them was so much a part of my childhood. But this road had a very special quality.

"There's glittering, sparkling gold dust in the joints of the roadbed," I said in awe. "This is a holy pathway. This place has such a wondrous ambiance. It's so peaceful and silent. It's like Christmas here." I fully expected a reindeer to suddenly come charging around the bend.

"This is wonderland, sir. I feel like I'm inside a snow globe. This is a fitting approach to the stable here in the heavenly realm. After all, it was the chosen birthplace on earth for our infant King."

"You're right. This is a holy pathway," the commanding general said emphatically as we turned the corner.

The path led straight forward at a considerable distance to another curve, this time to the left. I was so intrigued by the cobblestones and gold dust. "Commanding general, what are these stones made of?" I asked, bending down to touch the surface.

He turned back toward me and responded: "These are earthen stones from the great quarry of the east. They have been brought here to keep the horses familiar with earth terrain. We use this type of surface to train the young. The gold is a reminder that they are the royal steeds chosen and bestowed with honor by the King. They must always serve with humility, dignity and reverence for the Lord. Their fearless strength is His to command."

The Royal Stables

We continued forward and the moment we cleared the turn, a massive stable came into view. "These are the Royal Stables," the commanding general said with a tone of admiration. "Here is where the horses that guide the chariots are housed."

As we approached the stable, I was surprised by its similarity to the finest stables on earth. But this stable was a one-of-a-kind; it had a sacredness about it. Clearly, this was no ordinary barn. The frame structure was completely white with a dark green roof. The corners and window trim were painted a rich balsam green. A regal sign made from a single wood beam hung above the barn-like front door. The expertly inscribed letters were a royal blue trimmed in pure gold. At the very center of each letter ran a thin red line, like pin-striping, that highlighted the words, THE ROYAL STABLES.

An expertly carved emblem hung on the wall directly above the center of the sign. It depicted a cross, encircled by a king's crown. The cross was solid red. The crown was gold.

The Sign

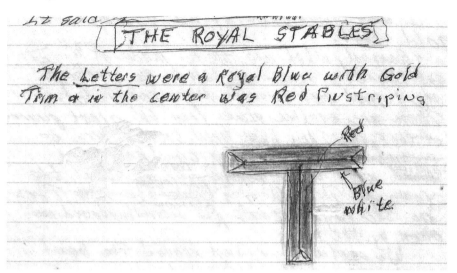

It said

THE ROYAL STABLES

The letters were a Royal Blue with Gold Trim & in the center was Red Pinstriping

Red
Blue
white

The Royal Stables and Symbol

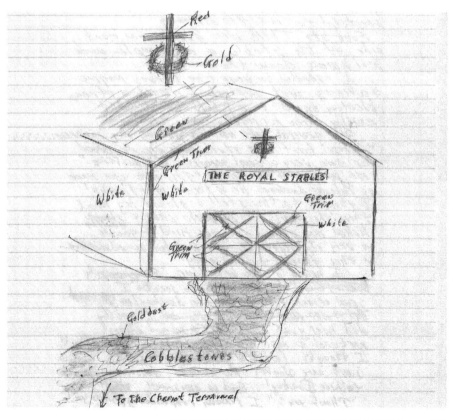

Red
Gold
Green
Green Trim
White
White
THE ROYAL STABLES
Green Trim
White
Green Trim
Gold dust
Cobblestones
To The Chariot Terminal

The angel guards slid the door open, and we entered the stable's inviting ambiance. I couldn't detect a light source, but there was a warm golden-honey glow throughout the entire stable. Horses' stalls ran along each side of the stable against the outer walls, stretching far into the distance. A wide-open center passageway provided ample room for ease of movement, grooming, tack and other necessary equipment. I expected to hear horses neighing and whinnying, but to my total dismay, instead I heard a strange bleating sound to my left and then almost in response, another from my right.

A Place of Honor

The commanding general was anticipating my consternation. "These first two stalls are reserved for two very special servants of the King," he explained, pointing to the left. "This one you know as Balaam's donkey.[42] His name is, *Ra'ah Dabar.* He is the *'one who sees and speaks.'*"

I stepped over to the stall and placed my hand through the rails. Ra'ah came and licked my palm. He was kind and gentle and very sensitive, certainly underserving of a horrific flailing by his undiscerning rider. His dark eyes were perceptive, no doubt seeing beyond the natural realm. I gazed in admiration at this amazing creature who became God's sentinel and mouthpiece.

When I finally turned away from his stall, I heard a voice behind me: "You are one who sees too."

I spun around and stared in shock at the donkey. "I really did hear you, Ra'ah!" I said, or asked, I wasn't certain which. *This all seems very natural to me. Here I am talking to a donkey,* I thought. *What a moment! And not just any donkey—an anointed, spirit-discerning, talking donkey!*

"God, You are awesome. Thank You so much," I finally responded in delight.

"God bless You!" I declared, watching the sparkle in this beloved creature's eyes.

"He has," Ra'ah replied.

I turned toward the stall on the opposite side of the stable. It was well supplied with fresh straw and had a wonderful fresh harvest aroma. Another donkey of medium proportion with a fine smooth gray coat of hair stood in the far corner. It was clear to me that he wasn't looking for attention. His head remained bowed as I approached the stall gate. I immediately sensed the humility of this amazing animal. His large dark eyes mirrored the sorrow of a thousand tears. He stood humbly before me.

"Who is this?" I whispered, fixing my focus on this meek beast of burden. "He is so precious. He exudes humility and glory."

"This is the colt that Jesus rode into Jerusalem," the commanding general explained. "His name is *Tapeinos*.[43] He carried the glory of God on his back and could hardly stand under the holy weight of his burden."

I crumpled to my knees, and huge tears tumbled down my cheeks. "Come here, lowly one. Let me touch you. You carried my Lord."

He walked slowly toward me with his head bowed. I extended my hand and stroked softly and gently along his forehead and down his neck. His strength was evident in every muscle and fiber of his body. No one would dare to push this donkey around. And yet he was the epitome of humility. It was his nature. He had been transformed. There was no rebellion or stubbornness left in him. For a few hours, in the middle of the crowded city of Jerusalem, this very creature became the Throne of the King of kings and Lord of lords. Total submission was his demeanor and glory.

I would have stayed in this spot for hours, but I could tell the commanding general was getting restless. Just as I was about to stand up, he spoke. "Someone here wants to greet you. He is waiting eagerly farther ahead in the stable."

I rose and walked alongside the commanding general deeper into the stable. The atmosphere was pristine, and the air was prairie fresh and mountain cool, the perfect temperature. The smell was intoxicating. If you love horses, animals and farms, you would want to bottle this fragrance. It was a perfect blend of leather, unvarnished wood, and fresh mown hay, with a hint of musk!

Each stall housed a single horse. There were many different breeds: strong and powerful workhorses, palominos, stallions, mares and ponies, Clydesdales, Arabians. The variety was all-inclusive. It was an equine display of God's creative genius and man's cooperation. I took special notice as we passed an entire section identified as, 'The King's Steeds.' A distinct anointing and holy presence set this section of the stable apart from the others by its regal atmosphere.

We had walked for about five minutes and covered a considerable distance. There seemed to be no end to the enormous facility. We passed several wings of the building leading off to the right and left at ninety-degree angles. Each of these corridors was filled with additional stalls on either side, just like the central corridor of the stable.

A Wonderful Reunion

As we passed the second intersection of adjoining wings, I heard a familiar sound about fifty yards ahead. A horse was whinnying and kicking the stall with its hooves. I quickened my pace and then began to run, charging ahead of the commanding general.

"Can it be? Spirit Wind!" I shouted with delight.

Before I could reach the stall, he thrust his head over the gate and looked in my direction. We were two best friends who hadn't touched each other since Frontier Town, finally reunited. I ran to him and threw my arms around his powerful neck and refused to let go of my grip. He responded by nodding his head in pleasure. Finally, after a massive hug, I withdrew my arms and stroked his flowing white mane with my fingers like a comb.

"Oh, Spirit Wind! How excited I am to see you again."

He lifted his head high in the air. I think he was introducing me to the other nearby residents of the King's stables.

The commanding general unlatched the gate, and Spirit Wind strode out and stood at his full stature.

"You are just the same," I said. "Just as beautiful, powerful, and anointed as I remember."

He pranced around me in circles, his tail slicing the air. His hooves pounded the soil and made the ground tremble.

"I wonder where you have been since we parted?" I asked. I knew I would not receive an answer, but I also comprehended that he had led many more spiritual pioneers into Frontier Town.

Spirit Wind slowed to a gradual stop beside me and nudged my arm in a playful way.

"I wish I could stay with you for a while," I said, stroking his side. "Maybe even go for a ride through the heavenly realms. But I am on the King's assignment. I must continue on."

He lowered his head in disappointment.

The commanding general spoke: "You may ride back to the entrance of the stable on Spirit Wind. I will meet you there." Then he vanished from sight.

Spirit Wind bowed, making it easier for me to mount. I settled comfortably. He whinnied and stood tall on his hind legs then took off in the wrong direction toward the far end of the stable. We galloped along the corroder like competitors in the Kentucky Derby. The stalls, flashing by, looked like the blurred view of scenery from the window of a speeding auto. In no time, we reached the end of the stable and Spirit Wind passed right through the wall carrying me along with him. We rose above the stable and turned back toward the entrance.

What an amazing view. I could see the entire angel encampment spread out before me. Its dimensions were massive. Order and perfection reigned. I spotted the location where I had entered the encampment and could easily trace my path through the troops to the chariot terminal and along the cobblestone road to the

Royal Stables. It was familiar territory to me now. Spirit Wind gracefully glided to a perfect landing in front of the stable doors where the commanding general was waiting. I dismounted and couldn't help noticing the smile on his face.

"Did you enjoy the ride?" he asked.

"Yes, sir!" I replied. "It was jubilant."

I turned to say goodbye to Spirit Wind, but he had already left. "A goodbye would not be appropriate," I realized. "We will meet again."

The vision of the archangel ended like someone had pushed the pause button.

My journey into the heavenly realms as the King's scribe is just beginning, I thought. *Today's revelation is a taste of what is to come. I wonder what tomorrow will bring?*

CHAPTER 8

The Armory

"Being a pneumanaut requires a different approach to reality," I said as I drove toward the church were the international prayer meeting would soon begin. The sanctuary will be filled with devoted intercessors and prayer warriors. International pastors and leaders will join us via the internet. The flags of their nations will surround us as visual symbols of those we are praying for. But this morning I was having difficulty keeping that focus. I felt the prompting of Holy Spirit to leave my physical environment and return to the heavenly realm.

"Physically, I am here at Heritage Fellowship in Jefferson City, Tennessee, but in the spirit, I am drawn toward the angel encampment in the heavenly realms," I said as I pulled into the parking lot. "Even though my earthly duties continue at their usual pace, it's impossible for me to function with total attention. This must be similar to the situation that John experienced on the Lord's day on the isle of Patmos. He was on earth and in heaven at the same time.[44] Today is no anomaly. That's for sure. It's Saturday morning, the sabbath day, and just like John I'm on earth and in heaven."

The moment I entered the auditorium I was surrounded by intercessors. The incense of their prayers had opened a portal into the heavenlies. I quickly took a seat and slid down onto the floor, pushing the chairs away to make room for my journal, Bible and computer. All around me, the saints were enjoining the mandate of Joel 2:28, but I was physically sprawled on the carpet. But in the spirit, the royal scroll was in my hand, and I was standing beside the commanding general in front of the Royal Stables.

The commanding general gave the order: "End time warrior, you have visited the chariot terminal and the King's Royal Stables. You have one more place to visit before you must leave the encampment and depart for another distant area of the heavenly realms. I will take you to the armory now. "Follow me!" he ordered.

Fiery Light Swords

In a matter of minutes, we were standing before a massive dome-shaped building that glistened like solid ice. The structure was made of crystalline, diamond-clear stones that were transparent halfway into their interior and then became opaque on the far surface. Lightening-like flashes of light rumbled and surged through the stones, triggering lasers that discharged from the surface and then shot into space in specific directions. They were apparently aimed intentionally. It looked like some sort of energy or power generator. The lasers fired at both intermittent and sequential moments. These supercharged power surges fired above the encampment and traveled out into the heavenlies. They carried such power that their penetration through any substance would be instantaneous. Watching this incredible display made me think of what Jesus said: "Everything will be tested by fire. Only that which is of God will remain and last."[45]

"These are the fiery light-swords of God,"[46] the commanding general explained. "They pierce the heavens and the hearts of men. No one can stand or defend against their power. These swords have eyes that see in the spirit realm. They carry the words of the Lord. The swords are formed in the Throne room. They are created when the King speaks. They are formed by His words. They are eternal and will never cease to exist. They are all-knowing. The utterances of the Lord are kept here in the armory and dispatched when and to where they are intended. They travel at light speed to individuals or nations, to slaves or kings. Nothing or no one can prevent or weaken their power."

My thoughts raced through the Scriptures. *"He sent His word and healed us."*[47] *"The word is like a two-edged sword dividing asunder between joints and marrow, soul and spirit."*[48] My entire body trembled. "This is fearful!" I said, my voice quivering. "The power of His Word strikes the fear of God in my heart and yet I am not afraid. I am strengthened."

"Yes," the commanding general responded. "His Word carries His essence. It is life and light. It cuts and opens and heals. It never ceases. The lasers are word-swords. Some carry prophecy or messages. Others are for healing or cutting away chaff.

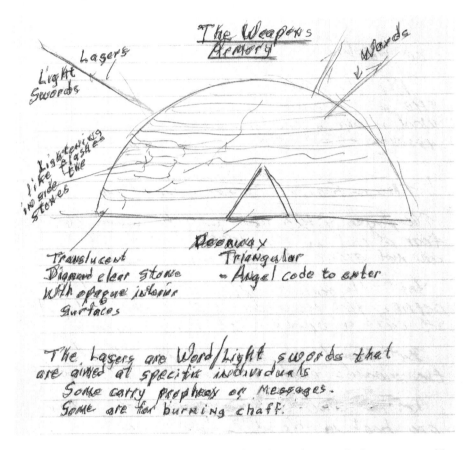

The Weapons Armory

Lagers

Light Swords

Wards

Lightening like flashes inside the stones

Translucent Diamond clear stone with opaque interior surfaces

Doorway Triangular - Angel code to enter

The Lagers are Word/Light swords that are aimed at specific individuals
Some carry prophecy or Messages.
Some are for burning chaff.

"But, Commanding General," I asked, "what about the swords that are carried by the angelic hosts? What purpose do they serve?"

"Come this way, Warrior. Their swords are stored inside the armory."

The Royal Scroll is a Sword

The commanding general spoke in some sort of angelic language. He uttered a verbal entry code. The armory lit up like a globe of intense light, then a triangular door opened in front of us. The instant I stepped through the entrance my pen began to vibrate. It was so strong that my arm began to shake. The scroll resonated with such power that a war song began to emanate from it. It became so hot that it glowed white. It was welded to my hand. It possessed a life of its own.

The commanding general observed and nodded: "This scroll was formed by the Master. All the scrolls issued to the royal scribes are made in the Throne room. They are spoken into existence by the King and designed for each scribe's assignment.[49] He sends them here to the chariot corps to await their dispatch to earth. God is at work preparing the scribes to receive them. When they are ready, mature enough, and equipped for their assignment, the angel couriers deliver a specific scroll to the scribe chosen to use it. It is their commission from the King. The scroll carries an anointing to release revelation. It is a supernatural pen, a container of documentation, knowledge and wisdom.

"The scroll you carry is extraordinary. It came to us with special instructions. It is an empowered pen. This scroll is charged with a specific authority to release heavenly revelation, strategies and peace. It carries the King's symbol and authority."

The scroll pulsed in my hand like a beating heart and then gradually the heat dissipated.

"It is the prophetic Word of the Lord that you are holding," the commanding general explained. "It is alive and powerful. It is a weapon beyond limit and sharper than any edge known to man. It cannot be imitated or duplicated." He spoke as one who understood authority. He touched his left shoulder with his right hand three times as he spoke. It was a salute to the Word.

"He is WORD!

"He is WORD!

"He is WORD!

"His Word creates. It gives life! It is all-powerful. No one dare question His Word. All the heavenly hosts, all the angelic army, cherubim and seraphim bow at His Word. His Word is our command."

"We love His Word just as much as you do, Commanding General, if not more," I responded, "but I am not sure you can love it as we do. We love His voice. His Word is food to our soul and spirit. He is the Word become flesh. Without the Word we are forever lost and in darkness. His Word is light shining in the darkness. He is the Word become flesh! Because of His Word, we have life. *In Him we live and move and have our being.*"[50]

Angelic Weaponry

"Look around you, Warrior Scribe, and see what this armory contains."

I turned completely around taking in the massive 360-degree enclosure from floor to ceiling. The walls were stockpiled with some recognizable weapons with familiar shapes. Others were totally unfamiliar to me. Bows and arrows were kept in one section. There were many different designs. They all had unusual colored bow strings that motivated me to think it was some otherworldly substance with great tensile strength and flexibility. I noticed a particularly interesting bow that was exquisite.

"Commanding General," I asked, "I have never seen such a design. How does it work?"

"Notice the tips are curved outward from the plane of the bow," he answered. "This enables it to be strung on the outside of the frame. Let me explain."

Arrows were stored in holders next to this bow. He lifted one: "Do you see this symbol? These are made for this specific weapon," he explained, running his hand along the shaft. "They can fly around the corners of solid objects and hit their targets. We call them 'spirit arrows.'"

Next to the bows were shelves of printed manuals for each type of weapon in the armory. Designs and nomenclature pamphlets and instructions on how to use the weapons and maintain them were divided into separate sections on the shelves. I chose a single volume and withdrew it from the stack. This manual contained an array of various weapons. I opened the book in the center. To my amazement the chapter was titled, "The Strategy and Use of Sound, Thunder and Light in Spiritual Warfare."

The commanding general said, "The power to release sound, thunder and light are assigned to the host's officers for strategic purposes."

I walked forward to another section containing slings.

"These are not ordinary slings," the commanding general explained. "They are used to propel hailstones and are weather related. In trained hands, they can sling a projectile great distances with amazing accuracy."

I turned from the circular wall of the armory to explore the center of the dome. An enormous collection of swords was positioned in the heart of the facility. Directly above them, suspended in midair, a flaming sword dwarfed the rest by its size and power. Its iridescent blade shone like polished silver. It flashed without moving. The hilt was embellished with exquisite jewels and at the very tip of the blade was a diamond point.

"This blade is made of a single diamond-like material. It is one of the hardest and sharpest materials in all of creation," the commanding general said. "This weapon surpasses all the other sabers. It is known as 'the Sword of the Lord.' All the other swords in the armory are fashioned in its likeness, but they are made of different metals for different types of combat. They are also called the Swords of the Lord to acknowledge the King and are to be used only for His purposes and glory. These swords are available to both armies: the angels and the saints. Every angel or human who wields these swords does so with the King's anointing and authority. The Lord is mighty in battle, and we fight with His weaponry. *The weapons of our warfare are mighty, to the pulling down of strongholds.*[51]

Scenes of Gideon's valiant small army, reduced from thousands to three hundred, flashed into my imagination. *"The Sword of the Lord and Gideon,"*[52] they shouted, striking fear into the hearts of the enemy. They were using supernatural weapons!

"May I touch the sword?" I asked.

"You already have!" he replied. "You have engaged the enemy, and he has fled on numerous occasions. Do you recall the moments when demons fled at the mention of Jesus by your command? When you wield the Sword of the Lord, you are affirming your identity in Christ, and your authority and anointed leadership result in the absolute submission and surrender of the enemy. Strongholds are destroyed! Lives are set free from bondage, possession, and harassment."

I knew the commanding general's words were true. I recalled moments in ministry of demanding demons to depart and speaking with authority into situations in churches and even nations using the Sword of the Lord.

I noticed an unusual object lying at the base of this section. "What is this?" I asked filled with curiosity.

"This is Moses' rod," he said, picking it up with great respect. "It was placed here in the armory to remind us that the King can use the natural realm just as we angels use the heavenly realm to form weapons of mass destruction that can even command the elements and they will obey. Never doubt that God can use what is in your hand for His purposes."

The Assembly of the Swords

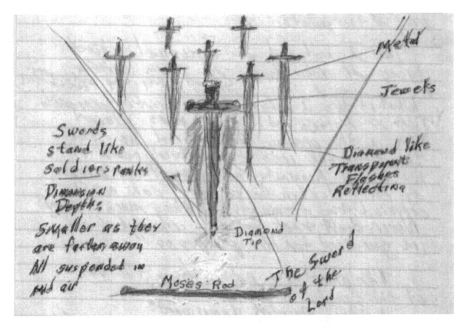

He placed the rod back at the base of the swords and then pointed downward. "You haven't noticed the floor yet. Look beneath your feet!"

The Angelic Wardrobe

I gasped in surprise. The floor I was standing on was made of an unusual amber-colored, semi-transparent material comparable to resin. Beneath me were all kinds of armor: shields, belts, armbands, leg and shoulder protective gear, footwear and helmets. All the habiliments and accoutrements needed for the chariot corps were stockpiled and ready for distribution. The array of combat clothing and armor were not traditional, even though some items had a Romanesque appearance. Every item was expertly designed and crafted for supernatural use. It occurred to me that getting sliced by an angel's sword may do more damage than just physical.

One section of this basement warehouse was devoted to clothing. Garments of all shapes and sizes were hung on clothing racks much like what you might see in a huge clothing store or costume department on a movie set. These were earth clothes of all different styles and were culturally specific.

The commanding general noticed my fascination. "These clothing items are available for earth assignments," he explained. "We must occasionally reveal our presence when we encounter humans. It's possible for us to blend in with the people and the culture where we are serving the saints. We are so good at disguise that people are unaware they are entertaining angels.[53] We often work in disguise and can draw our needed costumes from this inventory."

The commanding general paused. I sensed that he wanted to go into more detail and cite examples of angels working undercover in disguise. I couldn't help thinking about how angels appeared to Abraham on their way to Sodom and Gomorrah. They ate with him and talked with him. If it were not for Abraham's spiritual discernment, they would have been mistaken for a band of traveling nomads who stopped by the encampment to say hello.[54] We could easily mistake an angel for just another person. We need to be consistent with our kindness to strangers. You never know!

The commanding general's pause was intentional. He abruptly changed the subject. "You must go now, Warrior. Your time here in the chariot corps encampment is over. You may return in the future. You are always welcome here. For now, your tour in the encampment is over, but your journey has just begun. You are blessed and chosen.

"You are dismissed!" he said.

"Yes, sir!" I responded with respect, knowing that the archangel's authority came from the King who requires and deserves obedience and complete honor. I reached forth to shake his hand, but instead of responding in kind, he stepped toward me and in an unexpected and unmilitary fashion, he hugged me with such strength that the air burst from my lungs.

"We are here to minister to you. We are always nearby. Go in peace, Warrior, in the name of the King and for His glory!

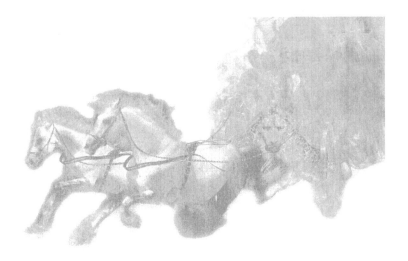

CHAPTER 9

Searching for the Right Portal

My departure from the chariot corps encampment was instantaneous. A portal opened right in front of me and in a flash I sped from the armory, descending at light speed back to the Hall of Pillars. To my surprise, I landed on a very different pillar than the one from which I had entered the encampment. It was larger than the first, which was nowhere in sight now. There were no guideposts or markers to identify my location. The pillars were much farther apart now, and they all stood under light tunnels, which were whirling like tornadoes or vortices of power.

The whirlwind of light above me diminished, and I was now able to see my immediate surroundings. To my left, a massive angel was standing guard. He spoke with certitude as if he expected my arrival.

"Welcome, Royal Scribe. You have arrived at my station. I guard this entrance to the encampment of the hosts. There are thousands of encampments and legions of angels here in the heavenly realm. Guards are stationed at each entry."

"Thank you for the welcome, Kaleb," I said and shook my head in disbelief at what I had just uttered.

"That's all right, Seer. You discerned my name in the spirit. I am Kaleb," he said. "I am the one who 'endures.' You can stay here for only a few moments. I have received orders that you must proceed quickly to the Library of Heaven. You may take a moment to rest in the spirit. I encourage you to look carefully at the royal scroll you carry. There are important markings on it now that you must remember."

"Yes, I should do as you say," I replied. "So much has transpired in such a short time."

I sat down on the white surface of the column and drew the scroll up to my eyes to peer inside. A chariot wheel was inscribed at the top of the inner surface of the scroll. *It's a perfect replica, identical to the one I saw in the hanger, and next to it is the emblem of the Royal Stables. I will never forget my exhilarating ride on Spirit Wind,* I thought.

Kaleb nodded as if he were discerning my thoughts but kept silent.

Reading around the cylinder in a counterclockwise direction, an engraving of the Sword of the Lord appeared. It contained a glistening miniature diamond just like the actual sword in the armory. Just by looking in the scroll and focusing on a specific icon, I could return in the spirit to its location in the realm of the kingdom. The scroll was a pathway or portal into the heavenlies. A spiritual map of my journey so far.

The heavenly realm is so vast, I pondered. *This scroll is more than simply a travel journal leading through the heavenlies. It is a passport that grants access, so I may fulfill the King's assignment as His prophetic scribe. It's a supernatural key that opens doorways.*

Real or Imagined? Yes!

What lies ahead of me? I can only imagine. But wait a minute," I realized. *"Isn't that how I got here in the first place? After all, God did tell me that my imagination is the page He writes on.*[55] *A pneumanaut cannot travel in the spirit without the faculty of Holy Spirit's anointed revelation flowing through his or her sanctified imagination.*

I'm not sure how long I sat on the pillar, meditating on the supernatural journey I had embarked upon in the heavenly realms. One thing was obvious to me. Like a perfect equation, each piece of my life fit together and led logically to the next step. It was all beginning to make perfect sense in my heart and mind. I saw the big picture of God's plan for me.

(As you're reading this, you may be wondering, 'Is this heavenly journey real or pure imagination?' The most accurate answer I can give is, Yes! It is real and it is comprehended in the human spirit as the King reveals His realm through the eyes of my sanctified imagination. I am a seer in the Spirit. Prophecy is seen and the voice of the Lord discerned through visual stimulation in the realm of the spirit. In the spirit I can fly!"[56] Please refer to my book, *The Imagination Master.*[57])

The Big Picture

This journey began when, out of desperation, I sought the Lord in the solitude of my own *secret place* on January 1, 2000. My prayer was a gut-wrenching cry for help. I knew that the thing I needed most in my life was intimacy with God. I prayed, "Lord, I want to be like Enoch. I want to walk with You and be Your friend." My transparent plea for love and intimacy with God turned out to be so deeply profound that I had no idea in that moment of its consequence or where its fulfillment would take me.

My intimate fellowship with Jesus began that day in the *secret place*. After months of sweet fellowship and life-changing revelation, He spoke to me one day: "Everything I have shown you so far, I want you to write in a book. Most of it is for my people." The resulting book, *The Secret Place: Passionately Pursuing God's Presence,* quickly became a best seller. Thousands of saints were hungry for deeper intimacy with God just like me.

Jesus continued. "What I have revealed to you so far is preparation, so I can now reveal My Kingdom to you," He explained. For the next year, he revealed the dimensions and nature of His Kingdom through visions and dreams. Our discussions, as we walked together in the Well of His Presence, were all recorded in my journal and became the basis of the second book, *The Hidden Kingdom: Journey into the Heart of God.*[58]

After the revelation concerning God's Kingdom, a drastic transition took place. In a matter of twenty minutes, the Lord downloaded a vision into my spirit. The vision depicted a scene on the main street of a town in the American West. He explained, "This is Frontier Town. This is where I bring my spiritual pioneers to train to be end-time warriors. I will introduce you to each of the buildings on Main Street. Be warned. Things aren't what they seem to be in Frontier Town."

In the rapid, non-stop pace of three weeks, an entire book-length revelation was recorded in my journal and became the basis for the third book, *Spirit Wind: The Ultimate Adventure.* Spirit Wind, an incredibly beautiful, powerful white stallion appeared each day to carry me into Frontier Town. The things I learned and discovered not only astounded me, but they also prepared me for what was to come.[59]

"Now I find myself sitting here on a pillar in the heavenly realms. This should not be a surprise," I said, gazing at the royal scroll in my hand and shaking my head in amazement. "This is exactly what Enoch experienced. His fellowship with God began with intimate walks together and culminated in such revelation and insight that Enoch became a royal scribe, a king, and the patriarch of pneumanauts. He walked with God and journeyed through the heavens. He measured the Garden of Eden and talked with the angels, both good and bad. He experienced such prophetic insight and revelation that he foretold the end times and the return of Christ a millennia before the events will yet occur.[60] I prayed to be like Enoch, and God promised me that He would come and walk with me just as He did with Enoch. God does not lie. Traveling in the spirit is possible, essential and my new normal.

So, here I am. I affirm and solidify the truth of my experience. I am sitting on a pillar inside a portal that opens into the third heaven, conversing with an angel and preparing to proceed further on my assignment as the King's royal scribe. This is amazing, unbelievably-believable, supernaturally-natural, humanly impossible but spiritually attainable, abnormally-normal behavior. So stay with me. We have much to see and do before this journey is over and we return to earth again. Remember, my imagination and yours are the page that God writes on!

Supplies for the Journey

"Jesus, You are so awesome and beautiful," I prayed. "Who am I that You would choose me for this journey in the spirit? I love you so much, Lord. I feel Your presence all around me. Heaven is Your home, Lord Jesus. This is where Enoch walked with You and talked with You. What an honor to walk beside You and talk with You in Your kingdom realm and witness the heavenly atmosphere. I am humbled and undone."

The Lord spoke, "I keep My word, son. I am answering your request. We walk together just like I walked with Enoch. You are My son and My friend. My love for you is far beyond your comprehension now, but you will experience it even more fully in the days to come.

"You are my appointed scribe. I have arranged and ordered your journey here in the heavens. There is far more than you can see or comprehend on this first visit. There will be many other journeys into the heavens in the future. I plan to reveal the royal forge to you on a future trip. It's one of My matrix makers, which creates more dimensions. But for now, you must focus on this assignment. Be careful to record what you see in the royal scroll. This revelation must be released into the earth now. I am preparing My people. The convergence of times and seasons, epics and entities is come. The spirit realm is aware, and My Spirit is hovering over the earth to incubate the end and the beginning.

"Carry this scroll and guard it. It must be delivered to My Church."

"Yes, Lord. With all that is within me, I will do Your will. Grant me Your grace, Father."

"I have granted it to you and grace upon grace, My son."

As He spoke I could sense a host of angels gathered around the pillar witnessing our conversation. Their loyalty to the King was total, and their determination was resolute.

"These mighty warriors are with you," the King said. "Everywhere I send you, they will be there. Now it is time for you to proceed on your journey. Keep your journal well and the scroll will record the message.

"I know that you love the Word. You are faithful to hide it in your heart. Now you will see how much I love the Word. I am sending you to the Library of Heaven next. Many things that you see will astound you. Many of My servants are being summoned to the celestial library now for further training, knowledge and resources.

"I bless you on your way. Be strengthened and renewed in My joy."

Searching for the Portal

The Lord's presence faded and I focused again on my surroundings. "Kaleb, I must be on my way. I've delayed long enough. The King is sending me to the library."

"Travel in His light, Warrior." He pointed into the darkness in a northwesterly direction in earth terms. "Go this way when you leave."

"How will I know which pillar leads to the library?" I asked.

"Do not be concerned. You will know when the time comes," he answered. "Travel in the heavenlies always begins with a leap of faith. You will return here again sometime in the future before the Great War begins. You are always welcome in all the angel encampments throughout the realm of His Kingdom, Warrior Scribe. Go now in His light!"

So now another test lies before me, I thought. *Each step in the heavenly realm, penetrating further and deeper into the Kingdom of Heaven, is a journey of faith.*

"I want more, Lord! Show me your hidden treasures in the darkness. Allow me to access the treasures of the *secret places*. I lay claim to Your promise to King Cyrus. *"I will give you the treasures of darkness and hidden wealth of **secret places**, So that you may know that it is I, The LORD, the God of Israel, who calls you by your name… I form the light and create darkness."* (Isaiah 45:3,7, NASB)

I gathered the royal scroll to my breast, pressed it tightly against my heart, and leapt forward off the pillar into the darkness in the direction of the unseen pillar and the doorway into another dimension of His heavenly realm.

Straightaway, I realized that what I thought was deep darkness was not the absence of light but an atmosphere that is familiar to those who travel in the spirit. My spiritual eyes were becoming accustomed to this environment. In the spirit, I could see in the darkness like a soldier on earth with night vision equipment. The words of David, the King's general, flashed into my thoughts:

> *Where can I go from Your Spirit? Or where can I flee from Your presence? If I ascend to heaven You are there. If I make my bed in Sheol, behold, You are there. If I take the wings of the dawn, if I dwell in the remotest part of the sea, even there your hand will lead me, and Your right hand will lay hold of me. If I say "Surely the darkness will overwhelm me and the light around me will be night." Even the darkness is not dark to You and the night is as bright as the day. Darkness and light are alike to You.* (Psalm 139:7–12)

The dark realm that pervades the atmosphere and dimension of space where the columns exist actually aids in making the portals into the heavenlies more visible. I was able to see more clearly and became aware that I was moving in a celestial light around me that I hadn't noticed when I first entered the door of the Unfinished House. I was glowing with a phosphorescent light.

Many beings were now visible to me that I was unable to distinguish on my first venture through the darkness. Angels, saints and other creatures were traversing the dark expanse just like me. Pillars rose into the atmosphere from beneath the darkness and were visible in every direction, but they were much farther apart than I first observed. A chariot flashed by, moving in the same direction as I was. Another chariot crossed in front of me farther ahead of my position, presenting no danger. Then, in an awesome display of synchronized skill, several chariots crossed in perfect formation and, once they were beyond the channel I was moving in, scattered in multiple directions, each one flashing off at high speed.

"This must be an intersection," I reasoned. "What should I do?"

My spirit clearly indicated to turn to the right. I adjusted my direction, turning about 90 degrees to starboard. I continued through the heavens making a slight 'S' curve first to the left and then to the right and finally back to a straight forward track like a military pilot would do, searching for any sign or indication of the pillar I was looking for. Finally, a pillar came into view ahead and to my right. An angel waved to me from the platform, directing me to land there. I adjusted my course and speed and made a perfect approach and landing on the pillar. He greeted me with enthusiasm.

My Flight Path

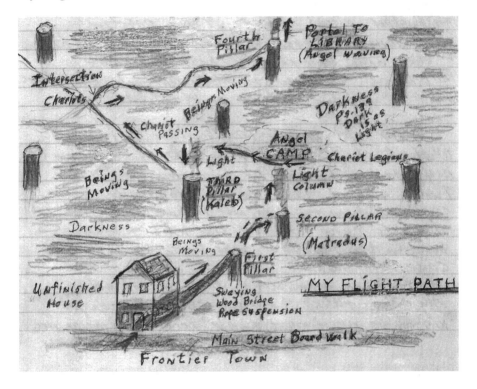

CHAPTER 10

Entering the Library of Heaven

"Welcome, Scribe," the angel said as I landed on the pillar. "I have been anticipating your arrival. I must confirm that you are carrying the royal scroll," he insisted, carefully examining the beautiful instrument. "It is genuine." He affirmed. "You are permitted to pass through this portal.

"Everything has been prepared for your visit to the Library of Heaven. You have been granted clearance to enter all the library sections except for the Hall of Times and Seasons that can only be accessed by the Father of Light. No one else from heaven or earth may enter. Otherwise, please explore and engage the library. It is unlike any other on earth or throughout all of creation. It supersedes the great ancient libraries of Alexandria and Constantinople and the most contemporary storehouses of knowledge, including the Library of Congress and the largest computer storage capabilities on earth, both in scope and capacity. It is a supernatural hands-on record and display of all knowledge."

So this is the real cloud storage, I chuckled. *But there is a secret chamber here that only Father can enter.* My thoughts quickly engaged the Scripture. *"Then they gathered around him and asked him, 'Lord, are you at this time going to restore the kingdom to Israel?' He said to them: 'It is not for you to know the times or dates the Father has set by his own authority.'"* (Acts 1:6–10,11, NIV)

The Anti-Chamber to the Library

"I'm getting accustomed to traveling in the heavenly realms," I said to the angelic sentry. "I have learned what to do." I lifted my arms into the column of light to worship the King of kings and Lord of lords. "All creation is waiting for Your coming, Lord Jesus. I worship You, Almighty King, Lion of Judah, Lamb of God!"

A rumbling sound cascaded through the light like a landslide of massive boulders coming toward me. It thundered through the portal and shook me to the core. Overcome with fear and awe, I proclaimed, "You are the Almighty One, awesome in wonder and power. Your beauty outshines the brightest stars. Your fire of love is hotter than a thousand suns. Who can stand in Your presence or comprehend Your ways?"

He spoke, "Come up here, My son! Enter into the abode of all knowledge, wisdom and creative power."

Instantly, I was transported through the portal and arrived at what appeared to be the anti-chamber or vestibule of the library. I figured that an angel would be waiting to greet me at the entrance, but much to my surprise and joy, Jesus was standing there to welcome me.

"Greetings, Dale. Welcome to My library. I have been waiting for this moment to introduce you to this great depository of knowledge, understanding and wisdom. It is much more than what you know as a library. It is more like a university. I have appointed the Spirit of Knowledge as the library steward. He will give you a personal tour, but you must move in the spirit. Allow your spirit to see and comprehend. Learn in your spirit-man because your soul and mind will struggle to comprehend. What you are about to see and hear are spiritual truths, words and exhibits that must be understood Spirit to spirit as they are explained by the Spirit of Knowledge.[61]

"The royal scroll that you carry grants you My permission to enter any section you choose except for one. That one is reserved expressly for My Father. The information and strategies contained within that area are top secret. No one must know the plans and tactics of Father's heart regarding certain end time matters. He has labored for ages to finalize them. What was, is, and is to come is prepared and will come to fulfillment by Father's initiation.

"Let Holy Spirit lead you as you explore the various halls of revelation. There is so much contained here. It is beyond a human lifespan to absorb. Only in eternity will you have adequate time and ability to search and fully comprehend the *source* of all knowledge and wisdom."[62]

As He spoke, I remembered my frustration when I considered visiting the Louvre in Paris with only one day left of my vacation. It was mind-boggling. What to see, where to go, what is on my priority list of must-see items?

This moment makes that experience seem insignificant. How could I possibly choose what to see and learn here in the Library of Heaven? Surely, Holy Spirit's guidance is crucial. I thought. I breathed a sigh of relief and let all my frustration go. *I'm just honored and blessed to have access. The Lord will guide my steps. I can come back here in eternity for a longer visit. I do love libraries, and this is the most important and greatest of all.*

"You may enter now. The Spirit of Knowledge is waiting for you inside," Jesus said. He immediately rose upward and disappeared.

Entering the Library

I stepped toward the mirror-finished, opaque double doors that led from the antichamber into the library. They were made of a silvery glass substance and framed in gold. Their simple beauty and function was stunning. Their allure was so enticing. An insatiable desire for knowledge and wisdom welled up within me. Solomon's directive pulsed through my veins:

> *My son, if you receive my words and treasure up my commandments with you, making your ear attentive to wisdom and inclining your heart to understanding; yes, if you call out for insight and raise your voice for understanding, if you seek it like silver and search for it as for hidden treasures,* then *you will understand the fear of the Lord and find the knowledge of God. For the Lord gives wisdom; from his mouth come knowledge and understanding; he stores up sound wisdom for the upright . . .* (Proverbs 2:1–7a, ESV)

"But wait?" I realized, immediately faced with a problem. "There's no door knob. How do I get in? There must be a code or key of some kind that grants entrance.

"What am I thinking?" I said out loud. "I have the royal scroll!"

I lifted the royal scroll up before the double doors. Some sort of locking mechanism clicked and the doors glided open automatically. I didn't hesitate. I stepped through the entrance. The doors closed tightly behind me. I could see out through the doors from the inside, but not from the outside in. Immediately inside the doorway, I stopped and stood still, quivering with anticipation, trying to take it all in.

Holy Spirit spoke, "Whoever passes through these doors comes to learn and discover God's wisdom and hidden knowledge. What is received in the library can be taken to earth because it is Spirit-breathed and Spirit-born. It is written in the heart and spirit of the person and carried back to earth as revelation knowledge."

"I am here to learn, Lord," I prayed. I felt like King David when he said, *"When I consider Your heavens, the work of Your fingers, the moon and the stars, which You have ordained; What is man that You take thought of him, and the son of man that You care for him? Yet You have made him a little lower than the angels, And You crown him with glory and majesty!"* (Psalm 8:3–5, NAS)

"I have no concept of what I am about to experience, Lord," I said. "I'm truly humbled to be invited here. This is more than my graduate or doctoral studies. This is attending class in which the **source** is the professor, and the knowledge is absolute eternal truth. The only reference needed here for authenticity and veracity is God himself."

A long hallway lay before me, leading toward the heart of the library. Its walls were a neutral color, plain and unadorned with no windows or natural light illuminating the way. Instead, an ethereal glow shimmered like heat rising from a highway surface on a summer afternoon. I could not see the other end as I began to walk quickly toward what I assumed would be another doorway. The passageway grew narrower the farther I went.

The Great Gallery

After a lengthy walk through the hallway, I approached the end of the corridor and discovered to my surprise there was no door at the end of the hallway, simply an opening. I exited the hallway into a cavernous circular gallery with a massive domed ceiling exceeding the scope and functional grandeur of the impressive Hagia Sophia in Constantinople. This was the central hub of the library and people as well as angelic creatures were moving through this cathedral-like concourse to learn and research. The busy scene reminded me of Grand Central Station.

A circular counter, obviously a reception desk, was appropriately positioned in the center of the library's main concourse. No one could enter, exit or transition from one area to another of this massive repository of knowledge without being observed by those attending to the library's business. I headed straight for the circular counter, knowing that what I was about to experience here in this royal palace of knowledge and wisdom would blow my intellectual circuits and propel me into a whole new understanding and revelation of truth and function from the King's viewpoint. Can you imagine the scope of information emanating from the Creator of all things in heaven and on earth?

The greeting I received was a balanced blend of formality and friendliness. "Welcome, Scribe. I am the Spirit of Knowledge. It is my duty and joy to instruct you and to reveal the mysteries and secrets of Father. Let me explain how the library works. Look around you!"

I turned to examine the library from the vantage point of its exact center. The gallery's entire circumference was occupied by unmarked doorways at equally spaced intervals. The interstices between the doors were non-descript and offered no help in identifying what was behind their walls. There were no signs or nomenclature of any kind. The doors evidently led into a different section of the library.

Each door had a different design to it. I had no earthly reference to compare with what I was seeing.

In a library with no markings and no way of telling where the various doorways lead, I thought, *I won't know what's inside until I enter each door.*

A shiver of delight piqued my exploring nature, which immediately rose to the challenge. *I can't wait to discover what's here? But wait. There's another enigma.* I squinted, *How do I get in? I don't see any doorknobs! But, alas, I am holding the key. The royal scroll will no doubt come in handy here in the King's Library of Heaven. It must be the key, just like it was at the entrance.*

The Spirit of Knowledge

My fascination with this tantalizing environment was interrupted by a voice from inside the reception center. The Spirit of Knowledge explained, " I see that you are intrigued by the various doors in this great rotunda. Each door leads into an exclusive hall in the library. Once you enter the door, you will encounter an entirely unique realm of knowledge and experience. There are classrooms in each section that apply to that subject area. You will find exhibits as well as pathways that will take you into supernatural realms of experience dealing with what you are studying. Your knowledge will increase exponentially. This is not just a tactile, hands-on interaction with the subject matter or merely a mental exercise. It is above all, spiritually imparted revelation knowledge, Spirit to spirit.

"You may have already noticed that although each door is unique, the door-ways and sections are not marked or identified here in the great hall. You must be led by Holy Spirit to choose the appropriate door. The King has prepared an itinerary for you and I will assist you. You have access to the entire library except for the Hall of Times and Seasons located opposite the entry hallway that you passed through when you arrived," he pointed with an expression of resolve at an imposing gold door. Obviously, no one would get past his watchful awareness of everything that transpires here in the library. His warning was firm and deliberate: "Do not, under any circumstances, try to enter that section of the library. It will cost you your life!"

His warning drove home the serious punishment for any attempt even to see into this hidden chamber of secrets. *This is the third time I've been forewarned,* I thought. *Out of the mouth of two or three witnesses a thing is confirmed.*[63]

"I will be available to you if you have any questions or need explanations or help," Knowledge offered. "You may call upon me at any time. Many other saints and angels are here now. Angels come often and saints are here more frequently than ever before. Some come for regular study and classes. You are free to speak with anyone, but remember, this is a library, so be sensitive to others. Several royal scribes are here on assignment, like you, who need total concentration."

The Gallery or Great Hall

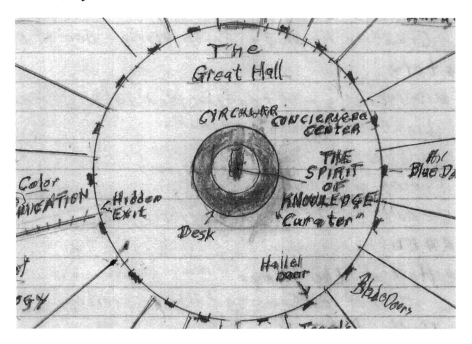

CHAPTER 11

The Hall of Languages

I turned a full 360 degrees, examining each door and considering the many choices that lay before me. I recalled a similar problem when I was a college student considering the multitude of available college courses when I registered for my freshman year at the University of Pittsburgh. The possibilities were overwhelming.

Where should I go? Which door should I enter first? I need some help. Reason and preference will not suffice, I thought in a quandary. *This decision requires discernment on a higher level.*

My spirit leapt within me. An entrance, three doorways to the right of the forbidden Hall of Times and Seasons, commenced to sparkle and glisten. Its surface began to cycle through different shades and hues of blue. It looked like watercolors being poured from atop it, flowing down like a waterfall. The scroll began twisting in my right hand. A blue flame glowed from one end of it. The royal scroll was acting like a compass. Its energy was so forceful that it turned my hand to point in the direction of the beckoning doorway.

"This supernatural scroll appears to have a consciousness of its own. It knows where I am and where I need to go. The King has programmed it," I said in wonder, marveling at the gold and silver cylinder pulsing in my right hand. "His ways are not my ways and His thoughts are beyond mine."

I spoke directly to the scroll: "My itinerary is encoded inside of you. You are guiding me to the first place I must visit in this depository of all wisdom and knowledge. My problem is solved. The Lord has preordained and ordered my steps through the celestial territories and the far reaches of the heavenly realms of His Kingdom, even down to the smallest details. God not only directs our steps on earth, but also He goes before us to guide us in the heavenly realms. *'The steps of a good man are ordered by the Lord: and he delights in his way.'*"[64]

"I don't think this means I must lead a robotic life and lack the freedom to explore," I thought, smiling. *"You promised me, Lord, that I would have time to investigate on my own and to spend extra time in some places when I want to. Once an explorer, always an explorer,"* I grinned with joy. *"God made me this way!"*

"This is it," I said, trembling with excitement like I had just boarded a roller coaster and was about to leave the station. "I am actually here. I have longed to see this place. I have always loved books and learning. My desire for wisdom and knowledge is insatiable." The Spirit of Knowledge nodded in approval but made no comment. In my heart and intentions, I was conscious of the great importance of my assignment. I immediately set out through the immense gallery, taking a direct path toward the inviting door.

"Each journey begins with the first step," I said, bolstering my courage and trying to harness my emotional desire to run at full speed across the great concourse. "Walk with purpose!" I told myself, gripping the scroll with focused intent. "I am on assignment. This is not a tourist trip."

Floating Letters
"What lies beyond this door?" I asked, standing before the entry with no clue how I would open it. The blue light emanating from the end of the royal scroll morphed and stopped when it perfectly matched the exact shade and hue of the door. I stared in amazement as the entrance became translucent. I stepped right through the membrane of color into the interior of this section of the library.

I was greeted by an intriguing phenomenon. Thousands of alphabetical letters were floating in the air in front of me. They appeared to form words communicating a message of some sort. I couldn't read the message because the letters were in languages unknown to me. I watched in consternation as the figures kept dissolving and reappearing in different scripts and fonts. Then finally the letters appeared in Hebrew. Somehow, supernaturally, I actually understood it. The message read, 'Hall of Languages.'

"Now I understand!" I nodded. "I'm in the 'Hall of Languages' of the Library of Heaven. This is amazing! It's the welcome message to identify this section for people of every tongue and nation, including the angels who speak many different languages. God is so awesome. And He certainly knows my heart and my love of words and their etymology. Why, I could spend the rest of my time exploring and studying in this single hall of the library," I said, relishing the possibility.

The Languages of Heaven

I passed beneath the floating letters of the entrance sign into a wedge-shaped room that increased in width the farther I walked. There were angels and saints on either side of the center aisle, laboring like scribes over numerous pages and manuscripts. An enormous book occupied each section. I stopped at one point to watch an angel lift one of these massive books that I assumed must be a dictionary of the language he was recording. He placed the book onto a device, and beams of light penetrated completely through the book, copying the entire volume in an instant, not page by page but all at once in its entirety.

I wondered why it was necessary to record this information manually. *Surely, God has an easier way?* I wondered.

The Spirit of Knowledge spoke, "Did you call me? Let me explain. You see, we need to collaborate. An angel and an individual are chosen to work as a team. We need the language written with human hands with proper spelling and inflection symbols. Once that is done, the word is spoken audibly and repeated by the angel. The writing as well as the words are recorded on the diction scrolls and then transferred by this mechanism to Word Central where every language on earth and in the heavenlies is preserved. The number of dialects increased exponentially when God created all the languages of the nations millenniums ago.[65]

"Language continues to evolve, and new ones are crafted more frequently than you realize as new universes are created, and the old languages increase in size. You can access every spoken, written or thought word here in this central depository of communication. It provides an instant response and will translate one language to another to assist you as you travel through the heavenly realms.

"Word and Spirit always move simultaneously. Some believe there is a single language in heaven, but that is not accurate. You still retain your earth-language here in heaven. Not only does every human tongue exist here, there are many angelic tongues as well as celestial dialects from the outer reaches. But the language of the Spirit is the common vernacular throughout the cosmos."

The Currency of the Kingdom

"Father loves words. Some words have special creative power. The currency of the kingdom is the words of God and the words of men and angels. All exchange in the kingdom realm is by WORD." (The Spirit of Knowledge put such emphasis on this point that I had to capitalize the letters of WORD to emphasize its importance.)

He continued, "Life force is the womb of creation. It resides and emanates from Father, Jesus and Holy Spirit. God disseminates life force by breathing or speaking and creates everything by His Word. Light is the medium and essence of Word. Light is the carrier of Word. Light and Word are the realm of communication. That is why you detect light beams and lasers here in the heavenlies. They carry and disseminate His Word. He is Light. His Word is Light, and it enlightens us.

"All languages reside in Father and originate in Him. He is even now creating new dialects and dimensions of communication. There are beings yet to be created and some that already exist that are unknown to man. Each one will speak in its own tongue. These new languages are or will be carefully and precisely recorded here for all eternity. I have often heard the King refer to this area of the library as 'The House of Words.'

"Remember this spiritual law: nothing happens on earth or in heaven unless it is spoken!" Knowledge said with definitive authority. His tone reminded me of the power of the utterances of the ancient Egyptian pharaohs: "So let it be written, so let it be done!"

"It is an irrevocable truth," I affirmed. Knowledge's words brought to mind James' metaphor concerning the power of the tongue. They serve as a clear warning of the consequences of what we speak.

Let not many of you become teachers, my brethren, knowing that as such we will incur a stricter judgment. For we all stumble in many ways. If anyone does not stumble in what he says, he is a perfect man, able to bridle the whole body as well. Now if we put the bits into the horses' mouths so that they will obey us, we direct their entire body as well. Look at the ships also, though they are so great and are driven by strong winds, are still directed by a very small rudder wherever the inclination of the pilot desires. So also the tongue is a small part of the body, and yet it boasts of great things.

See how great a forest is set aflame by such a small fire! And the tongue is a fire, the very world of iniquity; the tongue is set among our members as that which defiles the entire body, and sets on fire the course of our life, and is set on fire by hell. For every species of beasts and birds, of reptiles and creatures of the sea, is tamed and has been tamed by the human race. But no one can tame the tongue; it is a restless evil and full of deadly poison. With it we bless our Lord and Father, and with it we curse men, who have been made in the likeness of God; from the same mouth come both blessing and cursing. My brethren, these things ought not to be this way. Does a fountain send out from the same opening both fresh and bitter water? Can a fig tree, my brethren, produce olives, or a vine produce figs? Nor can salt water produce fresh. (James 3:1–11, NASB)

"We are destined to live the life we speak," I said, quoting from a book I read on angel armies. "Angels know it. Demons know it. But many people today do not understand it. Language is not only our means of communication, but also it is a roadbuilder, a bulldozer of energy, a force that we all must recon with and seek to control. Our future and our destiny are manipulated and determined by the words emanating from our hearts. We must speak to our future! We must control our tongue and steer the ship of our life with care and discernment. Even life and death are in the power of the tongue. Our words can injure and cut, or heal and restore."[66]

"You are a good student, Royal Scribe," Knowledge said, interrupting my thoughts. "You must come back here again. You will need the resources available here as you journey through the heavenlies and seek to communicate in the realms of the kingdom here and on earth. But now you must continue your assignment. You have much to see here in the library."

In an instant, I was transported from the Hall of Languages and found myself standing back in the great hall.

"I must be sure to enter this information on the scroll," I said, carefully recording the events and lessons in the Hall of Languages. I knew I had just scratched the surface of this inimitable part of the library. The volumes of etymology in this place must be incredibly alive with truth and revelation. The origin of words has always intrigued me. Thoughts of Tolkien, the philologist, raced through my mind as I recalled his amazing ability and skill to create unique original languages for his classic series, *The Lord of the Rings*.

CHAPTER 12

The Hall of Cosmology

I no sooner finished my notations when the royal scroll began vibrating in my hand again and rotating like a compass. It pointed to an entrance directly across the rotunda of the great hall. The door was pulsating with the same frequency. It changed color, cycling back and forth from black to white. In between each cycle, it transitioned through a beautiful velvet blue. I quickly crossed the great hall and stood before the supernatural door, mystified by its enticing invitation. The change from black to white was beautiful. It was soothing, and in a strange way, familiar. Its rhythmic pattern reminded me of the circadian cycle of night and day as it replicated this God-created sequence.

I'll wait until the light cycle begins, then I will step through the doorway, I strategized. To my surprise, suddenly the black faded into a beautiful golden-white, like a summer sunrise. I seized the moment and stepped through the entrance, trusting that the door would yield to my intrusion.

A View of the Cosmos

"Oh, my goodness!" I said in reverence. My gaze was frozen with wide-eyed wonder as I struggled to comprehend the immense scene before me. I was standing in a celestial observatory. Although I have visited several famous observatories on earth, this heavenly viewpoint was beyond extraordinary; it was truly extra-terrestrial. Even the Hubble telescope is like astronomy for beginners in comparison to this.

My eyes slowly adjusted to the darkness, but seeing clearly didn't help me fix my position. I was observing the heavens from an entirely different viewpoint. "This must be a kingdom realm, cosmic perspective of creation," I conjectured. "Here in this observatory, my planet is not the center of the universe anymore. My earthly paradigm is shattered and useless here. I can't get my bearings."

The cosmos was continually expanding and morphing. I felt dizzy, but there was nothing to hold on to, and sitting seemed inappropriate. The royal scroll began to emit a laser beam from both ends. The red and blue lasers fired from each opening and flashed off into the cosmos right through the ceiling—was there a ceiling?

I quickly realized that I could maintain my balance by looking at the scroll. "This is awesome," I said. "Not only is it a compass, but also it's functioning like a gyroscope. It must serve as some sort of a location device, but it isn't helping me to identify where I am in the cosmos. I'm unaware of the main reference point.

"Where am I, Knowledge? I asked.

"Welcome to the Hall of Cosmology," he replied. "This is where the angels and saints come to research and study the cosmic creation. You will discover new concepts here that you did not know existed. You may have detected already that direction and distance in the kingdom realm is not determined or measured by man's conceptions and devices. Earth is no longer your focal point of reference. Here in the Spacetarium, everything is centered on the Throne Room. All measurements and directions are determined by its precise location and centrality. Everything emanates from the royal Throne.

The Seven Dimensions

"In this observatory, you can discern every location in the cosmos. Here we use a seven-dimensional paradigm of creation or at least a part of creation. I say 'part of creation' because there are dimensions beyond what you call or are known as cosmotic-space. These realms of existence supersede your knowledge.

"Why would you think or determine that Father is limited to three heavens or a single cosmos?" Knowledge asked. "You know about the heavens and the cosmos, but have no understanding about what lies beyond the cosmos. Realms of existence, life forms and substances that occupy this post-cosmos realm beyond the outer reaches have never been seen or accessed by humans. Meager, incapable telescopes or astronautical attempts at observation or penetration are useless. This burgeoning region is cloaked in darkness. Only when Father decides to open these dimensions and regions of creation will you ever get to access them. I speak for the angels as well. For now, just embracing the cosmos is enough to keep us busy for eternity. But there is a beyond-eternity dimension waiting to be explored. Let's just refer to it as beyond-space. It is the frontier of continuous creation. The heavens are evolving in size and scope.

"Notice that this cosmic map of creation increases moment by moment as Father and His servants create new galaxies."

Father and His servants? What does this imply? Who is Knowledge referring to? I wondered. *Now I have another mystery to solve. God's ways are certainly not our ways,* I reaffirmed as an attempt to calm my overextended mind. I determined to learn more about this in the future.

The Chart Room

"Come this way!" Knowledge directed. "I will show you the chart room."

I followed him through the darkness toward a distant star. It sparkled and glistened, brighter than all the other stars in the spacescape. As we drew closer, I realized it wasn't a star at all. It was a portal into another section of the Hall of Cosmology.

We passed through the starway portal into another dimension of the hall. There were symbols written around the circumference of the doorway.

"What are these markings, Knowledge?" I asked.

"These are the names of the heavenly beings who are appointed by the King to patrol and guard the regions of the celestial realm. They are the seven commanders who rule over the seven navigation points of the plane or Seven-Gon (a seven-sided polygon).

"This is an amphitheater," Knowledge explained. Seats were positioned in tiers that encircled a center display area that contained an amazing hologram of the cosmos.

"Each student or observer in this room is provided with a precise individual view as they study and examine the cosmic hologram. They can manipulate the image suspended in the center of the amphitheater by using the screen in front of their seat. Everyone studies their own personalized hologram and can navigate through the cosmos here in the chart room. They can even file a pneumanaut flight plan for a celestial journey by using this amazing device.

"Sit here!" Knowledge directed, pointing to an empty seat near the entrance. "Let me give you a beginner's course on celestial navigation."

The seat was very comfortable and the computer-like keyboard was perfectly positioned for easy access.

The Seven Cosmic Pathways

Knowledge manipulated the keyboard, and with a few strokes a diagram appeared on the computer and was transferred immediately to the hologram in the center of the amphitheater. The image revealed a single plane with a center point and seven lines emanating from these foci in seven directions along the plane. These seven spokes created a navigational grid.

"This is the navigational plane of the cosmos," Knowledge explained. He stepped down into the center of the amphitheater onto the display floor and walked right into the hologram. He explained the grid's components from inside the cosmic simulator.

"There are seven directions in the circuit of the heavens that establish the cosmic plane," he said. "These seven radii emanate from the Throne of God, identified as the Alpha-Omega Point." Raising his arm, he pointed to the absolute center of the image.

"All the locations above the plane are Alpha positions, and all the locations beneath the plane are Omega positions. The seven radii are pathways leading from the Alpha-Omega Point, which is the Throne room of God. All travel throughout the heavenlies is authorized and approved by the King or His angel navigators.

"Each radius is identified by name. The first is Aphesh, then Sharet, Marsone…" Knowledge ran his finger along each line of navigation as he spoke. Moving counterclockwise, "This is Tridium, and here is Valasterium. Xeryon is here. The seventh is…" he looked at me and spoke like a professor who wanted me to know that this information was essential and would be on the test. He concluded with the seventh radius: "This seventh is Eternus." He spoke with an expression of humble gratitude. "The effulgence of God is the essence of creativity!" he commented, staring in amazement and wonder at the intergalactic expanse divided by the seven cosmic navigational spaceways."

The Star Heptagon

Knowledge continued, "By using these seven radii that proceed from the Throne of the King at Alpha-Omega Point, we can travel in any direction as far as the outer reaches and be able to pinpoint our exact location on the navigational heptagon.

"Let me enlighten you regarding the history of the heptagon.[67] This geometric form was studied millennia ago on earth at the school for scribes in Susa. In the first part of the second millennium before Jesus arrived, these astute scholars examined its shape with an inspired curiosity. They didn't realize they were looking at the navigational plane of the cosmos. They just knew there was something very special about this geometric shape."

He stepped toward me, "Let me show you." A single keystroke produced a geometric object inside of the hologram. "This is the Star Heptagon. It is the navigational locator for the heavenly realms. All galaxies and matter in the entire cosmos can be located and identified using this instrument. When you first enter the heavenly realms through the portals, you can find your way easily because you are familiar with those places. But you have only begun your journey here in the heavenly realms. Each visit will take you to new places and ultimately to the outer reaches.

"There will come a time when your journey will require a star guide. A personal Star Heptagon device is issued to humans who travel far into the heavenly realm and beyond the outer rims. Once you are commissioned for this journey, you must come here to obtain your star guide unit."

The whole concept of celestial navigation intrigued me. It never occurred to me that astronauts on space missions can't use magnetic points for navigation—neither can angels and pneumanauts. "It all makes sense," I responded. "Understanding follows revelation!"

The Cosmic Womb

"The concepts of celestial navigation, the plane of existence and the unfathomable expanse of the cosmic womb of creation are mind-numbing," I said.

"Wait a minute! Why did I say 'cosmic womb'? This is a *kairos* moment of inspiration!" I declared, stunned by my own words.

"You are so right, Royal Scribe." Knowledge affirmed. "The cosmos is only the beginning. It is the womb of further creation and the habitation of creative imagination that continues to envision and build new things and beings. In God, and by His decree, all things *created* and *yet to be created* live and move and have their being!"[68]

My curiosity was unquenchable. I just had to know. Questions spilled out in rapid-fire delivery. "What about the outer reaches? How long will it take me to reach them? How far is the outer rim? What kind of assignment from the King will require me to make these journeys into eternal distances that I know absolutely nothing about?

"I apologize, Knowledge, for my untamed desire to learn and understand, but I can't help it. This is more than any explorer could hope for or even dream of," I said. "Christopher Columbus was a novice compared to these possibilities, but he needed the same faith and resolve to go beyond what accepted thinking and current science dictated. Traveling in the spirit requires that same resolve. God is shattering my traditional world and cosmic view and transforming my mind. My paradigm is shifting from an earthly to a heavenly perspective."

"That's exactly why you are here," Knowledge said with an approving nod.

Cosmic Cartography

Knowledge pointed to a doorway opposite the entrance to the amphitheater: "The charts and maps of the cosmos are kept in the next section of the Hall of Cosmology. Follow me!

"This department," he explained as we traversed the huge room that housed the cartography of the cosmos, "specializes in the skyview from the surface of each planet. Over here is the area that catalogues every star by its original name.[69] There are charts and descriptions for every portion of the heptagon. Over there along the wall is a secret department where new cosmic construction sites are charted and identified.

"Did you notice the cosmic clock overhead? It displays the motions and mechanisms of creation. It does not measure time. It detects light and motion. All matter is measured, not by time as you understand it, but by cycles of light and motion. Mass exists in light and non-light. Its motion is measured and known as the cycles of the cosmos. All universes are coordinated and become a symphony of sound and light. They sing together. The sound of creation fills the heavens.[70]

"You may stay here in the Hall of Cosmology for a while if you like," Knowledge said. "Be sure to record everything you see and learn. It is critical to fulfilling your assignment, and it will be a great resource for others who will soon come into the heavenly realms. Be sure to tell them about this place," he departed as suddenly as he had arrived.

"My brain is numb," I said, rubbing my skull. "I don't think I can absorb any more, but what I have seen and heard is indelibly written in my spirit. I will come back here in due time." I determined, "Whatever due time is here in the heavenly realm."

New Realms of Reality

I turned back toward the door and stepped through the portal into the amphitheater. I made my way around the hologram and through the door into the dark expanse of the Spacetarium.

Doorways are amazing things. They are far more than a means of entrance and egress. They are dimensional portals that grant access to entirely new realms of reality. I learned this first in Frontier Town. It has become a part of my experience in both the flesh and the spirit. Every doorway is a new opportunity and launching point into revelation.

I believe that's why Jesus said, "I am the door."[71] He is a portal into the heavenly realms that gives us access to Father. He told us that He stands at the door and knocks. We must open it. I will always honor John the great apostle. He led the way! He was a pneumanaut who accessed the celestial doorway. He saw a door standing open in heaven.[72]

"I must tell the saints that God opens heavenly doors. We must heed His invitation and choose to go up and enter them," I affirmed.

I paused for a moment to take one last look at the brilliant stars glittering overhead and the huge expanse of the cosmos depicted in the Spacetarium.

"The Hall of Cosmology! Wow! I wish NASA could see this!" I said in admiration and stepped through the darkened doorway back into the busy activity of the great hall. Knowledge was speaking to another scribe at the central desk. An angel brushed by me and then several others eagerly passed by hurrying into the Hall of Cosmology.

The Navigational Plane of the Cosmos (The Seven Radii)

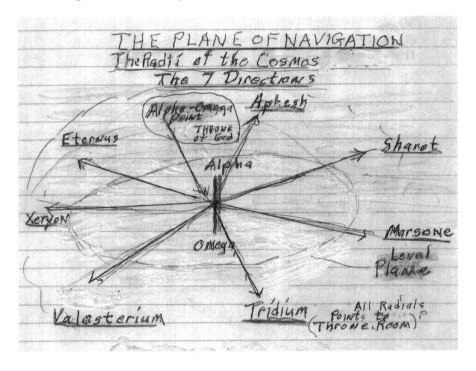

CHAPTER 13

Vessels of Peace and the Coming Convergence

A Promise Kept

"How long have I been here in the heavenly realm?" I asked. "I've seen heavenly beings that I read about only in the Bible. And this library, it's so different than what I envisioned on earth. Jesus, I am amazed and humbled that You would bring me here."

A flash of light surged through the great hall, and Jesus appeared next to me. "Hello, My friend. We have only begun our journey.

"I am keeping My promise to walk with you just as I walked with Enoch. You will soon meet him here in My Kingdom realm. I took Enoch to the far reaches, which are beginnings and portals into entirely new realms that I am creating with My friends. But you must first see and learn the basic principles of navigation in the cosmos and understand the ways of angels and heavenly beings.

"When this phase of your assignment is complete, I will welcome you into the Throne room to sit with Me for a season to see and hear and observe from the Alpha-Omega Point. This is the epicenter of everything that exists. Here is where you will experience My heart's passion like never before.

"I love you beyond your capability to comprehend My love in its fullness. And yet, certainly you know a measure of My love for you."

"Yes, I do know You love me, Jesus," I responded, overwhelmed by His faithfulness. "I live in Your love and depend on Your constant presence. You are my life, my guide; my very existence depends upon Your grace and Spirit. Paul said it best: 'In you we live and move and have our being.'[73] All things that exist on earth and in the heavenly realms cannot compare to You. I choose You above all else."

"I know," He replied. "And I chose you even before you were born! I will come to see you again soon. Guard the royal scroll and record as much as you can. You will not be able to document everything you experience because many things are a mystery to you. You may not even notice them as you pass through the heavenly realms. Don't try to analyze these things, just observe and record."

The Coming Convergence

"You are in the last stage of your training as an end-time warrior," He said with finality in His demeanor. "That is why you entered the heavenly realm through the Unfinished House in Frontier Town. It is your doorway into the heavens. The royal scroll you carry is intended for the sons and daughters of My Kingdom. The day is fast approaching when heaven and earth will converge for the final battle.

"My Apostle Paul was summoned here, but he was forbidden to share on earth much of what he witnessed.[74] It was not yet time. My Church had to grow and mature. Now is the time for the release of proceeding revelation and understanding from My Kingdom realm in the heavens. I am responding to the prayers of millions of saints who for millennia have beseeched Me to manifest My Kingdom in its fullness on earth. They have asked in obedience and faith just as I instructed them to pray, 'Your kingdom come, Your will be done on earth as it is in heaven.'[75]

"My Kingdom in Heaven is invading earth. But it will not happen as you suppose. I am inviting My saints to come up here first. Many in My Body are already hearing and responding to My invitation and are entering the heavenly realms in the spirit. Access has been granted to learn and procure supernatural kingdom resources for the coming culmination of the ages. Weapons, strategy and resources are being revealed and accessed. Strategic angelic communication and cooperation with the saints is being established. This alliance will evolve into eternal military and ministry partnerships and friendships. This is the process that will fully manifest My Kingdom on earth.

"You must understand why your mission is so essential. All the years since you asked Me if you could walk with Me and be My friend, just as Enoch did, I have been growing and grooming you spiritually for this moment. I have mentored you, just as I mentored Enoch. You are no longer an apprentice. You are a master scribe. But even more than that, you are My friend. Fulfill your calling and ministry. I am always with you. You are My beloved scribe.

"Now, continue your journey through My Kingdom realms," Jesus pointed to the adjacent door just as the scroll was twisting in my hand in that direction. "Enter this Hall next!" He commanded and then disappeared.

A Living Paintbrush

I glanced at Knowledge who was standing at the concierge's desk. He was occupied with new arrivals to the library. A small line had formed as men, women and children waited for further instructions. "Wait a minute," I gasped. A woman was standing in the que. She held a gold paintbrush. Its silver ferrule held the most incredible bristles at its tip. The brush was changing size and shape as she moved it in her hand.

I wonder if it morphs into a different shape to accommodate what her spirit is sensing? Her brush is an extension of her imagination. It becomes a part of her, I thought. *No doubt she has come to paint the heavenly scenes and beings here. She is amazing.*

I noticed that she was wearing some sort of broach on her blouse that looked like a miniature artist's palette. Colors dripped from it and flowed into the atmosphere like liquid mist. The colors infused the air with wondrous beautiful blends and hues. Rainbows were forming and dissolving around her.

"She is a living paintbrush in the hand of the King," I said, carefully recording with the scroll what I was observing. "She is the brush and the paint simultaneously. She paints in a similar way that I write. My words are my color palette, adding dimension and emotion to my thoughts. She must be here on assignment, seeking direction from the Spirit of Knowledge like everyone else who enters this facility. I wanted to rush toward her and greet her but hesitated. *I'm not sure that's appropriate right now,* I thought. I simply waved to her and turned to my left, away from the Hall of Cosmology toward the adjacent doorway.

"Thank You for guiding me, Lord," I prayed as I stood waiting patiently in front of the new entrance. Supernatural peace began to envelop me. It flowed all over me and into my being like a shower of warm oil. I was immersed in liquid peace.

"This is a baptism of peace," I uttered, surrendering to its soothing, calming effect. Every part of my being (body, soul and spirit) was transfigured by His awesome peace.

"You are the Prince of Peace, Jesus,"[76] I acknowledged.

A Vessel of Peace

A distant memory flashed into my mind. It was my first trip to minister in China. I was invited by a precious Chinese couple to come and visit them in their home. What amazed me most was the unique invitation they extended.

"Please come and stay with us," they offered. "We want you to be a part of our family." Imagine that. They were more interested in me becoming a part of their family than simply coming to teach and preach. They wanted to know the messenger of the King who carried the precious truth of the *secret place* and intimacy with God.

The usual preparations for such a long journey were filled with updating my passport, obtaining a visa and packing the appropriate clothes, books and notes. But in the midst of this important task, I became aware of the constant distractions harassing me. My life was literally cluttered with stuff.

"Lord," I prayed one morning, "I really need Your peace. There's just too much stuff in my life. I am distracted at every turn. I feel like Martha when I really want to be more like Mary who chose to sit at Your feet and receive Your Word instead of being distracted with the stuff in the kitchen.[77] In the midst of this chaotic troubled world and the diversions of my own personal environment, I desperately need to be constantly soaked and swim in the peace of Your presence. Lord, I long for more of Your peace. My prayer is that I would become a vessel of Your peace at the very core of my being. I ask that as I go to China, I may minister Your peace. When others drink from the river that flows out of my spirit, may they sense the presence of Your Spirit of peace within me."

I arrived in Guangzhou, China, excited down to my toes. I had always wanted to come to this mysterious country, and the explorer in me was functioning at full capacity. My eagerness to reunite with my hosts was a happy occasion as we shared the plans for the next few days. "We are going on a family retreat together," they said. "We are taking you up into the mountains to a very famous health spa.[78] There are thirty-six pools that are fed by thermal underground hot springs. Each pool contains a different added ingredient to soften and revitalize your skin and body. We want you to be a part of our family. We are even taking our son out of school, so he can be with us."

And so we left the hustle and bustle of the city for the serenity and beauty of the Chinese countryside and the lush verdant mountains. I tingled with anticipation as I stared out the window at the curious landscape unfolding around me. The resort seemed to grow right out of the mountain, carefully nestled into the rock faces and surrounded by pine and luxurious foliage. Our plan: check into our rooms, get our bathing suits on and meet at the pool.

Paths led from the main swimming pool into various directions. These narrow passageways lead down the mountain through the lush mountain foliage and flowers to numerous hot springs and bubbling pools of hot water containing surprising added ingredients: eucalyptus, milk, coffee, wine, natural spices and essential oils. By the end of the day, I had sampled them all. Exiting the milk pool, I realized that my skin was as soft as a newborn baby's.

The days went by quickly. Meals with the family were enjoyed around the table with laughter and happy conversation. Times of worship, prayer and sharing filled the early afternoon with spiritual encouragement and revelation from the Lord and, of course, the wonderful, luxuriating times in the various pools talking and sharing life together was priceless. By the end of the week, I was no longer the visiting expert speaker. I was a member of the family and a seat was always waiting for me at the circular table where we shared the savory bubbling hotpot. We returned to the city refreshed and united in the spirit.

The next afternoon, I was amazed by their young son's account of his first day back at school.

"How was your day in school, Joshua?" his mother asked.

"It was very good, Mom," he said.

"Tell us what happened."

"My teacher asked me what I learned on my vacation since he knew I was going to be with a professor from the United States."

"What did you tell him, son?"

"I told him that he taught us about peace."

My eyes nearly popped from their sockets. I was stunned. Never once during the entire time at the resort did I mention the subject of peace. I didn't even use the word. And now this little boy was a witness to something that was happening in the spiritual dimension. I was communicating peace from my spirit. God's peace was inside of me, and this nine-year-old boy sensed it. He was learning about peace by simply being in my presence. This moment stood out in my mind and stirred my heart the rest of the time I spent in China. God not only answered my prayer, but also He bore witness to it through those around me.

When I boarded the plane through the business class jetway for the long flight home, I needed some time to reflect on my answered prayer. Once we reached cruising altitude, the stewardess served a gourmet meal and then I settled into my comfortable seat. I hungered to understand and experience even more of God's peace.

Lessons from the Prince of Peace

Soaring over the ocean at 37,000 feet I prayed, "Teach me more, Lord. I want to understand the spiritual principles of Your peace."

Suddenly, I felt like I was the only passenger on the plane. *I am in the secret place, and He is here with me,* I realized. I felt a blanket of peace cover me. I had entered His classroom. I wrote the lessons in my journal.

"My son," He said, "My presence is always initiated by peace. Do you sense it? Without My presence, your peace is predicated upon external circumstances and inner emotions and thoughts.[79] I transform the outer and inner atmospheres. 'Peace, be still!' is experiential. Peace and stillness cohabitate. I spoke peace to the roaring waves and they became calm. I speak peace to the inner storms as well. My peace changes outer and inner conditions.[80]

"My peace is not of this world. It is illogical and denies explanation. It goes against man's perceptions of reality.[81] It is spiritual and physical. When I say peace, it is accomplished. In the world you shall encounter tribulation, but be of good cheer; I have overcome the world.[82] I brought peace to earth. But peace on earth does not mean the absence of war. There will still be wars and rumors of wars.

"It is My power and ability that gives you peace. It is a gift that must be received. But in order to retain it, you must let go of what you are holding on to! That which you insist on owning or possessing must be surrendered. This includes things, people, problems and circumstances. Let go of those things that cause worry, anxiety, and fear and receive instead My peace, which passes understanding. You must have detachment from the things of the world. Love of the world will destroy you. Detachment results in simplicity. It is a lifestyle that requires little and considers others first and loves everyone. It is unencumbered by earthly possessions and the need to control or possess others. It focuses on things above and not what is on the earth.[83] Birds do not worry and neither should you. I want you to be free from worry and full of faith instead."[84]

I felt such a hunger deep within me as He spoke. "I long for simplicity, Lord," I said. "I have a constant desire for quiet and stillness deep within my being.[85] When I am in the presence of others, I want to minister Your peace that resonates within my soul and spirit. Not the peace of meditation, but the peace of Your presence within me. I want to be an instrument of Your peace.[86] But I understand now it is impossible without abiding in You, the Prince of Peace, and allowing Your peace to flow into me and through me. This is true communion, oneness and singleness of heart," I realized. "I long for stillness and quiet intimacy with You."

"You cannot attain this without my Lordship in your life," Jesus responded. "My peace is governmental and relational. It is righteousness, peace and joy in

Holy Spirit.[87] There is no peace without surrender to Me. You must maintain right relationships with Me and others. I Am the PRINCE of peace.[88] I Am the peace giver, the peace maker, the peace provider. In Me there is no confusion, distraction, disorder, deception or divination."

"Lord, I want to be at rest in the very center of my being," I said. "I want my life and my environment to be peaceful. I am captured in the cacophony of this world's noise, clutter and detritus. I know that clutter is not only external, but also it is internal. Like the static on the radio, it garbles the sound and makes it unintelligible at times. This is how my spirit and mind become when I am constantly bombarded with external stimuli. My mind is like a phonograph needle stuck in the groove of a record album on a turntable. My thoughts are ceaseless. They just keep going around and around."

"Dale, that is why the *secret place* is so vital to your spiritual well-being.[89] The atmosphere of the *secret place* is life giving. The pervading power of My presence in the *secret place* creates an atmosphere that promotes the impartation of spiritual wisdom and understanding. It unclutters the atmosphere spiritually, mentally and physically for clarity and ease of communication. Distraction is dissolved by peace in your spirit and your environment. That's why I told you to close the door. You must separate yourself from the world outside.

"I Am the source of true peace. I Am the Vine and you are the branch. Peace is the essence and consequence of abiding in Me. This is the place of complete rest and peace where you must dwell.[90] Like the branch receives life from the vine, so do you receive life and peace as you abide in Me. It flows from Me into you, just as the life force flows from the vine to the branch. You are in Me and **I Am in you**. My peace is within you because I Am in you. Peace is the essence and consequence of abiding in Me. This habitation of abiding is the place of complete rest and peace. This is where you must dwell, My son. I Am perfect peace.

"Holy Spirit is peace," He continued. "Peace is not an emotion; it is a state of being. It is not dependent upon how you feel. It is an inner state of continual rest and trust in Me. It is the surrendered place. It is the place of resolution, the resolve of the spirit-man infiltrating into your consciousness.

"Peace means rest, but that does not mean inactivity. Rather it means ease of function, clarity of purpose and great fruitfulness. A branch does not struggle on the vine. It rests! When you operate out of the peace I give you, not only do you minister peace, but also you allow My grace to flow freely in you and through you. Great fruit is produced in your life.

"Above all else, don't seek peace, son. Seek Me! Abide in Me and I in you. This is the great divine mystery, the eternity of complete unity. This is the center and the synergy of the Trinity. It is the Godhead manifested: Father, Son and Holy

Spirit. The peace I speak of is not earth-born or earth-maintained. It originates in the Godhead, three in one, total unity and total freedom of expression. It is the place of honor and love. There is no competition, no contest and no disagreement. There is only honor and unity.

"You must live in the world and not be of it. Fear and a troubled heart will erode your peace. Let My words abide in you. Live in the moment. Be where you are. One-day living is a sufficient lifestyle. Do not be concerned about tomorrow. It will take care of itself. There is only today. It is a gift. Live fully in it, son. You are daily. Don't get ahead of yourself. If you will seek Me daily, I will integrate today with the entire matrix of My plan for your future. You will be fully prepared for tomorrow when you get there. It is simply a result of obeying Me in the now. Your now-obedience has consequences that reach into your tomorrows. It sounds simple and it is. One of the exercises of peace is to seek Me in the present to ensure your future success.

"But you must realize that abiding in Me is both a constant state and an action. It is both active and passive. It requires rest and resistance. Rest in Me and resist all that would detach you from Me. It is an act of will and spirit. It is letting go and holding on all at once.

"I love you, son. Even from your childhood, I have drawn you near. I have put within you a spirit of peace and have equipped you with all that you need for now and will equip you further for all that you will need in the days to come. Abide in Me. Wherever I send you, speak peace to the place and people. If they do not receive you, when you depart, take your peace with you. If they reject you, they are rejecting Me for you are My ambassador.[91]

"My peace I give to you. Not like the world gives peace. Don't let your heart be troubled and don't be afraid. Fear and a troubled heart will erode your peace. In the world you will encounter tribulation, but be optimistic and joyful. I have overcome the world and so can you."

"Thank you, Lord. Help me to understand in my spirit-man the lessons you have taught me, Holy Spirit. I claim your promise spoken through Isaiah the prophet: *You will keep him in perfect peace whose mind is stayed on You, because he trusts in You. Trust in the Lord forever.*[92] I love you so much, Jesus."

CHAPTER 14

The Hall of Communication

My longing for inner peace still remained, although the memory of my return trip home from China faded from my conscious thought. I focused on my surroundings in the great hall. "That was then, but this is now," I remarked, soaking in the ambiance emanating from the doorway in front of me. "I want to stay in this deeply satisfying shower of His peace, but I must pass through this doorway. If this is my experience at the entrance, what incredible revelation must be waiting for me inside this supernatural dimension of the King's Library of Heaven?"

Painter's Paradise

I lifted the scroll to touch the doorway, but the scroll and my hand passed right through it and an invisible force sucked me inside the hall. Colors flashed and swept by me like great broom-sized strokes from a paint sprayer. The air was heavy with the scent of oil and spices. Colored pigments burst into the atmosphere like exploding bags of finely ground flour, dusting the air with an effusion of color that stayed suspended in mid-flight and then gradually disappeared. Angels were playing in the colors, mixing and swirling and stirring their room-sized color pallet. Their wings were covered with heavenly paint and pigment.

"These colors are so pure," I observed. "They seem to have a distinctive composition different from those on earth. They're powerful, uncorrupted and unalloyed. These must be Spirit-Colors," I said, amazed at my choice of words. "Conceivably, I am looking at the source colors from which all others derive their origin." The rainbow of color zoomed around me like a ballet of brilliantly clad parrots joyfully displaying their plumage.

Everywhere that I looked, color was flying and floating in the atmosphere, but there were no canvasses or surfaces to capture the paint. The atmosphere itself was the canvass. I watched as one angel moved his arm through the air like a windshield wiper. The colors dissolved, creating a clear space for his masterpiece. Then he simply gathered the pigment he wanted by catching it and placing it onto the canvass of air. The atmosphere was both the palate and the canvass.

"I'm standing in an artist's paradise," I whispered in awe, breathless with the beauty around me.

The Power of Color

"What is your name?" I asked one angel as he mixed and blended the paint on his new canvas.

"My name is Arneold," he replied. "I am from the artisan's tribe of angels created by the King to serve His pleasure. I am the administrator of the Hall of Communication. Our names are given to describe our character and destiny. My own name, Arneold, means 'eagle power.'

"The names of the colors are intentional as well. They communicate far more than identity. Colors have great power and influence in the spiritual realm. They carry enabling qualities that enhance or diminish the spiritual atmosphere. The King chooses colors and combinations that communicate and accomplish His will. Let me illustrate this. Come over here, Royal Scribe, and touch my canvas."

I moved closer and touched the canvas with my index finger. The paint was fluid and hot to the touch. Power surged up my arm as I moved my finger into a red angel-brushstroke. The instant I withdrew my finger, the paint on it turned to fine powder, but it still retained its brilliance.

"This is Volcanic Red," Arneold explained. "It possesses a molten energy field. Now touch here!" he pointed. I placed my finger on a blue spot. "This is Lagoon Blue."

"It's so soothing!" I responded.

"Notice the blue-green combination. I love it," Arneold said. "I just mixed it so you could see it. It is actually a perfect reflection of one of my favorite places on earth."

"It's amazing, Arneold. It's beautiful and it really affects my emotions and even my physical being. I want to stay here in this artist's paradise and paint for years."

"That's what everyone says. It is so beautiful. But there are those who actually come here just to paint. It is their assignment."

I immediately thought of the anointed artists I know personally, such as Mandy Adendorff.[93] "Do you mentor these gifted artists?" I asked.

"Of course," he replied. "A few of them come often to gather supplies and regularly paint here in the Hall of Communication. But this is only the entrance. You must go farther inside this hall. You will discover the Father-Colors as you go deeper."

"Thank you for the demonstration, Arneold. This is a wonderful place. It's so full of vivaciousness and energy. This is a dimension of creativity, a playground of artistic evolution. I absolutely love it. I had no idea it existed until now. I am eager to discover the Father-Colors though," I said with anticipation. "I should be going."

Painting Studios

I walked through the swirling colors. They responded to my motion like rippling water. I passed through a doorway leading into an artist's work area. Small studios were located on each side of a center passageway. Each painter had their own workspace with an easel and other necessary supplies. Someone was painting sunrises and sunsets. Another individual was painting a portrait. There were creatures that I had never seen before that were breathing color like a living can of multicolor spray paint. I stopped to watch their creativity in utter amazement. One studio housed a being that threw colors in the air that instantly became a scene or schematic picture of an object, star or a galaxy.

"It's as if they are throwing the pieces of a puzzle up in the air, and the pieces are supernaturally joining themselves together to reveal the picture," I said in delight. "They are pouring the paint, and the colors mimic the imagination of the artist or even have a mind of their own."

The Mixing Gallery

I passed through another doorway into the third gallery of the expanding hall. Beams of light were cascading into the room with extreme power and blinding brilliance. A cloud of God's glory filled the entire space. Color poured into the room in such abundance and force that I couldn't remain standing. Caught in a stream of blue, I was swept off my feet and tumbled in the liquid light.

"Knowledge," I cried. "What is happening to me? What is this place?"

He appeared instantly. "This is the gallery where the Trinity-Colors are mixed. Light that is emanating from Father in the proceeding section is directed here to the Mixing Gallery. All color comes from the Father of Lights. He is Light. What you see here is the result of the 'I Am' qualities of His being. All color originates in Him and is part of who God is. We cannot create color, but we can make endless combinations by mixing the Trinity-Colors. We use these throughout the heavenly realm. Earth colors are limited thus far. But soon, new color combinations will begin to appear as the sons of God begin to manifest their diversity on earth and creation is unlocked.[94]

"The Trinity-Colors are as follows: Father's color is yellow, Son's is red, and Holy Spirit's is blue. These three are the source of all other hues. These Trinity-Colors are unalterable, irreducible and eternal. They are the progenitors of the seven Father-Colors. The Trinity-Colors are the first colors. The proceeding Father-Colors are secondary. The seven Father-Colors are unique compositions of the Trinity-Colors. When the Trinity-Colors are combined in various proportions and mixtures, the seven resulting Father-Colors are created. The results are red, orange, yellow, green, blue, indigo, and violet. On earth you refer to these as the color spectrum.

"These seven hues are the covenant colors or rainbow spectrum. They are specific blends of power, authority and communication that emanate from the individual Trinity-Colors. They manifest God's character. They function to protect, enhance, equip and enable all of God's creation."

The Gallery of Light

Knowledge pointed to another doorway that led farther into the Hall of Communication. "Let me explain further. Let's go into the Gallery of Light."

We stepped through another doorway. "All colors have three dimensions: hue, value and intensity," he explained. "The *hue* is the color's name. Its *value* is determined by how light or dark it is. Its *intensity* is the purity or strength of the color. The Trinity-Colors are absolutely pure. Their intensity is liquid light. They are so strong that they overpower all other hues.

"Father's identity, value and purity are manifested in His radiance. This is the glory-cloud that emanates from Him. The Son is the radiance of God's glory:

God, after He spoke long ago to the fathers in the prophets in many portions and in many ways, in these last days has spoken to us in His Son, whom He appointed heir of all things, through whom also He made the world. And He is the radiance of His glory and the exact representation of His nature, and upholds all things by the word of His power. When He had made purification of sins, He sat down at the right hand of the Majesty on high, having become as much better than the angels, as He has inherited a more excellent name than they. (Hebrews 1:1–5)

"The fullness of God is expressed through His glory-colors (Trinity-Colors): yellow, red, and blue. Color is much more than you realize," Knowledge insisted. "First, you must understand that color creates atmospheres. It can control mood. The appropriate discharge of a specific color or blend has the capability to control emotion, energy and productivity. It can sooth or excite, satiate or stimulate.

"Second, you know that God is the Light-Giver.[95] Color and light are the carriers of communication. Light is the conduit by which we communicate. Our words are carried on light. Color has the distinct capability of establishing and strengthening a covenant. For example, consider the rainbow.

"Color also has heat properties. It is a temperature regulator. When God manifests His glory, it produces intense heat and a burning fire of color, light and sound. You will understand this better as we proceed into the hall. There are times when Father manifests peace. The hues of blue and green are released in the spirit realm. Other emotions such as joy, sadness, knowledge, wisdom and revelation are all stimulated by the Father-Colors. The King loves color and has used it intentionally on the canvass of creation. The two predominate colors He chose for earth are blue and green.

The Crystal Prism

"Follow me," Knowledge instructed. I gasped in astonishment. The beauty and intricacy of what filled my vision was staggering. A giant crystal prism, so big that it filled the entire wall in front of me, flashed and sparkled as the light in the room splashed across its surface and cascaded back into the atmosphere. Smaller, diamond-like crystals embedded in the prism behaved like functioning fountain heads of liquid light. Angels were rotating these jewel orifices like showerheads. Each slight movement produced new shades and intensities of the color flowing out of the nozzles. Their movements were precise and often very miniscule. Once they adjusted the nozzle to produce a different shade, the angels recorded the nozzle setting information on a tablet that looked like a color chart. Then they held the chart up to the prism in front of the nozzle to obtain a color sample. It was captured onto the page, providing a color swatch along with the precise formula used to create it.

I was standing in a shower of pigment. My skin was bathed in this technicolor display. So many different colors streamed out of this fountainhead—thousands, perhaps millions, of shades and hues, too many to comprehend or categorize. It was incomprehensible and strained my artistic capabilities. I was on color overload. There were so many that I had never seen before. I stared at the mechanism in awe.

"A fountain of color with an adjustable diamond nozzle head—I'm taking a shower in liquid color!" I blubbered, wiping my hand across my arm. "I'm a living canvas covered with color from the very *source* Himself! I wish I had a mirror right now. I can feel the color. It's hot or cold, sometimes like the noonday sun or a cold desert night. This is more than amazing. There's simply no adequate way to describe it. It must be experienced."

My shower was suddenly interrupted. "We must pass through the prism of color," Knowledge directed. "Come with me!"

The Gallery of Essence

We stood directly in front of the center of the color prism. In seconds, I was melting into the stream of color emanating from the epicenter. My body absorbed the energy, and I flowed upstream into the colors, right through the prism and into a chamber with no walls. Only two dimensions existed in this unrestricted space, and a single invisible barrier that seemed impenetrable divided them. On my left was total black, terrifying darkness—so black that it struck fear in my heart. But I had a mysterious and very compelling desire to enter it.

On my right, pure light—so pure that I knew instantly that any attempt to approach it would put my life at risk. A nuclear explosion can't compare to this light-energy. "Where are we, Knowledge?" I asked.

"This is the Gallery of Essence," he replied. "Light and darkness dwell here. These are the ethers where Father dwells. He manifests His presence in light and darkness.

"Light and darkness are the same to Father. He uses light to transfigure and rearrange molecular structures and life forms. But it may surprise you to know that God created the darkness and uses it as a veil to hide Himself when He approaches."

My curiosity was ignited. I knew that the Scriptures often speak of God's relationship with darkness. Various passages scrolled rapidly through my memory:

It happened that when the priests came from the holy place, the cloud filled the house of the LORD, so that the priests could not stand to minister because of the cloud, for the glory of the LORD filled the house of the LORD. Then Solomon said, "The LORD has said that He would dwell in the thick cloud." (I Kings 8:10–12, NAS)

As the sun was setting, Abram fell into a deep sleep, and a thick and dreadful darkness came over him. (Genesis 15:12, NIV)

These words the LORD spoke unto all your assembly in the mount out of the midst of the fire, of the cloud, and of the thick darkness, with a great voice: and he added no more. And he wrote them in two tables of stone, and delivered them unto me. And it came to pass, when ye heard the voice out of the midst of the darkness, (for the mountain did burn with fire,) that ye came near unto me, even all the heads of your tribes, and your elders; And ye said, Behold, the LORD our God hath shewed us his glory and his greatness, and we have heard his voice out of the midst of the fire: we have seen this day that God doth talk with man, and he lives. Now therefore why should we die? for this great fire will consume us: if we hear the voice of the LORD our God any more, then we shall die. For who is there of all flesh, that hath heard the voice of the living God speaking out of the midst of the fire, as we have, and lived? Go thou near, and hear all that the LORD our God shall say: and speak thou unto us all that the LORD our God shall speak unto thee; and we will hear it, and do it. (Exodus 20:18–21; Hebrews 12:18–29)

Then said Solomon, The LORD hath said that he would dwell in the thick darkness. (2 Chronicles 6:1)

The Lord reigns, let the earth be glad; let the distant shores rejoice. Clouds and thick darkness surround him; righteousness and justice are the foundation of his throne. Fire goes before him and consumes his foes on every side. His lightning lights up the world; the earth sees and trembles. The mountains melt like wax before the Lord, before the Lord of all the earth. The heavens proclaim his righteousness, and all peoples see his glory. (Psalm 97:1–6, NIV)

*Thus saith the LORD to his anointed, to Cyrus, whose right hand I have holden, to subdue nations before him; and I will loose the loins of kings, to open before him the two leaved gates; and the gates shall not be shut; **I** will go before thee, and make the crooked places straight: I will break in pieces* *the gates of brass, and cut in sunder the bars of iron: And I will give thee the treasures of darkness, and hidden riches of **secret places**, that thou mayest know that I, the LORD, which call thee by thy name, am the God of Israel.* (Isaiah 45:3, KJV)

About eight days after Jesus said this, he took Peter, John and James with him and went up onto a mountain to pray. As he was praying, the appearance of his face changed, and his clothes became as bright as a flash of lightning. Two men, Moses and Elijah, appeared in glorious splendor, talking with Jesus. They spoke about his departure, which he was about to bring to fulfillment at Jerusalem. Peter and his companions were very sleepy, but when they became fully awake, they saw his glory and the two men standing with him. As the men were leaving Jesus, Peter said to him, "Master, it is good for us to be here. Let us put up three shelters—one for you, one for Moses and one for Elijah." (He did not know what he was saying.) While he was speaking, a cloud appeared and covered them, and they were afraid as they entered the cloud. A voice came from the cloud, saying, "This is my Son, whom I have chosen; listen to him." When the voice had spoken, they found that Jesus was alone. The disciples kept this to themselves and did not tell anyone at that time what they had seen. (Luke 9:28–36, NIV)

Darkness and Light

"So, light can actually dwell in the midst of darkness and be shrouded by it?[96] This is truly a mystery," I said, confused by the conundrum.

"Clouds and darkness are God's *secret place*. The phrase *secret place* can actually be translated 'cloud and darkness,' and the word 'shadow' can also mean 'cloud' and 'darkness,'" Knowledge explained.

I proceeded to walk forward through the center of the hall, straddling what to me were two totally different, conflicting milieus. The juxtaposition of light and darkness existing together was contradictory to everything I knew about the two dimensions. My left foot was treading in total darkness while my right was ensconced in brilliant light. This dichotomous pathway forced me to face two obvious questions: "God is light and in Him is no darkness at all, and Jesus came as a light into the darkness of the world's sinful citizenship. Despite how hard it may try, the darkness cannot overcome the light. How can these two totally different contexts be the same to God? How can this stalemate exist? God dwells in both!"

The sensation of walking in both dimensions at the same time was exhilarating and mysterious. I was connecting the two fields of light and darkness like a human fuse in a high-powered electrical circuit. I grunted and jerked uncontrollably.

"This is like walking a metal tightrope connected to an electric generator," I stuttered. Each step brought a new surge of power shocking my entire body. My muscles quivered and my head flew back. With each proceeding step, I kept grunting involuntarily and repeating, "Light and glory. Darkness and mystery. Light and glory. Darkness and mystery!" As I approached the far side of the room, the light and darkness moved away from each other, and the intensity of the atmosphere diminished.

"What's happening?" I asked, bewildered by my experience.

"You are embracing His manifest glory and mystery," Knowledge answered. "You have entered the realm of union with God. This is what Moses experienced on the mountain in the cloud and in the glory. He was transfigured into God's essence. His glory does that. You become one with Him.

"Remember, God dwells in light and darkness. You cannot choose one or the other. You must have both. Without darkness, there is no light. All color requires light and darkness. Black, deep darkness veils the King and is the canvas for the heavenly realms. Light radiates from the Father of Lights; the darkness is used to hide Him. Black and white are not colors; they are identifiers that express essence.[97] Jesus does not evoke darkness, but He uses the darkness as a dwelling place. It is light to Him, but darkness to us.

"You will eventually visit the heavenly capital, Royal Scribe. There is no darkness there, only shadow.[98] Jesus, our King, is the only *source* of light there. His essence and glory illuminate the entire holy city. It is awesome to behold."

I struggled to wrap my mind around this concept, to no avail. *Just record it on the scroll,* I thought. *This is a spiritual truth, not a physics lesson.*

Vibration

"We should advance farther into the Hall of Communication now. Follow me into this last section," Knowledge prodded.

"This entrance is unlike any other," I said, staring at the unusual portal. The door was circular instead of rectangular. It was made from some sort of skin-like membrane sewn onto the doorway with leather-like laces.

"Look, it's vibrating!" I said, glancing at Knowledge with a quizzical frown.

"Place your palm on it," Knowledge suggested reassuringly.

I reached my hand forward with caution and placed my palm on the membrane trying not to disturb the surface of the doorway. My experience playing the tympani drums in the high school orchestra came into play. There is a distinct skill achieved by the musician who can feel the timbre of the instrument through his hands and affect the tone and resonance of the drum simply by touching it. My caution was rewarded. The surface felt exactly like a drumhead. The exact moment I touched it, I felt like I had just put on an expensive set of Bose headphones. Music and sound reverberated into my soul and spirit.

"Stay where you are! Keep your hand on the speaker, and you will be translated into the chamber. This is the entrance to the Chamber of Sound," Knowledge instructed.

The Chamber of Sound

Knowledge was right. The vibration and sound transported me through the entrance into the chamber. People and angels were floating in what I can best describe as non-atmosphere.

"Notice that this chamber is directly connected to the Gallery of Essence were light and darkness exist. All sound frequencies emanate from the light and are carried and streamed along their waves. Here in the heavenly realm, the volume, range and frequency of sound are limitless. You can hear only a limited range of sound on earth. But here in Heaven, sound is not bound by atmosphere or limited in scope or scale.

"You must be mindful that sound has creative or destructive power. Just like color, its force can shatter and its softness can calm. Father releases sound when He speaks. His voice can be like the sound of thunder. He speaks out of the fire and the cloud.[99] He sounds like the wings of the cherubim.[100] His voice is borne by His majesty glory.[101] The Lord thunders from the heavens, and the voice of the Most High is like hail stones and coals of fire.[102]

"The voice of God is upon the waters; the God of Glory thunders; the Lord is over many waters. When He raises His voice, the earth melts. When He utters His voice there is a tumult of waters, and He causes the clouds to ascend from the end of the earth; He makes lightening for the rain and brings forth the wind from His storehouses in the heavens."[103] Thunder is an audible sign that God's purposes are engaging and intersecting time and earth and affecting history. When Jesus hung on the Cross, the crowd said it thundered![104] Saul fell to the ground when he heard Jesus' voice.[105] When God speaks, the ground shakes and heaven and earth take notice.

"Sound and light are used to create!" Knowledge explained. "Language is controlled and manipulated sound. Father created light first. He used sound and light to shape the cosmos. He spoke and it was formed from nothing except His word-sounds and light. Sounds are stored here in the Chamber of Sound and then released at the direction of Father, Son and Spirit.[106] I have heard sounds that can confuse or that are so pure and clear that they are like laser beams refracted off crystals with color and liquid essence like the purest of oil. The anointing is so strong that it causes the sound to pierce through any substance. On earth, a single frequency can shatter a crystal goblet. Here in heaven, such sound power can extinguish or create entire universes with a single tone.

"Some sounds here in heaven are unlike any on earth. You can hear them in the spirit realm but not by your physical abilities. In this place you must listen with your spirit-man."

I focused on listening in the spirit. I could barely discern a very low rumbling sound deep within me. It wasn't clear, just beyond my spirit's audible reach, but I knew if I practiced listening in the spirit, I would eventually hear more heavenly sounds. *After all,* I reasoned, *if we can speak in the spirit, we can also hear in the spirit.*

My focus was broken as the royal scroll began to vibrate in my hand. It was pointing toward the entrance. "I need to go now," I said to Knowledge. "But before I do, please explain something to me. When I first entered the door to this section of the library, I thought I had entered the galleries of color, but then I entered the Gallery of Light and the Chamber of Sound. Why are the color, light and sound components together here in this area of the library?"

"Because this is the Hall of Communication," he explained. "Color, light and sound are the components that God uses to communicate. The triad comprise sight and sound. This trinity is the core of all communication. In its purest form, communication transcends language, deeming it unnecessary. Communication at this level is Spirit to spirit. But Father, Son and Holy Spirit speak audibly when necessary or preferable."

"The Hall of Communication," I repeated. "Now I understand…" As I was speaking, I was instantly translated into the great hall and found myself standing at the circular reception desk looking at Knowledge.

"That was awesome," I said.

"I know," he replied. "But you're just getting started."

An Incredible Gift
My hand brushed across my side, and I felt an object hanging on my belt. I was shocked. It was a palette knife.

"Wow! Look at this," I said with joy, like a child on his birthday.

I withdrew the artist's tool with delight. "This metal blade's like a polished mirror," I said, admiring its quality. "It's so sensitive to the touch, so flexible. Do you see how it reflects images and colors? This is not a typical painter's palette knife. It's supernatural. I can feel the anointing upon it. This is a sanctified painting *instrument* and it fits perfectly in my hand."

Knowledge smiled: "He made it just for you. I saw Him place it under your belt. He didn't want to distract you at that moment because of the flow of revelation. Notice the handle. The gemstones were chosen with great care and intention."

I examined the gemstones embedded in the handle. They sparkled as though they were alive. A garnet, a yellow diamond and a sapphire were set in the olive wood handle. "The three-fold hues," I uttered, "the Trinity-Colors." My hand trembled as I admired the irreplaceable instrument.

I turned the knife over, suspecting what I might discover. I was right. Seven gemstones were positioned in a straight line along the length of the handle. The Father-Colors gleamed with creativity and virtue. "I'm holding the source of covenant authenticity," I trembled, feeling the power and authority of the painting instrument in my hand.

"What an incredible gift!" I said, my heart bursting with love for my Father. "Thank you so much, Abba. What a precious gift. I will cherish it always."

I did not see Him but His voice revealed the joy of the Giver of every good and perfect gift.

"You are welcome, son, but I want you to use it, not just admire it. Paint for Me. Holy Spirit will anoint you. Paint the heavenly vistas as well as earth's panoramas. I bless you and anoint you as one of My artists. Enjoy it and use it. Use your heart and your imagination to paint with it. Like a child, play with it to create what you see. Dream with it. Imagine with it. It is My gift to you for you to imagine, create and worship Me with. Let it sing and play with light, sound and color."

"Thank You so much, Father. I can't wait to start painting. I have learned so much here."

I could feel Father's joy.

I looked back at Knowledge: "It's really mine! He made it just for me. He wants me to paint for Him."

"I know," he responded, "but don't take it too seriously. It's not a job! It's for your and His pleasure."

Knowledge took on a more serious expression: "The Lord has determined your itinerary and on this first visit, you must experience a few things here before this part of your assignment is complete. Are you ready, Royal Scribe?"

"Yes, I am!"

The Pallet Knife

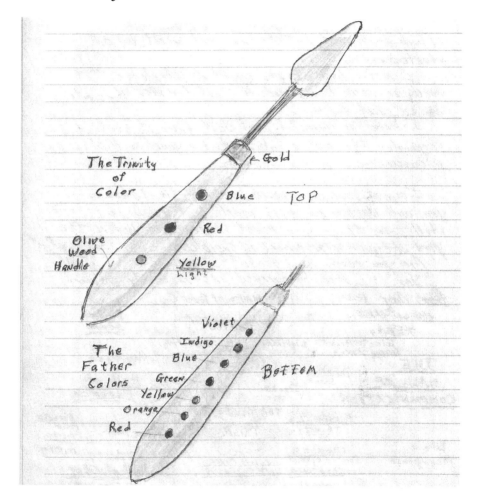

The Hall of Communication

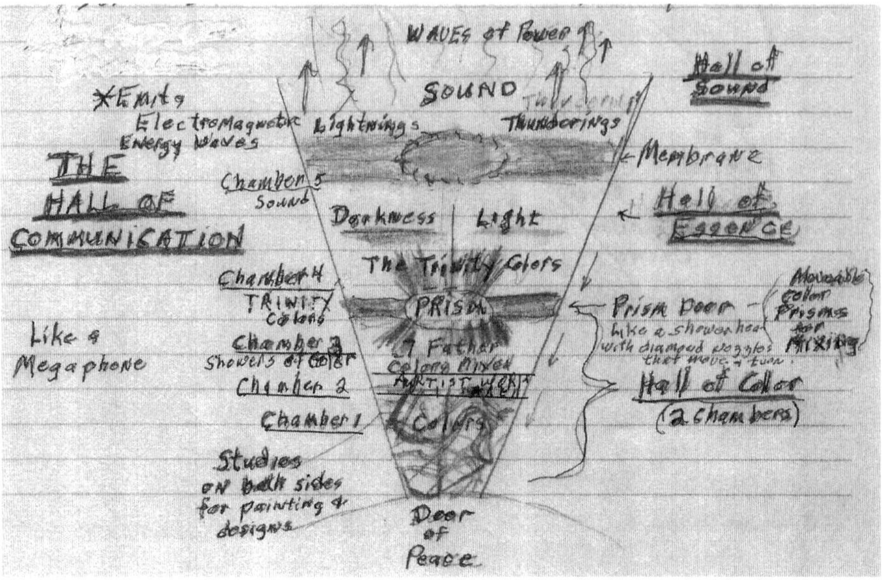

WAVES of Power
SOUND
Hall of Sound
*Emits Electromagnetic Energy Waves
Lightnings
Thunderings
Membrane
THE HALL OF COMMUNICATION
Chamber 5 Sound
Darkness
Light
Hall of Essence
The Trinity Colors
Chamber 4 TRINITY Colors
PRISM
Prism Door
like a showerhead with diamond nozzles that move & turn
Movable Color Prisms for Mixing
Like a Megaphone
Chamber 3 Showers of Color
Father Colors Mixed
Chamber 2
ARTIST WORK
Hall of Color (2 chambers)
Chamber 1
Colors
Studios on both sides for painting & designs
Door of Peace

CHAPTER 15

The Hall of Remembrance

It's better to wait for direction than to launch out on my own, I thought. The words of a dear friend and mentor came to mind: "Don't try to make things happen for yourself by your own initiative. Don't manipulate circumstances. Wait for God's initiative and be aware that every opportunity that crosses your path may not be an assignment from God. It may be a distraction from your true mission."

This truth certainly applies to my current situation, I realized. The view from the reception desk offered a multitude of choices. I was faced with the need once more for clear guidance. Something, or someone, prompted me to turn intuitively toward a door near the entrance to the library. The royal scroll confirmed my selection. I approached the entrance to another new and mysterious area of God's royal library with lightness in my step and joy in my heart.

"My spirit is happy, Lord. I feel like I'm walking on a cushion of air," I said. "I've already experienced so much here in the library, but I am eager to learn more, Jesus. Teach me Your ways. Reveal Your thoughts to me. I am here to search Your heart, King of kings and Lord of lords. You said treasures are hidden in the heart of the king and the wise man draws them out."[107]

"I Am about to reveal to you a sacred treasure here in the library. It is very precious to Me. Enter through this gate!" He replied. The golden scroll vibrated as He spoke, affirming the fact that He said 'gate' and not door.

The 'Hallel' Gateway

I stood before the entrance wondering what to do next. A deep desire began to rise up inside of me. I couldn't suppress it. The pressure was supernatural. A river of worship and praise began to flow through me. It exploded like a geyser rising out of my spirit.

"Lord, You are awesome and holy. Your Word is truth. You are absolute righteousness and altogether lovely. I bow before You. I humble myself in Your awesome presence. You are like the morning dew that wakens the day with freshness. You shine like the sun, casting out the darkness. You are worthy to be worshiped and adored. Savior, Redeemer, Friend—all the earth and the heavens sing Your praises.

"Thank you for redeeming me from sin and shame. Thank You for giving me new life. Thank You, Master, for choosing me to serve You as Your scribe. I love You so much."

The words tumbled out from my heart like gifts to the King; they were priceless pearls of worship that are the only thing that can satisfy His thirst.[108] To my total surprise, my thanksgiving activated the gateway. It swung open to reveal a hall filled with mist.

"This is not smoke or fog," I said. "This is His holy presence. An amazing aroma stimulated my entire being. "His presence is perfumed," I uttered in delight and took a single step through the entryway. "I feel like I am stepping into a bath of warm fragrant oil. It's like liquid love. Spirit of Knowledge, what is this atmosphere?" I asked.

"I thought you might recognize it since you have experienced it before. This is the Hall of Remembrance. You have just entered through the 'Hallel' gateway.[109] You can enter this passageway only by praise and thanksgiving. You are standing within the cloud of His presence. The aroma you detect comes from the holy incense burned upon the altar of incense that is located here in the Hall of Remembrance. Father loves this fragrance. This royal incense is continuously burned here in heaven by the Aaronic Priests who are here because of their faith in their Messiah. They are among the redeemed from God's chosen people, Israel. They continue their messianic priestly duties here, except for the offering of sacrifices, which are no longer required because of Jesus' crucifixion as the Lamb of God. Angels have joined them and also burn incense on the Golden Altar before the Throne of God.[110]

"Father, Son and Holy Spirit come here to walk in this environment and to talk with those who are here. This is like the holy atmosphere that the priests created in the wilderness Tabernacle amidst Israel's camp and also in the Temple in Jerusalem. It is precious to God. His sense of smell impresses and activates memory. He often comes here to revisit His servants and share again the intimacy they cherished in the Holy of Holies where He dwelt in their midst within the incense, fire and cloud above the mercy seat. Jesus will forever be our great High Priest according to the order of Melchizedek."[111]

Israel's Journey

"Follow me through the hall, Royal Scribe!" Knowledge commanded.

The scene was surreal, like a journey back into the past. Oil lamps placed at frequent intervals flickered along the pathway. They cast a timeless glow through the mist and over the stones, leaving shadows that made them appear like puzzle pieces masterfully placed together. The pathway followed a circuitous route through the vapor and shadows. It led through an ancient eastern city, or was it a replica?

"This is not a Disney World attraction," I reminded myself. "This is a sacred section in the Library of Heaven. I must pay careful attention to every detail. Could this be old Jerusalem?" I wondered. Then it dawned on me. My love of history captured the significance of this moment. "I'm walking through an authentic diorama of Israel's history."

Images flashed into my imagination. I sensed the presence of Abraham, Isaac, Jacob and his sons. Places and people flashed by like a documentary of the families, clans, tribes and the nation of God's choosing. Nations that either hated or blessed Israel filled the screen of my mind. Wars and struggles and peace and prosperity were all part of the landscape.

"You are right, Royal Scribe. This is the journey through Israel's past," Knowledge explained.

I focused on the details alongside the pathway. Rubble began to appear as we continued deeper into the sacred hall. Potsherds at first, then tent canvasses, water pots, carts and wagons and farm implements lay scattered everywhere. This was the detritus of history. Many weapons appeared in certain places along the pathway. My journey provided clear evidence of a unique culture and society. I felt like an archeologist discovering proof of the veracity of the Scriptures. When archeologists dig to uncover the past in Egypt, they call the earthen-mound a 'tell.' But no digging is required here. *What would these objects tell us if they could speak?* I pondered.

Uncut stone altars emerged along the way, serving as distance markers of a long-ago spiritual pilgrimage. Each one chronicled a God-encounter moment in the lives of Abraham, Isaac and Jacob as they journeyed by faith in obedience to God's direction. A multicolored robe lay unfolded near the opening of a cistern— Joseph's coat of many colors, I assumed. Turning a bend in the circuitous pathway, an enormous mountain made of mud and straw bricks bordered the road on both sides. I gasped at the sight. "Oh, the human suffering and untold years of forced slave labor. The sheer size and immensity of this brickyard is a silent witness to the agony, sweat and tears of bone-tired slaves forced to labor in the blazing sun of Egypt to satisfy Pharaoh's insatiable appetite for greater and grander tombs to transport him to the afterlife. This is truly the first holocaust of the Jewish people," I said, aghast at the human cost of a single pyramid. "Slavery in Egypt was beyond cruel."

A Baby's Lifeboat

In the distance, a light shined through a narrow passageway. It grew brighter as we proceeded through the stockyard of bricks. To my amazement, the massive wall of bricks on my right decreased and gave way to a river bordered by reeds and papyrus. A tiny raft of woven reeds floated near the shore; it was crafted skillfully and was the size of a small cradle. An infant's wool swaddling cloth lay crumpled in the bottom of the miniature vessel.

"These are the props of history," I said. "Out of the Nile, which gave life to Egypt, would come the deliverer of the people it enslaved. This was no mere boat; it was an ark of deliverance! God heard their cry and answered their lament. Moses was God's gift to the suffering offspring of Abraham. He arrived in an ark, the response of God's mercy and covenant faithfulness."

The Applied Blood is Still Fresh!

We were much closer to a glistening passageway ahead of us. Light coursed through the entrance like a beacon streaming from a lighthouse providing safety for all who could see it. It beckoned with a power beyond normal luminescence. This light was supernatural. At last, I was close enough to see that it was blasting through a doorway.

Knowledge spoke with a boldness and an anointing that was prophetic. "This," he proclaimed, "is one of the actual doors from Egypt! It was brought here by the angels of death. This is a Passover door. Look!" he pointed. "The blood of a lamb is still fresh on the doorposts and lintel just as it was on the night of Passover when it was applied. It has never dried! The Lamb of God remains the only way of salvation!"

I looked in reverence at the glistening crimson blood soaking the doorframe indelibly with the mark of redemption. "Without the shedding of blood, there can be no forgiveness," I said with a fresh realization that it is and always was the blood of the sacrifice that restored us to communion with God.

"The blood of the Lamb shouts through the halls of history. It is the only means of forgiveness of sins," I said again, with a deep sense of gratefulness and humility. "The blood of the lamb delivered Israel from death and slavery. The blood of the Lamb of God, Jesus of Nazareth the Messiah, delivers us from slavery to Satan, sin, death and eternal damnation. The image of this Passover door will forever be etched in my heart next to the cross of Christ."

By faith I stepped forward into the stream of white light and entered the ancient doorway not knowing what was on the other side. The power of God swept through me in waves, each one carrying an awesome increasing assurance of His mercy. I was infused once more with supernatural peace.

"I thought I understood portals and how they function, but this one is different," I uttered in astonishment. "I am totally and eternally protected. No amount of earthly security can match this incredible experience. You are my safe place, Lord. You are my protection! I need no other. There is no greater power on earth or in heaven than Your shed blood, Jesus."

The Aqua-Tunnel

My rapture was suddenly interrupted. My right foot landed in ankle-deep water and within a few steps, I was treading on dry ground. The sound of wind and waves crashed around me. I was walled in on both sides by staggering, huge walls of fomenting, tormented waves. Only one way was available: forward. It led down into a dark angry blue chasm between watery cliffs. The sea canyon floor was completely dry as I marched through the aqua-tunnel.

I pinched my arm to remind myself that I am in the Library of Heaven. "It all seems so real. But wait a minute. It is real!" I affirmed. "This is not a dream. This is God's account of sacred history and I am living it. I am travelling on the path of Israel's spiritual pursuit of the fulfillment of God's promise. This Hall of Remembrance is not a parched, unemotional, intellectual history lesson. It is alive! I am seeing it. I can feel it and smell, hear and taste it. And yes, I can even touch it!"

After several minutes of walking, my feet were on desert soil again. Knowledge pointed right and we turned south. Time sped up and in moments we were approaching a massive mountain. The fearsome sight made me tremble. Thunder rumbled a warning to all who approached. Lightening lit up the sky with such bolts of power that the hair on my arms stood up. A dark roiling cloud covered the summit, preventing any attempt to see what lay within its black billows. Any effort to see beyond its fringe was fruitless.

The Chosen People

"We have just passed through the Passover doorway entrance that leads into the *three dimensions,*" Knowledge explained. "We must ascend the mountain. Then you will understand what I am saying. But before we begin the climb, I must share with you some information about the Hall of Remembrance. Each time you enter this section of the library, you will learn more about Israel. You will have time to speak to the Israelites and ask questions. You will meet families and individuals from every tribe here. There are places that Abraham, Isaac and Jacob frequent, as well as Moses, Samuel, Elijah, David, Ezra and Esther, just to mention a few. All are welcome, from the least to the most renowned.

"The Jewish people come here to fellowship and remember the goodness and kindness of Yahweh and marvel at His wondrous works on their behalf. Their often repeated phrase is, 'Do you remember when…' The hall is often crowded with Jews and gentiles alike. Each one is qualified to enter through the blood of Jesus. They are all loved and regarded the same by Father. Every person here in the realm of the kingdom reveres Israel's journey and continues to profit from the lessons that our forefathers learned throughout their lives. But all sorrow has been wiped away. Joy fills the kingdom. Love and peace prevail. There is neither Jew nor Greek, bond or free, rich or poor, male or female that determines your qualifications to enter the realm of God's Kingdom. It is only through the Body and Blood of Jesus that you can enter. But you don't lose your identity as a person here in heaven. You bring it with you. You are an heir and joint-heir with Jesus Christ, your Brother. You are all sons or daughters of the King.

"Father chose Israel as the spiritual womb to prepare the way and bring forth His son on earth. They are His chosen people for a reason. He continually honors and keeps His covenant with them and will do so for all eternity. We must never forget the role they have fulfilled in God's plan and strategy to restore mankind to Himself. Jesus is the King of the Jews. He is the King of all kings. Every individual from every tribe and tongue and nation will bow before Him and confess that Jesus Christ is Lord, to the glory of God the Father."[112]

I was humbled by the great honor that God has bestowed upon His chosen people, Israel. "This Hall of Remembrance is not so much for Him," I uttered. "It's for me. It's for all of us!" I fell to my knees, so overcome with gratefulness for these chosen ones. Tears of repentance began to trickle down my cheeks. "Oh, Father, I am so sorry for undervaluing my Jewish brothers and sisters."

Possessing the Inheritance

I felt a hand resting upon my right shoulder. I turned my head to see who it was. A man was kneeling beside me. His head was bowed in prayer. He stretched his left arm around my shoulder and drew me close to his side. It was a fatherly gesture that melted my heart. He said nothing. His head was bowed in prayer. We knelt side by side, the warmth of our bodies mingled. Our hearts where synchronized in surrender and love for Jesus. Our tears mingled together and fell to the rocky hillside at the foot of the mountain of God's glory-cloud.

I didn't know who he was. I do know that overwhelming love exuded from him. I truly loved this man I had just met. He was more than a brother or a best friend. We were one in the Spirit, soulmates in the realm of God's Kingdom.

We must have prayed and communed with Father for hours. When, at last, we felt Holy Spirit release us, he turned to me. His face was aged but not tired, and bronzed by years of exposure to the desert sun. He wore a perfectly bound white turban. A strikingly beautiful broach immediately grabbed my attention. Its place of prominence on his turban in the center of his forehead made me know this was more than a mere piece of jewelry. It had the look and luster of a military medal awarded for special achievement. The medallion depicted two adjacent healthy, green palm trees standing by a pool of water. A mountain range filled the background. The palm trees were composed of rich jade with garnet trunks. The water was aquamarine and shimmered like the rippling surface of a pool. The mountain range was a multicolored mosaic—a mixture of dark browns, black and golds on a background of eggshell white.

Who would possess such a regal insignia? I wondered.

As if on cue, the stranger answered my question. "I am Caleb," he said. "I am like you. I have endured to possess the fullness of my destiny. I asked for and received the high ground. It was my reward for believing that nothing is impossible for Yahweh. Faith and a good report secured my future, even though I had to endure 40 years of wandering with the faithless to possess it. It was so difficult to remain in the column of people going in circles year after year and getting nowhere, wandering away the years until we buried an entire generation. But Joshua and I survived to possess the promise.

"You have endured like us. You have entered the spiritual high ground, the heavenly realms. We are one in the Spirit. I love you, Royal Scribe. When you return to earth, tell the saints to be fearless. They must endure to possess their inheritance. Age and station are not a factor. We may begin as a spy for the King, but if we are faithful, we will be among those who possess the mountain tops for Him. Passion, faith and confidence in God are what matters. Keep your focus on the eternal, all-powerful One. The angels join us to conquer and possess. I could tell you so many stories of the battles and victories won on the mountains. Perhaps in the future."

Caleb's Broach

"Will you climb with us to the mountain top? We can talk as we go," I asked.

"Yes, but I can go no farther than that. I have other things that I must attend to."

Knowledge, Caleb and I ascended the mountainside together. Caleb answered so many questions as we walked and talked. At times, we paused to catch our breath and then continued our journey upward toward the massive thundering cloud of glory above us. He did not hesitate to describe his journey through the wilderness and the forty years of excruciating mental and spiritual pain he endured. "All the while," he said sadly, "I tried to encourage others as best I could."

But then, like the rising of the morning sun, his face lit up with joy as he spoke about the miraculous crossing of the Jordan River and the great victory at Jericho. The details he gave were priceless, even to the actual describing of the shapes and colors of the stones used to build the memorial altar on the western shore of the river.

"What a day it was," Caleb said. "From morning to evening, the caravan crossed the Jordan on dry land until all of Israel was across. I remember pausing to look back toward the distant shore and the mountains beyond where Moses' journey had ended. I wondered, with deep love and appreciation, if he was watching us. He must be, I decided. I had the exhilarating hope that he was not dead, that I would see him again on this side of the river in the Promised Land."

As we approached the cloud, Caleb stopped and turned to face me. "Royal Scribe," he said with military respect," I must leave you now. Your journey ahead is so important. The revelation is vital information for the Church. I have others to meet and much to do. Come see me again!" he shouted back as he descended the mountain and was almost out of sight. "I often come to the Hall of Remembrance to reminisce with my family and friends. I'll see you here," he shouted and was gone from view, disappearing around a huge outcropping of boulders.

The Doorway of Revelation

Knowledge had been silent the entire time, but now he pointed upward to the swirling dynamo of blackness that roared with fear-inducing power.

What veiled mysteries must lie inside this numinous barrier? I pondered, trembling with emotion.

He broke his silence and spoke with definition: "The cloud is a doorway of revelation that leads into the three dimensions: the dimension of the Prophets, the dimension of the Priests, and the dimension of the Kings. This is the three-dimensional revelation of the Son of God who dwells in the cloud. These are His three eternal offices.

"Go now, Royal Scribe, but remove your shoes before entering the veil! Record on the golden scroll what you see and hear in the cloud."

I stood still, wondering why Knowledge would not accompany me, but hesitation was not an option. I sensed I wouldn't be alone. Understanding would be forthcoming.

I approached the cloud with trepidation. "I must enter. I want to," I confessed, "but what is it like in the cloud of His glory? Will I live to tell about it? Can my body endure the fullness of His presence?" I tried to correlate this moment with the experience of others before me. "Others have entered this cloud in the flesh," I said, encouraging myself. "Moses stood on this sacred mountain and in the Holy of Holies along with the high priests. They were in the cloud. Israel was led by a cloud and a pillar of fire. And what about the elders who could not stand to minister when God's Shekinah glory filled the temple? Don't forget that Peter, James and John witnessed His glory on the Mount of Transfiguration. And I know that Jesus ascended in a cloud and will return in a cloud. It seems to me that I can't get close to Him without entering the cloud! It is evidence of His presence, a covering of mystery we are invited to penetrate. But it contains an all-consuming fire!"

I tried, but my mind couldn't fully persuade me, even though others who went before me survived. My hands shook with uncontrollable tremors. The massive dark cloud was an arm's length away. I felt so small. The ground shook. The rumbling thunder exploded as flashes of shattering light emanated from within it and shot out at laser speed, scorching the air with electricity.

Immutable energy! I thought, dumbstruck by the power. I rapidly rubbed my hands along my forearms to calm my flesh, which felt like sandpaper. Then I heard it, a fluttering, buzzing sound like thousands of bees swarming around just inside the cloud. *Angels' wings!* I thought, encouraged by the sound of their presence.

The royal scroll became so hot that I dropped it. "Oh, Lord," I gasped. "The scroll. I'm so sorry." I bent to retrieve it. When I stood up, I was at the very surface of the cloud. I could breathe its essence. It was cold and hot at the same time. It was irresistible, yet so awesome that the presumption of daring to enter struck another blow of fear into my heart. But in an instant all fear was gone. His voice drew me into the cloud. I immediately knew I could. "God is here!" I uttered.

One step, a single action of abandonment and trust, and I was standing alone in His presence inside the cloud of His glory. I couldn't see anything but mist, but His presence was all around me and inside of me. Light was escaping through the pours of my skin. I was being transfigured.

"This must be what happened to Moses, Elijah, and Jesus on the mountain. God's presence changed their appearance and they radiated Father's glory," I said in amazement as the light poured into me and through me. I felt something changing deep inside of my being. The best way to describe it is that God was changing my DNA. The process was transforming me so completely that if I remained in the cloud, I knew I could never return to earth again.

"The process has begun," Father said. "This is a taste of eternity and what it is like to have a glorified body. You cannot stay in the full manifestation of My glory cloud much longer. Your assignment has just started, and you must return to tell My people what you have seen and heard. If you stay here you can never return.

"Proceed through the cloud of My glory. I want to show you what I revealed to Enoch and Moses. Ahead, you will enter the three dimensions that emanate from Me. The origin and authenticity of all ministry in My Kingdom is birthed and released in My presence." As He spoke, lightning and thunder accompanied His words and proceeded through the cloud ahead of me and beyond it. His words were preparing my pathway.

Kingdom Protocol

"Ahead of you are the three dimensions of protocol and function in My Kingdom," He explained. "They are the eternal offices of the heavenly realm. The angels know, acknowledge and have great respect for these dimensions of function and authority. You may proceed! Enter the three dimensions. My son is waiting for you there."

I walked through the cloud. Light continued to pour into and out of me. As I approached the far side of the cloud, the brightness around me diminished. I felt such heat in my body that I thought I would melt. Sweat dripped from my forehead onto the royal scroll and sizzled as it dissolved into steam. I arrived at the edge of the cloud and with one final step I found myself standing on a glass platform. Jesus was seated on the observation deck and rose to greet me.

"I have been waiting for you, Royal Scribe. I am going to reveal to you the three dimensions of kingdom life. You must realize and understand that I rule these dimensions. I commission My servants to fulfill their responsibilities by way of these offices and aptitudes. Every one of the saints here in the realms of the kingdom must serve in all three capacities. I am releasing revelation and greater insight to My Church in this age, so My disciples will begin to function at a higher level in the three-dimensional kingdom offices as My return draws near and the battle increases."

He paused and gazed into my eyes with such discernment that I felt like I was a microfiche of information under a magnifier. He was discerning and interpreting my spiritual DNA. His expression changed as He detected certain things. Then He spoke. "These are the three dimensions: the Prophet, the Priest and the King."

The moment I heard His words my spirit responded as though He had highlighted these three identities with a supernatural highlighter inside of me. The words were affirmed in my being and my DNA responded, igniting the divine code imprinted in my spirit, soul and body. My Creator and Redeemer was affirming my identity and function.

"I am a prophet, priest and king!" I asserted with confidence.

He smiled in approval. "Yes, you are! You must begin to walk in each of these offices. This is the fullness of kingdom ministry. All My sons and daughters must embrace their identity and function in these three dimensions. These are the three-fold offices that I brought from My Throne to the earth when I came the first time. I Am the Chief Apostle.[113] I was sent by My Father to bring the ministries of the prophet, priest and king to full manifestation and revelation knowledge. I Am the Chief Prophet. I Am the High Priest according to the order of Melchizedek.[114] I Am the King of all kings and Lord of lords.[115]

"The full experiential knowledge and function of these three offices resides in Me. I have brought you here to show you that these roles and functions are the full expression of how I operate. My Father appointed Me to fulfill My duties by operating in the three-in-one expression of His Word, His Holiness and His Government. The prophet-priest-king trinity is a reflection and manifestation of Father. Do not be enamored by the gifts of the Spirit or the five-fold ministries.[116] They are important, but they do not determine your true calling. They are operative graces intended for ministry and the equipping of My Church. But the three-fold offices are identity issues. You are identified as My priests, prophets and kings.

"He who sees Me, sees the Father. He who sees you, sees Me, for I am in you and you are in Me. You are transformed by My glory and presence in your being. You have become like Me in three-fold function. You are My royal priest, My prophet, and My functioning king in the realms of the heavenly kingdom and on earth.

"Earth and heaven recognize and operate by rank and authority. You have already witnessed this when you toured the angelic chariot legion encampment. I am sure you recognized that My Archangel Andrew carries great authority among the angel armies. No one messes with Andrew, the mighty warrior. He is also very humble. He never boasts of his valiant achievements and victories in battle. He never emphasizes his rank or function. He doesn't even reveal his name to anyone.

"Andrew's loyalty to me is absolute. When I created the angels, I gave them free will just as I gave it to mankind. They are not puppets serving Me like robots. They are beings of a different nature than man, but they can also choose. Lucifer sadly demonstrated this part of their nature when he rebelled against Me."

"A-a-andrew," I stuttered in surprise. "When I met him I discerned that his name was important, but he never disclosed it to me."

"His name means 'warrior, strong and mighty one.' He prefers the Chinese version, 安德鲁. When you see him again, speak his name in Mandarin. He will know that I told you to do it."

The Plane of Three Dimensions
Jesus turned to observe the view from the balcony. He pointed toward the vast plane that stretched out far into the seeable distance. I was expecting that each of the three dimensions would have a separate section or level, something like a campus with three schools. To my surprise, there were no divisions or boundaries—just one large open plane. *Never presume you understand something just because you hear it or see it,* I thought. *I learned this law in Frontier Town.*

Multitudes of people were dispersed across the vast expanse. They gathered in groups, from thousands to hundreds to smaller groupings around campfires, springs and wells, olive groves and oases. Far to the right, along the perimeter, a large body of aquamarine blue water sparkled as the light glistened and reflected off its shimmering surface.

"This is absolutely beautiful," I said. "I feel such peace and serenity. There is no conflict here. No tension or striving. Everyone seems so content."

"Yes, you are right!" Jesus replied. "Identity produces that. When you know who you are and that you are greatly loved and accepted by our Father, nothing can unsettle you. Competition and striving disappear."[117]

Gazing out across the panorama, I noticed individuals who attracted the attention of others as they walked among the people. Something distinguished them from the rest of the crowd. They were accompanied by angels who walked alongside of them, engaging them in conversation.

"What you are observing," the Lord said, "is the process of mentoring and discipling. I assign seasoned and mature priests, prophets and kings to come here to teach and train the saints. There is also a section for heavenly beings to be trained and taught regarding kingdom rank and protocol. The seven spirits also teach and mentor here. Wisdom, Understanding, Counsel, Might, Knowledge, and the Fear of the Lord have schedules and regular assignments.[118]

"Each saint is monitored and discipled by a prophet, priest or king depending on their weaknesses and strengths. Everyone must be mentored by the Spirit of Might though. My saints have not yet fully entered into the authority they should be exercising. This is essential in the coming age."

Jesus pointed to a large gathering of thousands. "Samuel is teaching them," He said with a look of satisfaction. "Notice that each one is carrying a scroll. These are given to each individual to be used here in the realm of the kingdom. They are journal scrolls for taking notes and recording lessons that are taught on the Plane of Three Dimensions.

"Let me emphasize a very important principle. You must understand this well. The purpose of the five-fold ministries of apostle, prophet, evangelist, pastor and teacher is to provide for the equipping of the saints for the work of ministry. These five gifts are not an end, in and of themselves. The work of the ministry is the three dimensions of prophet, priest and king. These are the universal offices that exist on earth and in all the heavenly realms.

"You must recognize that you are called to function as my prophet, priest and king. All the other gifts, anointings and callings are intended to release these three dimensions in and through you. My Word, My holiness and My authority are *the kingdom ascendancies.*"

The Three-Dimensional Kingdom Ascendency

"You must tell My people what you have seen here on the mountain. Encourage them to come up here to the library and visit the Hall of Remembrance to be mentored on the Plane of Three Dimensions. It is time for my prophets, priests and kings to arise in the earth to rule and reign with me. The three dimensions of the Son are invading the cosmos through My Body.

"You will soon see the manifestation of My glory as the saints arise to occupy their rightful offices as my ambassadors in the earth and in the heavenly realm. Human pride and arrogance will be shattered by the release of My Word, authority and holiness. This is the age of the three-dimension invasion. No one can stand. All must bow."

Jesus stopped speaking. Silence enveloped us. "It's snowing again," I whispered. "I love it!" Soon the balcony was covered in a blanket of white.

Jesus waved His hand through the falling snowflakes and laughed in delight. "I never cease to delight in these flakes. They reflect my creativity. I never make two alike. Imagine that, Dale. From the first snowfall till now and forever, no two alike. I know that you know that, but isn't it awesome? I love making snowflakes.

"I love you, Dale. It brings such a joy to Me to have you here." His eyes were so full of life and happiness. He spontaneously hugged me.

My heart leapt with joy. "Thank you, Jesus. I feel so complete, so accepted and loved."

He stepped back and pointed out over the Plane of Three Dimensions. "Before you leave, notice the gathering in the center, far in the distance. That is King David teaching. I love him so. He knows my heart." Then Jesus disappeared.

Weighty Revelation

I stood alone on the platform gazing off toward the distance at David's gathering. *Oh, if only I could go and join them. I want to hear David's voice and learn from his experience as the king after God's own heart,* I thought. In my enthusiasm, I impulsively stepped off the balcony toward the gathering in the distance. Instantly, everything disappeared. I was promptly transported back to the great hall in the library and found myself standing in front of the *Hallel* gate.

"Wow!" I gasped in astonishment. "That was some experience. I have so much more to learn in the Hall of Remembrance, but I'm just getting started. I have to come back here for more teaching and mentoring."

The royal scroll was noticeably heavier than when I first received it. "Interesting!" I said, humming quizzically like Sherlock Holmes as I processed the clue. "I guess the revelation becomes weightier as it accumulates inside the scroll. I dare not look inside right now. It's still recording the information I just received inside the Hall of Remembrance."

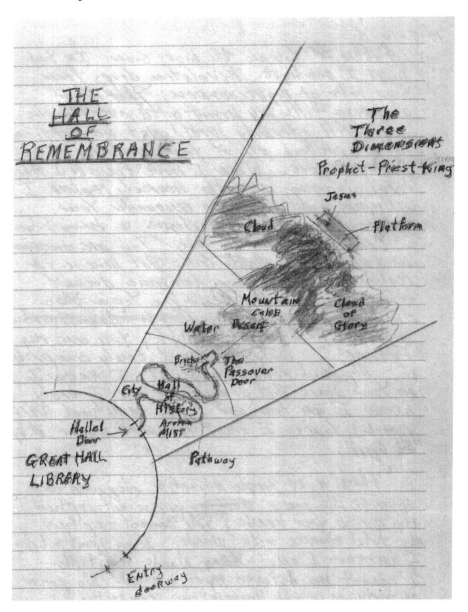

CHAPTER 16

The Royal Hall of Scrolls and Records

How can you measure the value of revelation? Without it we would perish in ignorance. What this royal scroll contains is priceless, but I have only scratched the surface of knowledge and understanding here in the heavenly realms, I thought, admiring the golden scroll in my right hand.

"Father, You are the light giver. In Your light, I see light. Revelation drops from Your robe of righteousness. Your oil of gladness fills my heart with overflowing joy. All eternity would not be sufficient to comprehend the totality of Your wisdom, knowledge, power and love. This first journey into the heavenly realms as Your scribe has made me eager to encounter more of Your awesome creativity, strategies and knowledge.

"On earth we often sing, 'You are awesome in this place, mighty God.' But here in the heavenly regions, 'awesome' is inadequate. It doesn't even come close to describing You and Your dwelling places. I am humbled to think that You are my Father! My spirit comprehends it more fully than my mind can grasp it. I know intellectually that I am Your son, and my spirit-man knows completely. It must! My spiritual DNA matches Yours. I am born of Your Spirit."

His response confirmed my inadequacy. "Many have tried and failed. No single adjective is adequate to describe Me. You cannot capture the air in your hands or slow down light. Neither can you capture the fullness of Who I Am with words. I Am Spirit and Life. I Am that I Am. Words limit Me. I Am undefinable and without limit. No being, whether by intellectual prowess or any other human or angelic effort on earth or in heaven, can comprehend all that I Am.

"Know this, My son. I Am for you and not against you. I have planned your future with ultimate value and intention. I love you and will never stop loving you. There is absolutely nothing you can do or say that can cause Me to stop loving you. But what I love most is when you come to spend time with Me. I long for and desire intimacy with you. Our time together in the *secret place* causes My heart to overflow."

"Me too, Father," I responded with delight. "I love being with You. Without Your presence, I am incomplete. Nothing can compare to it. Thank You for walking with me like You have with Enoch. Thank You for giving me permission to record our journeys together."

"My son, you have more than My permission. It is your calling and service to Me," He replied. "I have ordained you to be one of My royal scribes. Even before you knew it and recognized the anointing and flow of revelation, I was preparing the golden scrolls to serve as your journals. When you received the first scroll from My angels, you stepped into your calling, gifting and assignment.

"You have been faithful, and now you are carrying the fourth golden scroll from the Well of My Presence. When this journey through the heavenly realm is finished and you have filled the scroll, your first assignment will be complete. Two more assignments still wait to be fulfilled by you. These must be finished before I call you up here to serve me throughout the cosmos and in the outer reaches.

"Be faithful and obedient. Your reward is more than you can imagine."

"Father, serving You is reward enough! My heart bursts with joy, and I am humbled and honored to serve you."

A Word of Caution

"One word of caution, My son. Do not compare yourself with other scribes who serve Me. Much revelation is being released. Do not question or criticize your fellow scribes. There are many ways to see and perceive in the realms of heaven. What and how others see and describe things is up to Me. Just as you must be faithful to record accurately what you see and hear, they must do the same. Experience and revelation is in the eyes of the beholder. Just as the Scriptures reflect the personalities and anointings of those who wrote them, the scribes I have called and anointed for this age reflect what they see and experience in the realm of the kingdom through their individual personalities.

"There will be times when others see and experience what you have or will see. What they describe or hear will be similar to your account. This should reassure you and affirm the authenticity of the revelation. But you must remain faithful to record what you see and hear, not copy or try to imitate what others see and hear. Do not be influenced by other scribes and visitors into the heavenly realms and be led away from the revelation I am releasing to you. Guard your heart and always walk in a spirit of humility. Pride will cause Me to restrict and resist your access into the heavenly realms of My Kingdom."

"How do I stay humble, Father?" I asked with heartfelt sincerity. "I truly want to."

"You must always realize and know that it is not your ability, knowledge or spirituality that has qualified you for this assignment. I chose you! It is all My doing and for My purposes. I sent others to equip you and call you into this dimension. You were willing to come and obedient to My call. Never take credit for the measure of revelation or the calling you walk in. Always point and direct people to Me. Do not use the revelation or anointing to draw people to you or to force open doors for ministry. I will open doors for you that no man can open. I will send you where I want you to go.

"I Am calling My people close to Me. You are My royal scribe, anointed by Me to record the vision. You see what I say. My message is always about My love for all mankind. Point people to Me. Never seek self-recognition. Give me all the glory and accolades. I will affirm you; that is all the approval you need. You must not seek others for approbation. My pleasure and 'well done' is your greatest reward."

"Thank you, Father. I needed to hear this. By Your grace, I will guard my heart against pride. I will give all the glory and honor to You. I love You so much. All I need is Your presence and approval, Abba."

"You have it, My son."

He departed. I breathed a deep sigh of fulfillment as the fullness of His peace filled my whole being. I felt such affirmation and satisfaction in knowing I am pleasing to my Father. If I could only capture this moment, breathe it in and hold the atmosphere in my lungs. But alas, I must exhale. But even that is a spiritual sigh of contentment and joy. Satisfaction filled me to the core.

"Nothing can compare to pleasing Father," I said with profound contentment.

An Aqua-View

"The royal scroll…" I said, feeling its movement in my hand. "I've been lost in His presence, and now the scroll is behaving differently. It's pointing upward toward the ceiling." To my surprise, the dome shaped ceiling was moving like the screen of a planetarium. But instead of depicting stars and space, I was looking up from beneath the water at the surface of the ocean. Waves moved across the half-globe and crashed against the top of the walls of the great hall. At times the oceanscape grew calm and semi-transparent. I could not see through it, but light penetrated from above and was refracted into the great hall.

"This is like being a scuba diver submerged in the ocean," I said, astounded by the aqua-view. Shimmering light beams from above pierced through the water. Hazy yellow sunrays danced around me.

"The entire great hall looks like a giant world underwater. Life is surging; it's moving all around me. This is incredible," I uttered, taking in the breathtaking scene. "It's so beautiful, like living beneath the oceans. Why would Father create this supernatural ceiling?" I answered my own question: "He did say the earth will be filled with the knowledge of the glory of the Lord as the waters cover the sea.[119]

"This is an appropriate covering for the royal library," I said, gazing around in awe at the inundated world of knowledge. This repository of supernatural knowledge is a manifestation of God's glory. His grandeur is revealed to us here in these sacred halls of knowledge. Here in this rarified atmosphere, we experience the depths of His majesty and wisdom."

A Surprise Greeting

The scroll began to move again, slowly shifting to point toward the Hall of Times and Seasons and then rotating like a compass needle to the left. As I crossed the hall, I waved to the Spirit of Knowledge. He was talking to the Spirit of Wisdom and the Spirit of Counsel. He waved back at me, but did not speak. Apparently, their discussion was very important.

I would love to eavesdrop on that conversation, I thought. *I wonder what the topic is?*

An unusually strong magnetic pull began to emanate from the royal scroll as I approached a specific entry door. A palpable force was attracting the scroll to this section of the library. The scroll acted like a homing pigeon returning to its nest.

I was startled by the sound and jumped back in shock as the door abruptly flew open.

"Come in, Royal Scribe. I have been expecting you. I am the Scroll Keeper and this is the Royal Hall of Scrolls and Records. No doubt you've heard of me. My name is Luke," he said, extending his hand to me.

"Luke," I replied, grasping his hand while still reeling from the sudden encounter. "Of course, the Scroll Keeper. That makes sense."

"And this is my assistant, Barak," he continued, pointing to an angel who was wearing glasses.

"A privilege to meet you, Barak," I acknowledged, "but why are you wearing glasses?"

"These are not glasses so that I can see. This is a visual instrument that accesses the catalogue of the entire library of the Royal Hall of Scrolls and Records. There are an infinite number of items kept here. Every scroll, book, article and parchment in the library is listed. I can access it easily by its title, author, scribe, subject, date or location. All this information is instantly projected on my optical scanner lenses when I call for it."

I looked past Luke and the bespectacled angel, eager to see what lay before me. The entire area was filled with resource material. Scrolls of all sizes filled the shelves along the walls and were displayed in rows on finely grained, honey-colored, highly polished olivewood bookcases in the center of the room. These cases looked more like tall wine racks for different sizes of bottles except that they were designed to securely hold the scrolls snugly upright in separate cradles. The room seemed endless. "This looks like 'Scrolls-a-Million' only bigger," I said, grinning. "It's huge. I can't see how far back it goes. Maybe miles."

Luke promptly responded to my amazement. "Here in the Royal Hall of Scrolls and Records are many galleries. We will give you a quick tour to introduce you to the resources available to you as a royal scribe. You will not have time to read or research on this first visit, but you may return at any time in the future to explore, study and write. Many scribes come here and some spend entire seasons here. We provide housing for those on assignment. What is learned and discovered here is taken back to earth and to the outer reaches into the 'beyond.' Few have gone that far, but that is beginning to change. You will go there in the future, Royal Scribe. But for now, pay careful attention and record what you see and hear in this section of the Library of Heaven. You must learn it well."

No Overdue Fines

My thoughts raced back to an unforgettable time in my early childhood. A friend introduced me to the Carnegie Public Library near our home in Pittsburgh. The austere stone building with its foreboding Greek columns frightened me beyond scared. Entering was like walking into a gaping dinosaur's mouth, but I bravely overcame my fear and proceeded. Thankfully, I wasn't swallowed up in the intimidating prison of books. It wasn't so fearsome after all. I immediately signed up for my first library card and proceeded to select five or more children's books.

I couldn't wait to check them out and take them home. The problem: nobody explained that I had to return them. After more than a year, I found out. I was scared stiff I would be put in jail for keeping the books. My solution: I took them and set them on my friend's front porch. I never did find out what happened with those books. I am so glad the rule-keeping head librarian didn't send the police after me. I lived in fear for months, waiting for the ominous knock on my door. Only much later in life did I discover that the library has forgiveness days on which you can return overdue books without a fine. Phew! That's what I call grace.

"Can you check the scrolls out?" I asked.

"No, but you will not need to," Luke said. "Things are *imparted* here. What you learn here, you will never forget. The first thing I should tell you is that the spirits of Wisdom, Knowledge, Understanding, and Counsel all have offices here. You can speak with them at any time or even make an appointment if you desire."

"Awesome! How do I do that?" I asked.

"Just invite them. They will come when you need them."

"Wow! I'm certain that their advice and insight is incredible and essential."

"You have no idea how important it is," Luke replied. "There is so much here in the library beyond your comprehension. Mysteries, secrets, formulas, mathematical equations and physics are just the beginning. Do you think you understand chemistry? Wait till you see some of the scrolls. One of my most favorite areas is the section on 'light.' Being a physician, I have spent a lot of time studying 'light.' It's the source of all life, you know? That is partly why He is called Light. But that discussion is for another time. Let me introduce you to the Gallery of Scrolls."

The Gallery of Scrolls

We walked slowly through the colossal gallery. I stopped, from time to time, to take a closer look at items that intrigued me. The expertly crafted shelves held scrolls of every size and shape. Some were so exquisitely bejeweled that I could only imagine their value and the priceless contents recorded on them.

"I feel like I am walking through a museum of priceless works of art. No that's not right," I paused. "'Museum' isn't the right description. A better one is 'heritage.' Why am I feeling this way?" I asked Luke.

I noticed that Barak was smiling.

"Because each scroll represents the work and life of one person. This section is the 'legacy' area," Luke explained. "These scrolls are the journals and documents of saints who have fulfilled their assignments. Did you notice how the shelves rise to the very top of the ceiling and some go through it. That's because Malachi, who is the one appointed to tend these shelves, is constantly adding new material. These are the journals of God's people. They contain dreams, visions and prophecies given to them.[120] Their conversations with Jesus, Holy Spirit and Father are all written in their individual scrolls. Each scroll bears the name of its writer. How sad it is that some of the journals only have a few pages of entries, while others are completely full."

As Luke spoke, a cloak of remorse enveloped me. "Luke, so many times, I have neglected my journal," I said, dropping my head in disappointment. "The dreams I never recorded; the prophecies I simply disregarded. They're gone now. And yet, my journal is a precious treasure to me. It may not be perfect or complete, but it is my spiritual biography. In it I've carefully recorded my conversations with the Lord word for word. My prophecies are written to confirm and correct my daily spiritual walk and encourage me to fulfill my destiny and assignment. When I re-read the dreams that have changed my life, they are still as vivid and fresh today as they were sixty years ago. I still find encouragement and new meaning in them."

"So many of the saints neglect this vital part of their spiritual discipline," Luke replied, with a pleading tone. "Please continue to encourage the saints to write their visions and dreams and record their conversations with the Lord in the *secret place*. This is one way we leave our legacy for others to profit from for their own spiritual journeys. Our journal is an encouragement to those who follow in our footsteps. Had I not done so, my own books would never have been written."

"Well, after all, you are the scribe who wrote Luke and Acts. Who knows better than you how important keeping a journal is?"

"Follow me!" Luke ordered, as we approached a massive cedar door.

"The cedars of Lebanon," I considered, breathing the pungent air infused with the aroma of fresh cedar wood. A masterful carving on the surface of the door depicted a wooden chest. I stopped in my tracks. "This chest!" I declared. "I've seen it before at the Well of His Presence! This is like the chest the angels use. It contains supernatural scrolls. I will never forget the moment when the angel opened it and selected the golden scroll prepared for me. He presented it to me to use on my journey into Frontier Town. I wrote everything I saw and heard with that supernatural pen."[121]

The Gallery of Royal Scrolls

"You're right. That's exactly what this carving exemplifies. Well done, Royal Scribe," Luke said. "You are very observant. It identifies this section of the Gallery of Royal Scrolls."

We stepped through the doorway into another dimension. The section was filled with a mystical atmosphere that engulfed the space like a diaphanous cloud. The entire room was transformed into a spiritually charged realm. The level of prophetic anointing was noticeably stronger than I was accustomed to.

The gallery was filled with carefully preserved gold, silver and clay scrolls. Some were plain with no markings or adornment. Others were a combination of all three. Toward the center of the room, there was a section of priceless, beautifully adorned scrolls engraved with designs and symbols and embellished with various gemstones: diamonds, rubies, emeralds, sapphires, pearls, amethysts, onyx and other gems that I didn't recognize. These stones were expertly set on or embedded into the surfaces of the prized scrolls. One stone was unlike all the others. It changed shape, morphing into different symbolic configurations as though it were communicating a message. Sometimes, its surface was faceted and then it became smooth and highly reflective. When smooth, a starburst flashed inside of it. The exploding colors defied description. A dynamic, orgasmic celestial display was encapsulated in the stone.

"It's like seeing atoms birthed and burst as they are split by an unseen force," I said, struggling to comprehend what I was observing. "This gem must be of heavenly origin?" I asked, mesmerized by the living stone.

The Father-Stone

"This is the Father-Stone," Luke replied. "It's His stone. All other gems find their derivation from the Father-Stone. It is grown in the King's quarries. It is unlike other stones that are formed on earth, but some of the same elements come into play: light, pressure, heat, cold, sound, color and composition are some of the forces and constituents Father uses. But there are other factors we are not privy to. These secrets are hidden by Father. No one knows except the Creator. We think it must relate to the life force and origin of the universe, but we can only guess. This stone has been known to speak.

"One thing we do know: all of the lesser jewels are created from pieces or parts of the Father-Stone. All earth gems derive from some aspect of the Creator's formula, but only He possesses the Father-Stone. It is positioned in the center of the King's crown. Here in the Gallery of Royal Scrolls you see it in a much smaller size. It is here because the King comes to endorse the scrolls of the royal scribes with the Father-Stone, the royal emblem of the King of kings and Lord of lords. Father crafted and created it for His Son. It is holy and pure. The scrolls that bear the impression of the Father-Stone are authentic and sacred. It is His imprimatur."

I viewed the stone with the same regard as the sacred Ark of the Covenant. "It is holy and pure!" I kept repeating. "I thought I heard angelic voices responding antiphonally, "The Creator, He is holy and pure." I stared as the Father-Stone morphed from transparent to translucent and then opaque. It could govern the light by absorbing it or dispersing it partially or totally. It sparkled like a diamond, and it could change the refracted light into completely different hues and light beams, which emitted sparkling dust into the atmosphere.

"Look, Luke, it's alive! It absorbs and reflects light at will. It's every stone in creation reduced into one single expression of radiance and energy, and yet it is more. It's worshiping the King!"

"Yes!" Luke replied. "All creation worships Him. Stones play an integral part in this constant universal chorus of praise. In my opinion, I think Jesus spoke specifically about the stones because they seem so inanimate and lowly, mere rocks, weapons of destruction or building material. You see, I was there in Jerusalem when Jesus referred to them. It was a hot, dusty day in the city. We were near the place where the road goes down the Mount of Olives. Jesus was riding on a colt and a rowdy crowd of followers was lining the route, shouting joyfully and praising God at the top of their voices. They were overwhelmed with joy. Children were dancing, clapping their hands and shouting hosannas. Some were cutting branches from the palm trees and waving them in the air. It was a royal procession for sure, but humble in its appearance. The man next to me bellowed in my right ear, 'Blessed is the King who comes in the name of the Lord!' It still resounds in my heart. The crowd kept proclaiming, 'Peace on earth and glory in the highest!'

"The Pharisees were spying on the entourage, hanging back at the perimeter of the crowd. They couldn't take it anymore. Their ire was unmistakable and angry hatred distorted their faces. 'Teacher, Rebuke Your disciples!' they demanded, shaking their fingers at Him with fierce angry religious bigotry.

"And then he said it, 'Listen to me!' He shouted back, refusing to quiet a single voice. 'If they keep quiet, the stones themselves will cry out.'[122]

"I thought at the time that He was just using a metaphor. Only later did I truly learn the full meaning of what He meant when I first saw the Father-Stone. The stones speak. They can worship the Creator. I determined in that moment that I would never allow a stone to take my place in worship and praise."

I doubted if I could turn away from the sacred stone, but inquisitiveness burned in my heart. "Can I stay here a while and examine the royal scrolls?" I asked.

Luke spoke with a sense of urgency. "I'm sorry. We must move forward. There is so much more in the Royal Hall of Scrolls and Records for you to witness."

My curiosity was undeniable. "The first three golden scrolls from the Well of His Presence must be located somewhere on a shelf in this gallery. I'll return in the future to search for them," I determined.[123]

The Gallery of Designs

We made our way through the immense section until we came to a colossal wall constructed of heavy sand-brown quarried stones. It looked like a scene from the hidden city of Petra in Jordan. It stretched across the entire width of the Royal Hall of Scrolls and Records, dividing the Gallery of Royal Scrolls from whatever lay beyond it. Two ancient marble pillars supported an archway in the center of the wall. They stood like sentries, guarding the entrance. No one could pass beyond them without acknowledging their superior form and strength.

"These columns, Luke," I asked, sensing a significant spiritual meaning to their intentional placement, "they serve a greater purpose than just holding up the archway, right?"

Luke nodded, reaching out to run his hand along the left column. "Feel its texture and integrity," he commented. "It is without fault or blemish."

I was astonished by the smooth marble surface and magnificent grain and quality of the stone. "Michael Angelo could find no fault in this," I said. "There isn't a single crack or defect."

"That is a well-chosen analogy, Scribe. This left column is known as the Pillar of Perfection and Beauty. The right column is the Pillar of Function. Together, they support the archway and provide an entrance into the Gallery of Designs. All of God's designs are perfect, beautiful and functional."

He pointed forward, "Let's enter!"

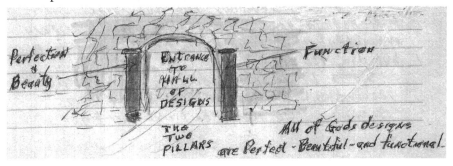

We stepped under the archway, passing between the columns that define all authentic kingdom design: perfection, beauty and function.

"All of the King's architectural plans and drawings are kept here," Luke explained. "Do you remember when Jesus brought a few of them to earth to show you when you were exploring the Hidden Kingdom? I read about it in the royal scroll you wrote. The Hidden Kingdom scroll is in the Royal Hall of Scrolls and Records, alongside the others that you have written."[124]

"It's really there!" I interrupted, unable to restrain myself. I felt like I would explode with joy. "Thank you, Luke. It's really in the Library of Heaven! It is acceptable to Him! That's all I desire—to be pleasing to the King.

"Oh, Yes!" I responded to Luke's question. "I remember the very moment they brought me the chest containing the plans and drawings. I saw so many of them: the plan of Creation, the Garden of Eden, Noah's Ark and the Tabernacle with its accoutrements and habiliments. The drawings themselves are glorious and so holy that some are untouchable. I had no idea they were kept in a place like this here in the library for others to see and examine.

The Hexagonal-Pyramid Crystal Monitor

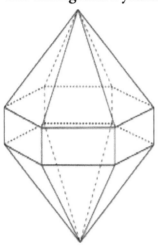

My attention was abruptly arrested by a giant-sized, pure crystal suspended in midair in the center of the gallery. It was shaped like a lead pencil on steroids, blown up to the size of a school bus. The hexagonal shape had six faces. But unlike a normal pencil, it was sharpened on both ends. Its top and base were hexagonal pyramids. The six faces met at the points of the apex and nadir.[125]

"What is this?" I asked.

Barak replied with professorial exactness: "It is the exhibition screen. Any item or architectural drawing here in the Gallery of Designs can be instantly transmitted to one of the many screens on the crystal. The eighteen surfaces allow multiple viewers to access it at any one time. Each screen can be divided further into multiple screens as well. We keep the originals in their respective chests for the viewers' protection. They are sacred and holy and cannot be touched without harm. You remember what happened to the priests who transported the Ark of the Covenant on an ox cart? When Uzzah tried to keep it from falling by touching it, he died.[126] So here in the library, the documents can be studied safely on screen or copied for use here. There are many identical crystal monitors throughout this section of the Royal Hall of Scrolls and Records to accommodate as many as may come to study.

"Very seldom do the original items leave the library. But when they do, it is only by the King's permission and command. The architectural drawings that Jesus brought to earth for you to see were the actual original plans. Aren't they incredible?

"Noah's Ark is one of my favorites. He had quite a task building the ark as he followed the Lord's designs and specific instructions. Noah's work ethic was outstanding, and he followed every detail of the plans with the utmost attention to accuracy. It's a good thing. Every inch of the ark was needed to survive the coming deluge. We consider Noah to be a master builder. You will appreciate his insight and inventiveness when you get to meet and talk with him.

"Let's continue. There is so much more to see here in this gallery," Luke prompted.

We turned away from the main display screen to look deeper into the room. Many isles led from the main section of the gallery on both sides of the central passageway. I immediately detected a strange phenomenon. The light in the room emanated from two sources, the display screens and the storage drawers where the drawings and schematics were kept. Several people and angels were working among the rows of file drawers that looked like those used in an architect's office—very large and flat, able to accommodate a complete set of drawings for a project. Some of the drawings were works in progress. Whenever someone opened a drawer or door, light cascaded out of the compartment.

"Why does this happen?" I asked Barak.

"The plans and drawings are anointed and sanctified. They are holy and carry the authentication of the King's seal. Some are scrolls, others are made of metal sheets that are malleable. Sometimes they are so thin they become translucent. They are embossed with a laser pen by the scribes here in heaven. They reflect the glory of God. There is no need of any other light here. His glory illuminates the hall.

"One of our assignments is to bring all the King's designs and architectural plans here for eternal storage. But the Lord recently instructed us to prepare an entirely new section that will be designated for the creative designs and plans of the saints. God is releasing an end-time anointing to unleash the creativity of His people, not only on earth but also throughout the heavenly realms. It has already begun. He made us in His image. We are created to create."

The River of Revelation

As we approached the farthest wall from the entrance in the Gallery of Designs, I could hear water flowing. At first it was a low soft sound, but as we drew closer I recognized the distinct sound of a stream or perhaps a river babbling and singing its way across the entire gallery from left to right. I was beyond curious. "Why a river?" I asked.

"This is where the Word is kept," Luke explained. "The Word is encircled by a pure river of revelation. Inside this circle you will see and even access the Journal of the King. My scrolls are kept here alongside Matthew's, Mark's and John's. Paul's journals and letters are next to ours. The original biographical and historical documents that comprise the Holy Scriptures are kept within this compound of divine disclosure. Are you ready to cross the river of revelation?"

"I am so honored and humbled!" I responded in utter amazement. "What a privilege. I have read the Word all of my adult life. Now, in this moment, I get to see it in its original form in the handwriting of the scribes who wrote it as Holy Spirit inspired them."

We stepped into the stream of revelation. Visions and heavenly sounds pulsed into my spirit and flashed onto the screen of my imagination. It was like watching my life flash before my eyes in a second, but it wasn't my life I was seeing. It was the life of Jesus that I was envisioning. It was like a trillion-terabyte download occurring inside me in a millisecond.

I struggled to comprehend what was happening to me. *Is this similar to what the Israelites experienced as they crossed the Red Sea or entered Canaan by a supernatural crossing of the Jordan River? What did they see and hear in that moment?* I wondered. *I am standing inside the circle of the river of revelation that circumscribes this entire section in the Royal Hall of Scrolls and Records. I feel like I am in the epicenter of the Word. It must be so! It's impossible to access this area of the Hall without crossing the River of Revelation. This body of living prophetic water must be crossed to enter the full experience and reality of what it encircles and protects. I think I've stepped into the realm of the 'more-sure' word of prophecy,* I thought.[127]

I turned to get a panoramic view of my surroundings. The sound of the rushing river of revelation was like wind blowing through the trees. Angels were moving about over this sacred circle, coming and going with determined expressions of intentionality. They were departing from the center of the enclosure to deliver the Word they carried.

The Golden Chamber

"This is astounding," I uttered as my eyes surveyed the scene before me. In the center of the gallery, a golden chamber with an iridescent glow radiated supernatural power. It had three rectangular sides or faces, each sloping toward the top.[128] But unlike the ancient pyramids, there was no point at the apex. Instead, light streamed out of the opening like a laser and shot through the ceiling of the gallery and into the cosmos beyond. The light beam moved back and forth like a laser pen, writing something on the scroll of the cosmos.

"This is more than a repository of holy documents," I acknowledged, overcome by the awesome power it evoked. "This is the supernatural pen that Holy Spirit uses, a golden scroll of epic proportions unlike any other ever created."

I discerned three entry points into the triangular chamber, one on each face at its base. Light emanated through each portal. Gemstones of various sizes and shapes were flying out of these gateways, tumbling and bouncing along until they splashed into the stream of revelation.

"The bottom of this stream must be covered with gemstones," I said. "Just think about it! We can go treasure hunting for spiritual revelation that's just waiting to be discovered and retrieved from the river. Revelation waits for those who pursue it. We must come to the river!"[129]

"Luke!" I exclaimed, trying to decode the scene. "Please help me understand this. I am overwhelmed with the majesty and holiness of this place. But all along, Scriptures keep flashing into my mind. They all appear to have a similar theme. I proceeded to quote several texts:

For no prophecy was ever brought about through human initiative, but men spoke from God as they were carried by the Holy Spirit. (2 Peter 1:9)

In the beginning was the Word, and the Word was with God, and the Word was God...and the Word became flesh and dwelt among us, and we beheld His glory, the glory as of the only begotten of the Father, full of grace and truth. (John 1:1,14)

He who has seen Me has seen the Father. (John 14:10)

And there are also many other things that Jesus did which if they were written one by one, I suppose the world itself could not contain the books that would be written. (John 21:25)

From infancy, you have known the holy scriptures, which are able to make you wise for salvation through faith in Christ Jesus. All scripture is given by inspiration of God and is profitable for doctrine, for reproof, for correction, for training in righteousness, that the man of God may be complete, thoroughly equipped for every good work. (2 Timothy 3:16)

Be diligent to present yourself approved to God, a worker who does not need to be ashamed, rightly dividing the word of truth. (1 Timothy 2:15)

The sacred things belong to the Lord, our God, but the things revealed belong to us and to our sons forever, that we may observe all the words of the law. (Deuteronomy 29:29)

"What am I to make of this, Luke?" I asked, urgently trying to decode the message like Tom Hanks in the movie *The Da Vinci Code*. "There must be a connection between these verses and the actual scene before me?"

The Trinity of the WORD

"Come closer!" Luke instructed. "I want you to see…" he paused for a moment to inhale deep into his lungs, then continued with such reverence that it required all his breath, "…the WORD!" he announced with such force that I shuddered at the power of Holy Spirit streaming like a mighty river from within him. Luke's eyes flashed like mirrors reflecting the sacredness of the moment and the scene before us. The story was emanating from his heart as he pointed to the shimmering structure.

We approached the golden chamber with veneration. My pulse pounded in my chest. Heat flowed over my face because of the scorching discharge emanating like a blast furnace from the three openings. He pointed to the gold edifice and said, "This is the Trinity of the Word." His expression was one of total veneration and appreciation for its power.[130] "This entire structure is made of gold, which is purified to perfection. There is not a single trace of impurity or dross in this holy enclosure."

"This first surface of the 'Trinity of the Word' is the Old Testament face." He pointed and then drew back: "Look through the portal!"

A single glance forced me to cover my eyes. Pure white light glowed like liquid-fire in the center of the chamber. I staggered backward, grateful for Luke's steadying hand on my shoulder.

"The best I can explain it is, this is the Origin-Word emanating from Father. All other utterances are crescive. Everything else proceeds from or rises out of His Word-Power."

"Now follow me," Luke said.

We moved counterclockwise and turned the corner to the second surface of the pyramid. "This is the New Testament face," he explained. "Look again!" he instructed as he pointed into the flaming chamber.

"It's a gigantic ladle full of molten white-hot metal!" I shouted, covering my face instantly, almost incinerated by the heat. I stepped back. "Whatever this substance is, it's being poured into the center of the chamber at a constant rate. But look!" I pointed in amazement. "The ladle remains full even though a steady stream of the substance spills over the edge."

The luminous element flowed from the massive ladle into some sort of form in the center of the chamber. Yellow and red sparkling embers exploded outward, creating surging rivulets of shimmering fire that flew in every direction.

"Luke," I said with childhood wonder. "This reminds me of when I was a little boy living in Pittsburgh. I visited the massive steel blast furnaces along the river and watched them pouring molten steel into molds to make metal ingots. But this… this is something beyond superheated metal. This substance is supernaturally formed in the furnace of heaven."

Luke trembled as he spoke: "It is! This Word is poured into human vessels and then shaped and released to the world as the written Word of God."

He bowed his head and could barely speak. "I stood in this furnace, Royal Scribe," he said, and fell to his knees.

I rushed to his side, tears coursing down my cheeks. "Oh, Luke," I said, my heart bursting with compassion. "So that's what it takes to be a royal scribe who records the holiest scroll in all eternity. I had no idea of the cost and the sacrifice."

"It is nothing compared to the fruit of my service to my Lord. The satisfaction of serving Him far exceeds the cost."

He rose and stood unsteadily for a moment. When he regained his balance he spoke, "Come to the third face." Luke urged on, "If you think this is overwhelming, wait till you experience the next portal. You must see this!"

The heat from the opening behind us diminished as we moved toward the third side of the pyramid and turned the corner. The third golden face was supercharged with power. The hair stood up on my arms as I entered the face's energy field. Bursts of power were firing from the outer surface into the atmosphere.

"Shundo!" I shouted as one hit me and knocked me flat to the ground.

"This is the face of Holy Spirit," Luke explained. "His holiness, presence, and power can overwhelm you and often can cause you to fall down. Now, look through the portal inside the chamber!"

Supernatural power flashed inside the space. "This must have been what it was like in the beginning when God said, 'Let there be light,'" I presumed, awestruck by the sheer creative force of the living dynamo. "This is like watching creation happen."

The concentrated power of Holy Spirit was focused into the center of the chamber. He was engaging something or someone. Interchanges of energy and power radiated back and forth from the object in the center to the interior walls of the chamber and back again.

"I believe I'm observing the dialogue among Father, Son and Holy Spirit. Luke, I think they're communicating with one another. This is implausible to the intellect; it's way beyond my ability to even imagine. I am literally seeing a conversation occurring within the Trinity."

I stood staring into the chamber, captivated by the discourse. "I wonder what They are saying? Are these new truths and revelations from Father being released into the atmosphere and cascaded into the spirits of the prophets and teachers? Perhaps, it's revelation to explain the deeper meanings of the Scriptures already spoken? Could this even be a picture of intimacy with God that occurs in the *secret place*?"

A Lesson from Professor Luke

"Follow me to the bank of the River of Revelation," Luke said. "Let's sit awhile so I can explain to you what you have just seen and witnessed." He chose a delightful spot by the refreshing, crystal clear stream. I raised the royal scroll to be careful to record his words of instruction.

"This golden chamber is the realm of the 'Word,'" he began, carefully placing the emphasis on 'Word.' "This chamber contains the Word of God, the Journals of Jesus and the writings of Holy Spirit.

"The first face of the Word is the Old Testament side. If you enter through the portal into the chamber, you can access the Torah, along with the entire Tanakh: the law, prophets and writings. The journals of Moses, Samuel, Job and David, to mention just a few, are all there in their first edition, original state, form and substance. You can read all of their writings.

"The second face is the New Testament side. If you enter this portal, you will discover immediately that the Word is flesh. The molten glory of God is poured into the center. It is the WORD BECOMING FLESH AND DWELLING AMONG US. It is His Word communicated through and in human channels. The ultimate, defining word above all other words is 'Jesus.' Within this chamber, you can access all of the gospels, my journals, Paul's letters and the entire New Testament. It is at your fingertips. Again, these are not copies but the original documents. Communion with 'the Word became flesh' is priceless here inside the chamber of the Word.

"The third face is the realm of Holy Spirit's impartation. All of the Word is Spirit-breathed, formed and empowered—even 'the Word became flesh' is Spirit-conceived. When you enter into this chamber, you will discover writings that are mentioned in your Bible but were not considered or included. They are also found inside the chamber and can all be seen and read. Holy Spirit will illumine them. The Journals of Jesus are inside. Apostle John spoke of them in Revelation when he said, *'There are many more things that Jesus did and said. If all of them were written down, I suppose not even the world itself would have space for the books that would be written.'*[131]

"The laser beam emanating from the top of the pyramid is not only a pen, but also it is a portal as well. You can travel inside the laser beam to access the scrolls of the Word written with His Light in the outer reaches. Few have gone there to read or study the *progressing* Word of God written in the heavens. Perhaps, you will be among the first to travel there in the future, Royal Scribe."

"My circuits are already blown, Luke," I replied. "How much can one contain?"

"In your spirit-man your ability to see and remember is unlimited; God made you in His image.

"Do you have any questions, Scribe?" Luke asked.

"More of a statement," I replied. "Now I understand why those particular Scriptures scrolled through my mind earlier when I first observed this sacred compartment and then throughout our circumnavigation of the golden chamber of the Word."

"This always happens to each person who comes here," he said. "The Word in you is activated by the golden chamber of the Word. Did you notice that all the faces focus on the inside? This entire chamber is the centrality of the WORD. It is the beginning place, the Journal of Christ Jesus; it is the WORD in all its essence. That same Word lives within you."

We sat quietly together at the edge of the river. Obviously, Luke wanted to give me time to absorb the powerful revelation of the golden chamber of the Word of God. The royal scroll vibrated mildly in my hand as it recorded the vision. A resonating awareness infused my spirit beyond my natural state. The eternal truth of what I had just observed settled deep in my being like an immovable, unshakable foundation.

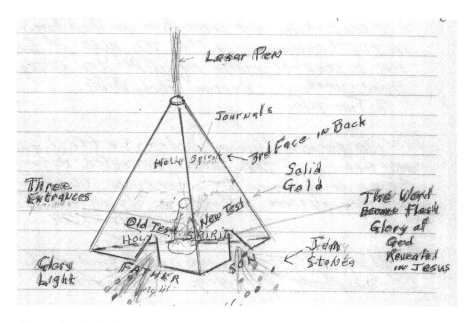

Gems in the River

"There is one more gallery in this Royal Hall of Scrolls and Records. It's just beyond the River of Revelation," Luke pointed deeper into the Hall beyond the river into the distance.

He proceeded to lead the way, stepping into the crystalline water to cross the river. I followed him into the water and then an idea struck me. *Why not pick up a gem while I'm here in the River? A mischievous impulse perhaps, but who can resist these delicious gemstones?* They sparkled like inexhaustible treasure lying on the bottom all around me, inviting retrieval. *But which one to choose?* I pondered. *They're all enticing.*

I bent to pick up an exquisite emerald. Its irresistible rich-green hue drew me to it.

Luke spoke, as if he had eyes in the back of his head. "Well chosen, Royal Scribe. Take it back to earth when you return. It will bring amazing insight to you. Trust me, it will reveal its secrets at the appropriate time."

"I will." I replied, embarrassed like a child caught in the act of mischief. "How did you know that I picked it up?"

"Everyone who comes here picks up at least one gemstone. Some leave with pockets-full and I've even seen people put them in their mouths and ears. Truth is, you can't get enough of the Word," he chuckled.

"I wish I had taken more," I replied.

"No problem. Just come back for more anytime you want to."

"Really? Anytime?"

"Absolutely. These words are for everyone, but there are few who make the effort to retrieve them. Once you have seen and tasted them, you are addicted."

The Lord's Secret Place

We walked along a pathway that eventually led to a cottage nestled in a beautiful forest. "This is a very special place," Luke explained. "It is one of the Lord's own *secret places*. He has many, but this one is special. This is where the King keeps His own books and records. We cannot go inside. He meets here with Father and Holy Spirit. The books here no one has ever seen, and some we do not even know exist. Their subjects and titles are a mystery."

He paused and then, placing his forefinger to his temple to capture his thoughts, continued, "But I can name some of the scrolls and volumes because He has spoken of them. In His *secret place* you will find *The Book of Remembrance*.[132] It is His prayer list. *The Scrolls of Idle Words* that have been gathered and noted by the angel scribes and delivered here. Every idle word of each saint is recorded and available to the King. (Matthew 12:36) An angel told me that they are carefully secured so no one else can access them. *"The Scroll of Accounting and Rewards* is also located here. It contains the results of each saint's stewardship over what Father has given them to do and care for.[133] Oh, yes! *The Catalogue of Creation* is here," he chuckled. "I am sure it would blow the mind of every evolutionist proponent. And, of course, *The Book of Hidden Mysteries and Secrets* is included here in the King's *secret place* personal library.[134] Jesus keeps His personal journal here as well. It is recorded in *The Scroll of the King's Journeys* and is automatically written in the golden chamber of the Word in the Royal Hall of Scrolls and Records. He loves to travel throughout His creation.

"Did I mention several other books and scrolls are kept elsewhere in the library? *The Book of the Covenant* is located in the Hall of Remembrance. You saw the *Book of the Wars of the Lord* when you visited the Strategy Room of Heaven. Do you recall? You were there with your angel companions on your first journey into the realms of the kingdom?"[135]

The scene flashed into my mind as fresh as the day I lived it. The impressive auditorium with assigned seats and the lectern that held the massive book with its two columns that coordinated the tactics of the army of the saints and the angelic hosts. "Unforgettable!" I responded.

Luke continued, *"The Book of Life* and *The Book of Judgment* are beside the Throne in the Throne room.[136] *The Seven Sealed Book* is kept by Father who sits upon the Throne. It has never been opened. Only the Son can open its seals. No one else is worthy.[137]

"The King's special angel envoy will bring *The Little Book* and will release the seven thunders when he roars like a lion. He is a mighty angel and will come clothed in a cloud. A rainbow will be on his head, his face will shine like the sun and his feet are like pillars of fire. The book he carries is written by the Almighty. This book may be small, but the power that it wields is mega-dunamis.[138]

"I must also mention the two important spiritual sources on earth that you must be aware of and recognize as authentic information stored in creation itself. The rocks and stones can speak and even the ground cries out."[139]

Every stone has a story!

A recent encounter burst into my memory like a scene from a movie. It was a *kairos* moment. I was in the waiting room at the doctor's office for an eye exam when my name was called. I was ushered into an adjacent room where three others were waiting to have their eyes dilated. I took a seat beside an older gentleman and initiated a conversation with the women sitting across from me. Her German shepherd was sitting peacefully at her feet. "Where are you from?" I asked. She willingly shared her story about how she and her husband moved to Florida. Before I could reply, the gentleman sitting next to me responded to her.

I immediately turned toward him and asked, "I notice you have a very strong accent. What is your nationality?"

"I am from Israel," he said.

"Which city?"

"I lived in Jerusalem."

"Oh, I love Israel," I responded. "Jerusalem is amazing. What is your name?"

"My name is Abraham."

I nearly fell off of my chair. *Could this really be happening to me?* I thought. *Is this Abraham? THE Abraham! His bearded face and brownish-tan, weathered skin certainly fit the description.* I was dumbfounded.

Abraham continued, "Yes, I love Jerusalem too. The thing about Israel is that every stone has a story."

I was shell-shocked by his insight and depth of passion and understanding of the nature of this sacred place. I stared into his eyes with admiration. *No doubt he reads the stones!* I thought. *He can hear the voice of the land stating its case for all who will listen to its witness.*

A voice from the nurse in the doorway (or was it an angel) put an end to our encounter. "Abraham!" she called. He rose and left the room.

Everything in me wanted him to stay. I had a thousand questions to ask. Only after he was gone did I realize I should have asked for his contact information, but it was too late. I never saw him again.

"Luke," I said. "Abraham told me that every stone has a story."

"He did it again." Luke smiled and Barak straightened his glasses and smiled in delight.

"We have come to the end of your introduction to the Royal Hall of Scrolls and Records, Scribe. Those who have never come to the royal library here in heaven think it is merely a collection of books, records, and scrolls of written materials, simply a place to keep documents. But you know differently. This is only one of the many halls here in the library. It is much better to think of this entire library as a university with many halls of learning. Each hall contains various galleries with multiple sections in every gallery. Please encourage others to come here to this part of the library and to enter the other halls as well."

"I will, Luke, I will. I promise."

Trust Holy Spirit

"Thank you, Luke. I have always loved your scrolls, especially your account of the birth of our King. I would love to know who the wise men were?"

His eyes teared with gratitude. "Perhaps you will meet them. The Magi can be found in the Hall of Kings."

I lowered the royal scroll to my side and gripped it tightly: "I hope I have recorded everything accurately," I said, looking for Luke's affirmation. "I want to serve the Lord with all of my heart and do a good job as His scribe."

"Trust the Spirit and follow his directions," he said. "If you do, you will not be distracted from your assignment and will fulfill your duties with accuracy. Believe me, I know!

"Enjoy the rest of your time here in the King's Library of Heaven. I really do mean 'enjoy.'"

"Come back soon," Barak chimed in cheerfully and blinked his eyes playfully behind his supernatural glasses. "I'm always happy to serve you. Just ask and I'll help you locate any item in the Royal Hall of Scrolls and Records."

"I will, Barak." I replied. "See you again. I'm sure I will be a regular visitor. I love books and have so much more to learn and discover. I guess I will have all of eternity to do so."

"Not really," he replied. "You will have lots to do besides coming here."

I put my hand in my pocket. "It's still here," I confirmed, turning the faceted emerald in my fingers.

The Royal Hall of Scrolls and Records

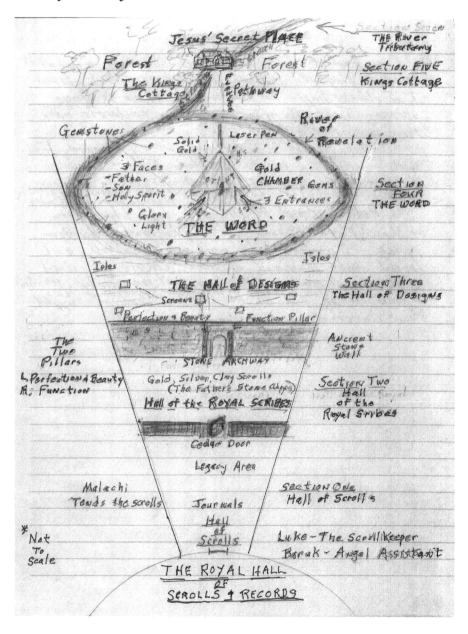

CHAPTER 17

Who's In Charge?

Barak and Luke disappeared from view as a sudden whoosh of air sucked me into a portal. It felt like I was inside one of those clear plastic tubes shoved into a pneumatic system. I was suctioned away from the Royal Hall of Scrolls and Records and transported to the concierge's desk in the center of the great hall. The spirits of Knowledge, Wisdom, and Counsel were all surprised by my sudden appearance and stared at me rather perturbed. I guess I had interrupted their conversation again.

Speak to Your Spirit-Man

A struggle was going on inside of me. My soul was warring against my spirit. A great pull was drawing me back to earth, and it kept growing stronger. I felt it earlier, but at first it was just a subtle desire to hurry back, so I could share with others what I have seen and heard in the heavenly realms. Now it was so much stronger; it was becoming a loud voice shouting in my head.

"I know the royal scroll is not even half full. I'm fearful that my assignment will be aborted if I allow my soul to dictate my decisions and action," I mumbled. I turned to the Spirit of Counsel. "What can I do to silence this?" I asked, explaining the battle going on inside of me.[140]

"You must command your soul to submit to your spirit," he responded. "Pride and self-serving motives are very strong in the soul realm, especially when it comes to revelation knowledge. You must humble your '*self*.' Assert your spirit. Speak to your soul and command it to be still and submit to your spirit."

"For sure, that's what's going on, but I thought I had done that before," I replied.

"You must do it again and again, as often as is necessary," Counsel responded. "Your soul realm is very strong. That's not a bad thing. But your spirit is the place of life and pre-existence. It is stronger and multi-dimensional. God speaks Spirit to spirit, not Spirit to soul. You must activate your spirit and command it to rule over your soul and body. Speak directly to your spirit."

I stood in front of the reception desk, determined to win this battle. The Spirit of Might appeared next to me, and the power of Holy Spirit rose up in me. I spoke with commanding power as the delegated authority of Jesus pervaded the center of my being.

"I am speaking to you, my human-spirit within me. In the name of Jesus, I release you and command you to have dominion over my soul, my mind, my will and my emotions. Every part of my 'self' must submit to you. My memories, my subconscious mind and thoughts must submit to you. I speak into my soul realm. I decree and command that you must and will obey and submit to my spirit-man. I will not be led or persuaded by your attempts to use my emotions, feeling and soulish thoughts to persuade or to govern my actions and decisions. I will not worship my mind or feelings. I will worship and exalt the Lord Jesus Christ alone and Holy Spirit within me.

"I declare that my body is the temple of Holy Spirit. I am bought with a price and I am redeemed by the blood of Jesus Christ, God's only Son. I am filled with Holy Spirit, baptized in water and Spirit, submitted and empowered by Holy Spirit and chose to be led by Holy Spirit. Soul and body, I have had enough of your attempts and constant pressure to rule me. I love how God has designed me. I am fearfully and wonderfully made, and before I was conceived He knew me and loved me. Now I restore and bring His divine order and alignment back into my being. I am first and foremost a spirit-being. I have a soul, and I live in a body. Flesh and soul, you will submit to my spirit-man.

"This I decree and establish in my life in the name of Jesus. In Him I live and move and have my being."[141]

A singularity was restored within me. "Things are set right again," I said. "The struggle is gone. This divisive raging battle is over. It's resolved. I no longer feel any time restraints or sense of urgency to return to earth.

"This assignment is not about me. It's about you, Lord, and Your plans and purposes. I am Your royal scribe to command. I am in Your service. I am blessed by Your love and grace and humbled that You chose me for this assignment. I totally surrender to Your will and leading. You said, 'A double-minded man is unstable in all of his ways.'[142] My intention and desire is to be single-minded, of one heart and purpose, and to will one thing;[143] Your will! I want to please You and serve You faithfully. My one desire, like David's, is to dwell in Your presence to behold Your beauty and to inquire after You."[144]

A hush pervaded the great hall. No one moved. Counsel, Wisdom, and Knowledge bowed their heads. I fell instinctively to my knees in honor and reverence to the King. "He's here!" I realized. "He's beside me." I felt His hand on my head, warm and gentle and comforting. Love poured out from Him.

"I came to bless you, My son," He said softly. "Peace, be still. You have travelled well in the heavenly realms of My Kingdom, son of the Highest. Your journey has just begun; do not concern yourself with where you will go. I will lead you. Everything here in the heavenly realm is revelation. Holy Spirit will guide you. Pay close attention to him. See and hear what I am saying and revealing to you. I love you, Dale. You are one of My royal scribes."[145]

"Thank You, Jesus." I replied. "I love You so much."

His presence and touch slowly faded. I reached to touch my head where His hand had rested. It was saturated by His anointing. "It's covered with oil!" I said, wafting the delicious aroma. "And this fragrance, it's so invigorating. It has the awakening scent of eucalyptus and lemon. But there's a subtle hint of sandalwood too. It stirs my entire being."

He Guides Our Steps

I turned my attention back to the task at hand. "Do you have a plan?" I asked Knowledge.

"He already gave you the plan. Follow your heart," he replied. "Holy Spirit is your guide."

I stepped back from the circular desk and surveyed the great hall. "It's time for me to proceed, Holy Spirit. There is so much I haven't seen. Lead me. Your word says, 'As many as are led by the Spirit of God, they are the sons of God.'"[146]

His response was instantaneous. Footprints appeared on the floor in front of me. I stepped forward, confidently tracing their path. They led to the outer wall of the great hall and then to the right in a clockwise direction. As I walked along the circumference of the wall, I passed one of the sections I had already accessed. The surface of the royal scroll glowed in acknowledgment. My unseen guide led me around the hall until his footsteps stopped between the Hall of Cosmology and the Hall of Communication. I was mystified by the curious location.

"There's no door here," I said in a quandary. "I'm standing between two halls. This doesn't make sense." The solid surface before me appeared impenetrable. "Help me, Spirit of Knowledge," I asked. "I'm stumped."

"Just wait here," he instructed. "Wait!" he said firmly a second time. "The pathway will be revealed."

A deep rumbling sound began to emanate from behind the wall, steadily increasing in volume. I placed my left hand on the surface were the sound originated. The royal scroll turned and pointed directly at the spot. At first, a small crack appeared. I watched in amazement as it widened, descending from the top to the bottom of the surface. A loud boom resounded through the circular hall as the floor shuddered under the weight of the massive object. An ancient stone doorway slowly slid open, scraping along the polished floor. The vibrations made my legs tremble. The door reached its limit and stopped, exposing a hidden passageway.

The Spirit of Knowledge spoke. "There is only one entrance into the royal library, but there are many exits, Royal Scribe. Your assignment here is finished for now. Follow the corridor!"

"Thank you, Knowledge," I responded. "May I call upon you again?"

"Of course," he replied. "We are all available. We are your mentors."

The Spirit of Counsel added, "Allow the King's blessing to continually flow over you like the holy oil of anointing you have just experienced. Proceed in His grace."

The Spirit of Wisdom encouraged, "Remember, Royal Scribe, that what Knowledge and Understanding are teaching you must be activated and applied. This is vital. They provide you with the raw materials of successful living and prosperity. They equip you to make right decisions during peacetime and in war. Your heavenly assignment is so much more than informational. It is transformational. It is meant to change you and the Church."

"By God's grace, what I am receiving here in the heavenly realms will be my new reality. As in heaven, so on earth," I said with conviction.

"This is why you have come, Royal Scribe," Wisdom affirmed. "This is the great invasion the prophets spoke about and the King foretold. Even now it is happening, although many do not discern it yet. They will continue in their old ways, but soon the Light will dawn on a new time and season. Father is about to open the Hall of Times and Seasons. I am forbidden to say more, but I must alert you. Be prepared!"

Liquid Light

Wisdom's final word echoed in my mind as I turned toward the supernatural door and stepped into the dark hallway. Stumbling along in the darkness, I used my free hand to trace the surface of the passageway in order to keep my balance. Finally, I could see a light shining in the distance and began to walk more rapidly. The light increased until I realized it was not a single light but a strong stream of light energy, a portal.

"It's so powerful," I said. "This stream of light must be flowing from an enormous source. It's irresistible," I shouted and began to run toward it like a child on summer vacation racing toward the water for that first plunge into the lake.

"Now!" I shouted, diving into the descending column of liquid light with total abandon.

In an instant, I landed on top of a pillar that had safety nets all around its edges. "Whoa! What a surge. Where am I? What is this?" I shouted, disoriented by the unusual design of the pillar. "This is really different."

An angel sentry spoke: "Yes, I know. We put the nets up because pneumanauts keep diving into the light and don't always land in the center of the platform. The nets make our job easier.

"I am Marcus. You have landed on an exit pillar from the King's Library of Heaven. This portal only opens in one direction, out. You have been sent here because this is the closest portal to your next place of assignment. Are you ready to depart?"

Checking the Scroll

"May I check the royal scroll first?" I asked.

"Of course. Be my guest," he smiled. "Most people are eager to proceed, but I can see you are a royal scribe. You may stay here as long as necessary."

"I must examine the scroll," I replied. "I sense that this is a critical point in the journey. I need to be sure I have recorded the details and conversations accurately."

I held the scroll judiciously, rotating the cylinder to examine the outer surface. "It's so exquisite," I whispered. "It's beautiful. It displays the creative nature of the King and speaks of His royal beauty and honor."

When I tilted the scroll to look inside, I was pleased to discover that a perfect replica of the concierge's desk in the center of the great hall was inscribed on the surface. An indigo vessel that looked like a giant lamp stood inside the enclosure. A curled wick in the pool of oil inside the vessel burned brightly. Its flaming light danced joyfully, illuminating the entire hall. Like a lighthouse beacon, its shafts of light swept around the circular wall, highlighting the various doorways into each area of the library.

The Concierge's Desk

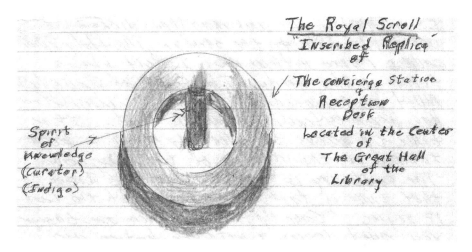

The Royal Scroll
"Inscribed Replica"
of
✓ The concierge Station
or
Reception
Desk
Located in the Center
of
The Great Hall
of the
Library

Spirit
of
Knowledge
(Curator)
(Indigo)

"The Spirit of Knowledge," I said. "This symbol represents him. He is the curator of the heavenly library."

The realization tripped a switch in my mind, and I began to trace my journey through the library by viewing my itinerary inside the scroll. Each engraving was a visual reminder of my experience: the Hall of Languages, the Hall of Cosmology, the Hall of Communication, the Hall of Remembrance, and the Royal Hall of Scrolls and Records. Then it dawned upon me. I never realized until now that the royal scroll is itself a portal into the heavenly realms, and I can return to each place in the spirit by looking at the inscriptions inside it. I can recall and revisit each location as often as I want. The itinerary recorded inside of it will also help me to give an account to those who will listen and who hunger to know what the King wants to reveal to His Church.

The Time of Times!

"It is time!" I declared. "This vital message must be brought to earth from the kingdom realm in heaven." I paused and then repeated the affirmation. "It is time! It is time! It is time! If you hear me, please understand that these are more than mere words. This is a mandate to the saints." Holy Spirit burned within me.

"Yes! The light of revelation must be released," Marcus said. "The Lord has extended the invitation. It is time to access the heavenly realm and receive training in the realms of the kingdom. The Church cries, 'Maranatha! Even so come, Lord Jesus.' The time of His return is fast approaching. But right now, the Lord is saying, 'Come up here!' You must see and learn things in the heavenlies before the final battle begins. The saints must be trained as prophets, priests and kings. It is time!"

"It is time, Lord Jesus," I affirmed.

Knowledge appeared next to me and reached forward to touch the royal scroll. He spoke with great insight. "Do not rush!" he said. "Allow Marcus' words to rest in your heart and bear fruit in your spirit. They will burn within you like embers of fire that will grow into a flaming torch in your spirit. Holy Spirit is igniting them right now.

"The revelation of this scroll will be like a sword penetrating into the religious and demonic realms. Unbelievers will be challenged and the true Church will be awakened. You must become the message, Royal Scribe. All of heaven is preparing for war. Kings are rising in the earth. The age of the seed of Satan will revive with fury. Giants will again wage war against us.[147] It will be like it was in the days of Noah, only much worse.[148] The great transfer of wealth has begun for a reason.[149] The army of the saints will be well supplied."

"We must war together, Son of Man," Marcus added. "We are united as God's army of saints and heavenly hosts. You will see weapons and strategies that have been formed in the Strategy Room of Heaven and the *secret chambers of war*.[150] The earth does not even comprehend such things. A single sound, a pure color or an atmosphere can destroy an entire army of Satan's seed. Our King is a mighty warrior. He is strong in battle, furious in power and might. He never loses! No weapon formed against Him, or us, can prosper.[151]

"The times and seasons are in Father's hands," he said. "Watch carefully in the spirit. The season is changing rapidly. We are about to enter a new time and a Time of Times. All of the heavenly realm is peering into the *chasm of conflicts* and waiting for the dawn of the beginning day."

Conversation with a Waring Angel
"How do you know these things?" I asked.

"I am Marcus," he replied. "I am a waring angel. I have fought in many battles for the King. I was part of the attack on Jericho and marched with the unseen battalion in the air above the trees. David heard the rustling and we attacked the Philistines.[152] What a victory we delivered that day.

"This is my assigned post for now. I guard this exit from the King's library. I will never allow anyone to pass by me and try to gain entrance illegally through the back door. It is forbidden. Access to the library is restricted. Saints can come as well as heavenly beings who are approved, but all must enter through the main entrance."

"Marcus, I feel such a heaviness in my spirit. It's not sadness; it's more like I am carrying a burden."

"You are, Royal Scribe. The Word of revelation causes a pressure in your spirit. It is waiting to be released. God doesn't just speak His Word. He sends it.[153] It is in motion within you. It is pressing upon your spirit. When you release the Word, it carries the anointing and power of Holy Spirit. When the prophets declare, 'This is what the Lord says,' they are releasing His Word. His Word in your mouth is just as powerful as His Word in His mouth. Always remember that it's His Word—the Word of power, life, revelation and truth."

"His Word is burning within me like holy fire," I said. "My face feels like a stove burner set on high.[154]

"Yes, His prophets are torches and trumpets in His mighty hands."

The Multi-dimensional WORD
The vision I received before my departure into the heavenlies flashed into my mind. "The monk was holding a lantern," I said. "I think I understand more clearly, Lord. The light is to enable others to see and discern the pathways into the heavenly realms of Your Kingdom. But it is also a lamp of revelation. It is the message You have summoned me to witness and record in the royal scroll. It is the prophetic Word that I must bring back to the Church."

"My son," the King responded, "there is always more to My Word than first appears, whether I send it by vision, dreams, prophecy or Scripture. My Word is multi-dimensional and affects many realms of understanding. It has layers of truth and meaning. A single word from Me is able to release an incredible degree of truth and insight, but this can only be spiritually discerned. My friend Paul understood this. He sought to speak spiritual words that can only be understood by spiritually enlightened people."[155]

The talking ceased. I sat silently for a long time considering the Word of the Lord. "I don't want to let a single seed fall upon unfruitful ground in my heart,"[156] I determined and bowed my head in prayer.

The Cup of Life
"I'm thirsty," I said to Marcus. "His Word made me thirsty."

"Here. Drink this!" he replied, handing me a cup of cool water.

"Oh, my goodness," I stared in shock. My hands shook as I reached to grasp the vessel with reverence. "This is the cup of life that Father made just for me.[157] How did you get it?"

"Father knew you would need it so you could be replenished during your journey through the heavenlies. He entrusted it to me ahead of time. I must confess that I looked inside. What an astounding life you are living, Royal Scribe."

Tears of gratitude moistened my eyes. "I'm drinking the water of life from the Well of His Presence from inside my own vessel. This is my life!"

Each gulp was delightful. I drank heartily and then licked my lips, savoring the last few drops. Then I saw it, a fresh engraving glistened inside my cup. It read, "The Library of Heaven." I was undone.

"Father, You planned this from the foundation of the world. Thank You, Abba. Thank You so much. You do all things well."

CHAPTER 18

The King's Royal Conservatory of Music

"I need to get going, Marcus," I said, standing to my feet. I stepped to the edge of the platform and peered into the vast darkness.

"Watch the net!" Marcus shouted. "God speed!"

"God speed," I chuckled. "That takes on a whole new meaning here in the heavens. Marcus really means it."

I catapulted off the pillar, clearing the net by a good ten feet. "That was cool," I said. "I had no idea I could do that. Kind of like an astronaut on the moon. I wonder why I never really thought about gravity in the heavenly realms until now. But wait a minute. Where am I going? Retreating back to the pillar is out of the question. I need to listen carefully. The Lord speaks in a still, small voice."[158]

I waited until I heard Holy Spirit say, "Go straight ahead! Listen for the sound. It will guide you."

"Listen for the sound? What sound?" I asked.

"You will know when you hear it," Holy Spirit replied.

"Okay. Now I can proceed with confidence. I am going to relish this journey. Traveling through the heavens is so amazing and inspiring."

I passed what looked like a waterfall of stars in the distance to my left. "Probably millions of light years away," I commented. Then I realized, "My vision must be magnified. It's supernatural. I have the ability to see great distances. I don't know how far, but my eyes are acting like a telescope. When I look in a certain direction, my eyes automatically focus. This ability must be activated when you are traveling great distances in the cosmos. I can't see like this when I'm not traveling or when I explored the angel encampment or the Kings' library. It makes sense, though. I can understand the need for greater visual acuity when I am moving at such a high rate of speed. Accurate depth perception is critical and measured in light years instead of miles or kilometers."

Listen for the Sound

I stopped abruptly. "What is that?" I asked. A very soft, almost undiscernible sound, barely a whisper, was coming from somewhere. I turned in every direction. "It's so faint, I can't tell which direction it's coming from. I should move in a circle, increasing the radius with each revolution like a search plane looking for lost survivors," I strategized. "I will eventually be able to determine where it's originating from."

I circled in ever-widening passes, flying over numerous pillars, none of which were emanating sound. Then I heard it. "It sounds like a trumpet. This could be the signal I am searching for. It's coming from that direction."

I set a course in the direction of Eternus.[159] The sound grew steadily louder and finally a pillar appeared in the distance. The sound was emanating from the portal above it.

"It is a trumpet," I affirmed. "It's playing a single note and it never stops. It's like a sonar beacon directing pneumanauts here to this portal."

I approached the pillar and gently landed on its sparkling surface next to the angel sentry who was guarding it. "I'm getting much better at landings," I smiled, congratulating myself.

The angel's face was glistening with powdery gold dust. Showers of miniature gold flakes where drifting down in the white light of the portal and landing on us. "It's snowing gold!" I exclaimed, awestruck with child-like delight. In moments, I was covered with gold specks. When I shook the royal scroll, it shed its gold coat and sent a blast of particles across the surface of the platform, exposing the pure white surface underneath the accumulated blanket of glory-dust.

The Music of the Spheres

"I heard the trumpet and followed its signal here," I explained to the angel doorman.

"Well done, Royal Scribe," he replied. "You heard the beacon of sound that helps pneumanauts traveling in the heavenly realms of the kingdom to find this pillar. This is the portal that leads to the King's Royal Conservatory of Music. This is where angels and saints come to study, learn, practice, and create the music of the heavenly spheres."

"Awesome!" I replied, totally intrigued. "I had no idea such a place existed. I love music. I love to sing. Do you know that I once directed a choir? I can also play several instruments as well. I love to worship and sing His praises."

"No, I didn't know that, Royal Scribe."

"Who are you?" I asked.

"I am the Staff Sergeant," he replied, laughing heartily. "No, not really. I'm just kidding. I love puns. You know, many of us angels have a great sense of humor, but humans don't always understand it.

"My real name is Penrose, from the legions of worshiping angels. My tribe studies here and we return often for classes. We never stop learning, composing and creating. Our greatest joy is being around the Throne of God. We love to come here to the conservatory to perfect our skills and craft. We are the King's lead worshipers and musicians. You will learn more about us in the conservatory.

"I welcome you, Royal Scribe. You may proceed through the portal whenever you desire. I must advise you that you will not be the same when you leave here. The conservatory of music is a place where you will grow exponentially in your worship skills."

This is a whole new method of transportation, I thought. *I am about to enter a portal that glistens with flakes of pure gold.*

I stepped into the center of the platform and raised the royal scroll into the lustrous column. Gold swirled around me like confetti and gently struck the surface of the scroll. Sound began to emanate from it. It released such a beautiful melody that I was deeply moved. It was so tender.

"Someone's playing the scroll," I said. The unseen musician drew his bow across the body of the royal scroll like an accomplished concert violinist and was playing it like a virtuoso.

The rapturous sound grew stronger and louder until it rose to such a crescendo that my entire being was resonating to the vibrations of the strings. "I feel like

I am one of the strings on the violin!" I declared. "I'm vibrating with pure music. I am becoming an instrument of worship in His hands."

Seraphim Guardians

I was so caught up in the heavenly solo that I forgot I was standing inside the portal. A sudden explosion of light flashed through the passageway, and I was caught upward through the golden shower and sped toward the conservatory of music. Light glittered all around me. The glory of God increased until it was difficult for me to see. Then they appeared!

"Look at those giant angels!" I said in astonishment. "They're on fire![160] They look like the burning bush. They are not consumed and so holy I'm afraid to come any closer. But I must proceed. I see a golden door behind them. It must be the entrance to the conservatory."

I stopped abruptly in front of them. The portal behind me faded and then disappeared. The gold flakes were gone and the light dissipated. *What shall I do?* I thought, too afraid to speak in their holy presence. I stood shivering and looked up into their faces. Strength and authority emanated from them.

The first heavenly being spoke, "We are seraphim." He said with such regal authority and power that I was actually blown backward by his voice.[161]

"Our purpose is to worship God around His Throne. The seraph speaking had six wings: two covered his face, two for covering his feet and two for flying. As he spoke, the seraph to his left spread his wings and drew them around his face tightly.

"We are created to be close to the King. We are His personal royal sentinels. We have been assigned to safeguard the access door to His Majesty's conservatory because His glory and presence is powerfully manifested here. You must enter with the utmost humility. The greatest danger here in the conservatory is pride.

"Satan came here often. He practiced his craft in the conservatory. It was his ability to create music and worship that made him think he could displace God. He was the Master's chief musician and the director of the conservatory. In his prideful lust for power, he rebelled against the King and was cast down. Through his popularity and persuasiveness, he influenced many to follow him. A serious rebellion created a major division among the angels. He intentionally and, oh, so subtly drew them away from the King. They became loyal to him and were complicit with his schemes to overthrow the Lord. Many of the angels were cast out of heaven along with Satan.[162]

"His fallen angel minions are banned from the third heaven. They worship Lucifer. They are full of darkness and deceit. Demonic influencers, they are bent on possessing mankind's affections and demanding their subservience. They will stop at nothing: stealing, killing and destroying their human prey. They delight to dwell in darkness, and inhabit places and living beings to torment and possess.

"But in all of his power, Satan is weak compared to the King's supremacy and authority. A single light beam of His glory can make Satan's minions flee. Regardless of their rank or position in the dark legions, they must bow before the King of kings.[163] They are obliged to obey God's servants.[164] They fight with the intensity of Satan's anger and wrath, but they cannot win, and they know it."[165]

Passing the Test

"May I see your scroll, Royal Scribe?" he requested.

I was reluctant to give it to him. "The King has entrusted it to me. I must guard it. I will protect it with my life if need be. I cannot let you have it," I replied in stubborn refusal, clutching the scroll selfishly to me chest.

"You must let it go," The seraph stated. "It is not yours; it is His. I must check the scroll before you can enter the conservatory."

He's right, I quickly realized. *It's not mine. It is the King's scroll. I am His royal scribe. Both the scroll and the scribe are His.*

"I will surrender it to you, Seraph, but my assignment is far from complete." I cradled the scroll, like a Templar Knight would present His sword to Jesus, and knelt before the seraph to vow allegiance to the King. "I bow to You and only You, Lord Jesus. All I am and have belongs to You."

I trembled in fear as the seraph reached to take the scroll. Waves of glory flooded over me. I held my position. My head remained bowed as the powerful, majestic angel examined the scroll. Once he had fulfilled his duty, the seraph's hand touched my shoulder. "Rise before the King, Royal Scribe," he instructed, "and take the royal scroll. All is well. You may proceed into the King's conservatory. You have passed the test."

"The test?" I asked, standing to receive the scroll.

"Yes, the test," he replied. "All who enter here must humble themselves and acknowledge who they are and who the King is. You must be willing to surrender everything, including your assignment, to Him. Do not withhold anything. You must enter with no idols and no personal agenda."

The commanding seraph opened the golden door: "Proceed, Royal Scribe! Someone will greet you at the entrance."

The Entrance

I could not contain myself. The scene before me was otherworldly. Puffy white clouds were everywhere. I ran forward and leapt through the gold doorway into the vast expanse.

"This is what David must have felt and acted like when he brought the Ark to Jerusalem!" I shouted gleefully. "But this is so unlike me. I'm skipping and dancing wildly, praising God with all of my might, just like he did.[166] This atmosphere is so refreshing and invigorating. It's like morning sunshine after a spring rain. The smell is delightful. I am so alive and bursting with joy."

I was so overcome with the desire to worship the King that I didn't keep track of how far I had moved toward the conservatory. As the clouds thinned, a very large, shining edifice, like a skyscraper, appeared in the distance. "It's really high," I said in awe, admiring the architecture and unique design of the structure. "I think it could reach the heavens." I realized the incongruity in what I said. "Wait a minute. I'm in the heavenly realms already!" I laughed. "This must be the King's conservatory." I approached the main entry with all of my discernment on high alert, searching for the smallest details. "I mustn't miss a single thing."

"Hmm? There are three adjoining doors and all of them are panes of etched crystal. Why three?" I ran my hand across their surfaces. "This center door doesn't swing; it slides open in either direction. But wait. The engraving on the inside of this door is the same design as the one on the barrel of the royal scroll. I'll bet these swooshes contain music too."

I raised my hand and flicked the center door with my finger to test it. It rang like a fine crystal goblet sounding a chorus of carillon chimes. The door slid open.

"That's some doorbell!" I declared. "Music is the visitor's entrance announcement."

The Foyer
I passed through the door and stepped into the delicious atmosphere of the main floor. The room was an inviting luminous foyer. All the exterior walls were clear glass. It was open and airy with a fantastic view of the surrounding exterior and the clouds in the distance.

Someone's approaching. Is this a cherub? I thought. *He sure is dressed differently.*

"Welcome to the King's Royal Conservatory of Music, Royal Scribe. I see that you are carrying the royal scroll that plays music."

"Thank you, sir," I responded. "It does have that amazing ability. I just discovered that it can sound like a violin. I think it has something to do with these silver swooshes on the surface."

"Yes! I know this scroll well," he acknowledged. "I oversaw its programing. It was sent here to the conservatory by the King with instructions to record several compositions that were made specifically for it. What you carry is much more than a scroll. It is a musical instrument, as well as many other things. You do not know how to play it yet. If you have time while you are here in the conservatory on this visit, we will teach you."

"I would love that, sir."

"You do not need to call me sir. My name is Pilar.[167] Wait here while I check your itinerary. I'll be back in a moment."

"What's a moment, Lord?" I asked, still in an investigative frame of mind. "There's no time here in the heavenly realms. Or is there? I mustn't forget the principle, 'I really don't know what I don't know.' Let's see. If a day is as a thousand years, well, a moment could be a year.[168]

"Does eternity have its own paradigm of coming and going, arriving and departing? Is there a way to measure the immeasurable and chronicle timelessness in the heavenly realms and the kingdom expanses? If we can't measure times and seasons, then past, present and future no longer exist in heaven, and any attempt to record events here is fruitless and impossible.

"Lord, I need revelation. You know the secret mysteries and have the power to reveal the answers. I tend to think in light years in this realm, but my thoughts are not your thoughts.[169] You are Alpha and Omega, beginning and ending.[170] What does that description of You really mean? Like King David, I am inquiring after you."[171]

My Conservatory Itinerary

Pilar returned accompanied by another angel. "I have checked your itinerary, Royal Scribe. The King desires that you have a guided tour of the conservatory, and at its conclusion we are to prepare a royal concert for you to attend before you leave. You are to be given the Ambassador's seat at the concert alongside the King."

"What? Who me? I can't even imagine what that will be like. And to sit beside the King? What an incredible honor.[172] Wait a minute," I realized. "Yes, I can imagine it! I need to keep reminding myself that my imagination is the page God writes on. He told me that Himself."[173]

The second angel introduced himself: "I am Petros. I have the honor of guiding you through the royal conservatory. We will begin at the top floor and descend through each level until we have arrived back here at the Royal Music Hall. Follow me, Royal Scribe. We have a schedule to keep."

He led me to my right toward a translucent vertical passageway that had no entry door. "This is the transition tube. Stay along the outside wall," Petros directed. "Step into the tube. Now!"

"Okay. But there's no floor."

"Just do as I do," he said.

The passageway was packed with people, angels and other beings. Petros explained, "Those who are in the center are all descending. Everyone who is going up keeps toward the outside. Simple, common courtesy makes transition between floors easier."

"This is otherworldly," I winced. "It's like riding in an elevator shaft with no car, no doors and no floor." We surged upward, caught in a stream of human and angelic traffic moving in both directions at the same time. Passengers kept disappearing right through the wall of the vertical portal. The crowd had thinned considerably by the time we approached the topmost level.

"We will exit soon," Petros said. "Just follow me." He faced the wall and stepped right through it.

"Here goes!" I declared, visualizing that an unseen bungee cord was attached to me. I stepped into the iridescent wall. My right leg went in completely as if through water. I could feel a slight resistance. The surface yielded to my motion, and I passed through into a regal foyer.

CHAPTER 19

The King's Heralds

"You are going to love this place," Petros said enthusiastically, his facial expression communicating sheer delight. "This floor houses the Academy of the King's Heralds. The angels who belong to the King's trumpet legion come here to learn and develop their skills. You don't just pick up a ram's horn and start tooting," he grimaced. "It takes practice. When the trumpeters have graduated, some are chosen to serve the King as a member of His signal corps."

Petros pointed toward the door into the academy. "This door is sound proof," he explained. "The signals and fanfares must be protected and secured with the utmost secrecy."

He stopped and looked up with admiration. Two trumpets were displayed diagonally on the wall. Each one had a flag attached to it. The flag on the right trumpet bore a red cross and gold crown on a white background that was identical to the emblem I saw at the Royal Stables. The banner was bordered in royal red. The left trumpet carried a flag with a royal blue background. The depiction of a head of a lion and a lamb were woven into the fabric.

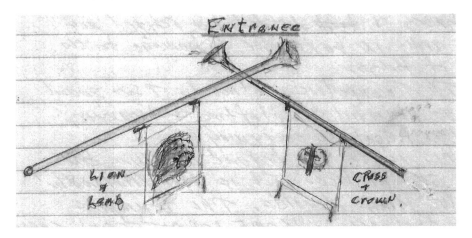

"The angels polish the trumpets often," Petros explained. "There are many banners. All of them are designed by the King. The herald chooses the appropriate banner to place on the trumpet, depending upon the nature and content of the proclamation.

"The heralds have great power and authority when they sound the King's messages. They announce and declare the changing of times and seasons and inaugurate Father's will and actions in the heavens and on earth. The sound of the trumpets signal the end and the beginning of times—and a time. They announce the arrival of the King. Everyone here in heaven and on earth must pay attention when the trumpet speaks."

The Academy of the King's Heralds

"Let's go inside," Petros said, stepping through the doorway.

Many hallways led from the entrance to deeper into the academy. "We'll go down this passageway," he said, pointing to the right side of the corridor. "These are practice rooms designed for each level or grade of musicianship," he explained like a seasoned tour guide leaving no information undisclosed. "Every student starts with the shofar. When they have mastered it, they advance to basic trumpet. Once they complete that level, they are given their very own instrument designed and inscribed by the King. No one else may play their trumpet. It has a distinct sound and it is made to synchronize and harmonize with the entire corps.

"Some trumpeters are assigned to the signal corps. Others become part of either the King's heralds or the royal orchestra. But everyone is commissioned to play before the Throne at the King's command."

Angels kept passing us in the hallway, carrying trumpets of different sizes and shapes. Beginning students carried their ram's horn shofars in blue velvet bags held closed at the top with a silver drawstring.

"I believe the King's heralds are rehearsing now. Would you like to listen?"

"Are you kidding? Let's go!" I responded enthusiastically.

The Practice Chamber

We reached the end of the corridor and stepped into open space.

"There are specific boundaries and limitations here," Petros explained. "This is the trumpet practice chamber. Its sound is directed toward the outer reaches. This entire space is designed so the heralds can practice in the actual conditions they will be called upon to perform in."

I detected a host of angels positioned behind us on what looked like the ramparts of a castle wall. The wall was shaped like the cone of a rectangular speaker, directing the sound outward. Parapets and platforms were lined with regal angels. The moment we entered, they raised their trumpets to their lips in perfect unison. On command, they erupted in sound.

The fanfare raised the hair on the back of my neck. Goosebumps covered my arms.

"How majestic!" I declared, standing at full attention. "They're incredible!" I shouted at Petros, but he did not respond. He was totally focused on the music, carefully listening and deciphering the message it carried. The tone and harmony were pure and distinct. The staccato was riveting. Then the angels would hold a single note without breathing for a very long time. "That's impossible for a human to duplicate—at least five or ten minutes according to earth time," I said, astonished by their ability.

Unexpectedly, the sound stopped, but the angels were still playing. "What's happening Petros? I asked.

"They have gone beyond the range of your ability to hear. Now you must listen in the spirit."

"Of course," I intentionally tuned into my spirit. "Oh, my! It's so cosmic—so magnificent and pure."

"Yes, it is," Petros said. "It is heavenly, isn't it?"

I watched and listened as the heralds began to signal to one another. One section would play and then another section would respond in an antiphonal trumpet chorus. The sound moved me so deeply that I became transfixed. I could hardly breathe as I listened in awe. "They're conversing with one another."

"They are trumpet voices of declaration and responses of affirmation," Petros explained.

The Royal Insignia and Fanfare

"Here comes the best part," Petros said ecstatically, poking my arm to be sure I heard him. "They are about to play the fanfare announcing the entrance of the King."

The music stopped. Every angel bowed his head and held that posture. The commanding angel shouted, "The Royal Insignia!"

In perfect form and synchronization, the angels withdrew flags from satchels hanging at their sides and placed them on the retaining rings located on the trumpets' shafts. The banners were regal—appropriate for the King. Gold brocade bordered solid purple. A single gold trumpet was embroidered with gold thread in the center of the banner. The phrase 'King of kings' was engraved along the barrel of the trumpet. The detail was exquisite. Even the hooks that held the banner were symbolic. They were designed like miniature replicas of the ram's horn or shofar.

The Royal Insignia

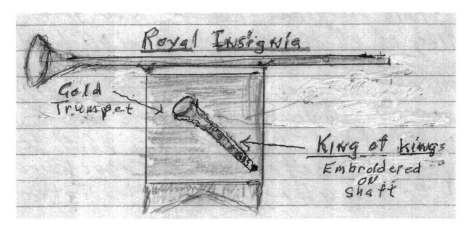

The commander raised his trumpet to his lips and sounded a series of precise notes. The other heralds responded to his signal and raised their trumpets, holding them at the ready. He played again, but this time with such power and authority that it sounded like crashing waves on the shore. "Daaaa datdatdat daaa, datdatdat daaaaaaa." On this cue, the royal heralds, at least a thousand trumpets, released a clarion declaration. Were it aimed earthward, the sound would shake the ground and every person would bow in preparation and honor of the King's appearing.

I dropped to my knees unable to stand as the sound penetrated into my bones.[174] "I know this is a rehearsal, but I can't stay standing. I exalt You, Majesty. You are holy and righteous. God of all creation, I lift my hands in surrender to You." How could anyone refuse to bow down when He enters? It is impossible to resist. I recalled Paul's words to the church in Philippi. *"Every knee shall bow, and every tongue confess that Jesus Christ is Lord, to the glory of God the Father."*[175]

The fanfare continued. It was so uplifting and honoring—regal in every way. "This is far beyond anything that earth can produce." I said in admiration. "It surely surpasses the skill of any military signal corps. It's a fitting fanfare to announce the entrance of the King. If the saints' cry is 'Maranatha,' then this must be the angelic response. The King's heralds are declaring, 'ENTER, LORD JESUS! ENTER IN!'"

The trumpet chorus ended with a flourish of soaring tones. The commander gave a signal and the angels responded immediately, lowering their trumpets and bowing their heads. Total stillness filled the hall. The silence was breathless. Then, one by one, beginning on the right, every angel in succession raised his trumpet to his chest and held it vertically against his heart with his left hand. The effect was striking, sending a stereophonic breast thump through the chamber like a drum roll. They held this position at attention until the commander, pleased with their performance, shouted, "At ease!" And then "Dismissed!" The rehearsal was over.

"Petros," I asked, "how come all of heaven and earth didn't respond? I fully expected Jesus to enter the room."

"Remember," he replied, "this is a practice area. Most of the sound in the conservatory is contained within strict boundaries. Otherwise, we would have confusion in the cosmos. Can you imagine the signal corps, the King's heralds and the orchestra all playing at the same time? That is why the conservatory is sound sealed, although there are some places, like this one, that have outlets into the heavenlies in specific directions. These designated areas are like signal channels. We use them to monitor and test the volume and distance of the sound."

Cosmic Communicators

"It's time to go. We must return to the portal now. There is so much more for you to experience here in the conservatory," Petros insisted.

We retraced our steps through the busy corridor toward the entrance and the transition portal.

My mind was on overload. *If this is only one floor in the conservatory, what do the other levels contain?* I pondered. *But it surely makes sense that the heralds command the top level. Their role is critical in the heavenly realms. Like prophets, they declare and release the will and purpose of God throughout history and all eternity.*

We must always be alert with spirit-sensitivity to listen for the sound of these messengers of God. They hold the sound-key to the portals of change and open the door to the new things that God is doing. They precede and initiate the King's strategies and are the cosmic-communicators who trumpet the revelation. Nothing in all of creation can stifle their decrees.

CHAPTER 20

The Academies of Voice and Percussion

The portal was crowded.

"Is it always like this?" I asked, bumping into an angel next to me.

"If you think this is crowded, you should be here when we are preparing for special events. We need ushers to guide traffic," Petros replied with a frown.

Storage Levels

"Some of these upper floors are storage areas," he explained as we dropped past them. "The one just below the top is where we store instruments of all kinds, many of which you have never seen or heard before.

"This next level is where the musical scores and compositions are kept. It is divided into two sections: instrumental and vocal. The vocal section has choral music for the heavenly choirs. There are many choirs here in heaven, and every angelic legion has its own choir. The saints also have their own choirs according to their tribes and tongues. Every nation comes before the King singing. But I must admit, I love the corporate choir. When all the choirs assemble together with the royal orchestra to worship at the appointed time, the praise and exaltation fills the cosmos. Even the stars join in the celestial ensemble."

"Someday, I'm going to hear it," I determined.

"Yes, you will," Petros responded, "but not today."

"Maybe I can join the choir or orchestra?"

"The Lord knows your heart's desire already, Royal Scribe."

Petros could not contain himself. He broke into singing. His face shone like an angel's should:

Praise the LORD;

Praise God in his sanctuary;
praise him in his mighty heavens.
Praise him for his acts of power;
praise him for his surpassing greatness.
Praise him with the sounding of the trumpet,
praise him with the harp and lyre,
praise him with timbrel and dancing,
praise him with the strings and pipe,
praise him with the clash of cymbals,
praise him with resounding cymbals.

Let everything that has breath praise the LORD.

Praise the LORD. "[176]

Every passenger in the portal joined in after the first line. Students and professors, from novices to masters, were united in one voice. I joined the chorus, my heart pounding with excitement. *Just think!* I thought, pinching myself to see if this was real. *Here I am, joining this heavenly chorus of encouragement. I will never be able to read or speak this Psalm again without recalling this moment.*

"Do you hear me saints?" I added in solo to the end of the musical declaration, "PRAISE GOD IN EVERY MANNER POSSIBLE!" with all the volume I could muster. Everyone in the portal looked at me in shock and started to applaud.

Petros spoke, anti-climatically, "All of the songs and hymns of the Church are stored on this level. There are hymns and choruses and symphonies of every kind of musical score and every genre. Even Mary's lullabies are here. Choir and choral arrangements and cantatas occupy one vast section. Another holds all of the music from Israel's worshippers; of special interest are King David's compositions. I trust that someday you will get to hear some of them. Oh, and yes, you will also find the Song of Moses in its original form and melody. It attests to God's righteousness and greatness.[177]

"I must tell you that an entire department is dedicated to Angels' songs. It's astonishing. You know, some of the heavenly creatures are created purely to worship Him. You haven't fully heard worship until you hear the seraphim crying, 'Holy, holy, holy!'" Everyone around the Throne is transfixed by their declarations. Their antiphonal pronouncements direct all attention to the Throne and Him who sits upon it. King Jesus is high and lifted up by their praises."

Isaiah's words scrolled through my thoughts. *"In the year that King Uzziah died I saw the Lord sitting upon a throne, high and lifted up, and the train filled the temple. Above it stood the seraphim. Each one had six wings and one cried unto another, and said, 'Holy, holy, holy is the Lord of hosts, the whole earth is full of His glory,' and the posts of the door moved at the voice of him who cried, and the house was filled with smoke."*[178]

New Songs
We continued down through the transition portal. "This floor of the conservatory houses the Department of New Songs," Petros revealed.[179]

His information instantly evoked a fond memory. The melodic Jewish refrain of a chorus we sang during the charismatic days sprung to life in my spirit. *"Sing unto the Lord a new song. Sing unto the Lord all the earth. For He has done marvelous things, He has done marvelous things. God is great, and greatly to be prai-ea-ea-ea-eased…"*[180] I recalled the scene vividly: guitars strumming, tambourines vibrating and pounding out the rhythm while we twirled around the circle, dancing enthusiastically with newfound freedom. We tossed our straightjackets of religious restraint right through the stained-glass windows of confinement and set our hearts and feet to worshipping in full-blown, party-mode celebration before the King.

Petros raised his eyebrows in surprise. "Good song!" he said.

"I didn't know I was singing."

"Oh, but you were," he smiled in approval, "and I could see your feet tapping as well. It's quite appropriate here. But it's not just the earth that sings. The music of creation, the sounds of the earth and planets, actually create a symphony of praise.[181] The ether oscillates like a string section.[182] When God conducts the cosmos, all of creation is involved. The trees clap their hands. The rocks sing His praise. The galaxies declare His greatness. The Instrumental Scores Department on this level of the conservatory is never-ending. The music charts of the universe are all kept here.

"I can't wait," Petros sighed, breathing deeply and slowly exhaling as he indulged in a moment of anticipatory reflection. "Creation's eager expectation will soon be fulfilled. God will reveal who His true sons are! Then, everything that exists will join in a cosmic, never-ending chorus of praise and worship with the set-free sons of God."[183] The portal grew silent. Everyone, including me, was contemplating the moment when the sons of God will be revealed.

What will it be like when God reveals who His children are? I wondered. *It must be more than the opening of a closed curtain as though He was revealing a portrait of His image. Our sonship will be manifested. This is a verb not a noun. We will be revealed, established and fully activated. God's sons will demonstrate His power and authority. Creation's expectant longing will once-and-for-all be fulfilled. This will be the mother-of-all demonstrations—God expressing Himself through His offspring. No wonder all of creation is yearning and aching for this moment with eager expectation.*

My thoughts were interrupted when Petros tapped me on the shoulder. "Stay alert. We will exit here, Royal Scribe. This is the Academy of Percussion," Petros announced.

The Academy of Percussion

I followed him into the foyer. It was like stepping into a gymnasium's locker room, minus the smell. We were greeted by a city-block-sized display of shelves and doorless lockers. I went into exploring mode. Mallets, with felt, cloth or animal-hide heads, drum sticks, and drum brushes of all shapes and proportions were neatly stored by type and size. Several large blue bins lying on the floor contained metal rods and mallets for striking triangles, bells, chimes and other instruments requiring metal tools. A closet at the beginning of each row of shelves contained white gloves, polishing clothes and multicolored containers of wax, oil and polish. An entire closet, stretching the width of the room at the back, was filled with drum heads and skins carefully hung or stretched on frames.

"Grab two mallets," Petros instructed, "and follow me. I know you're going to enjoy this."

The door to the Academy of Percussion was Chinese in design and symmetry. I stopped to admire the images painted on the surface of the entrance. "These artistic brushstrokes obviously tell a story," I said, hoping to prompt an explanation from Petros.

"You are very observant, Royal Scribe," he responded. "China's script is still basically logographic, comprised of some fifty thousand signs. Traditions of writing do not die easily. These logograms chronicle the development of percussion instruments and technique. The scribe used his ancient skill to paint these *hanzi* logograms.[184] He used the white and black contrast. Notice the borders of each panel on the door. The frames are inlayed with ivory lightning bolts on black ebony."

The First Percussion Beat

Petros passed his right hand slowly over the panels in the proper succession to reveal the chronology of percussion. "Each panel tells a story," he explained.

I traced the evolving drama like an enthralled youth looking at an illustrated children's book. Petros interrupted my storied journey and insisted I return to the first panel. "This is not a bookend to mark the start of the story!" he stated. "This is the very beginning. This is the initiation of percussion," he said, pointing to the panel on the upper right. "Look carefully! Tell me what you see."

"There are two hearts portrayed inside the panel," I said. "There is a line of force between them. I think it represents life. Life is flowing from the left to the right, pulsing from one heart to the other."

"That's right," he replied. "This is the inaugural pulse of God's creative masterpiece. It is Adam's first heartbeat responding to Father's life-giving breath. The beat of Adam's heart was established and set to match the Creator's. The first rhythm of creation occurred in the beginning moment when the convergence of eternal and human hearts pulsed together and signaled life. As long as the heart beats, there is life. It is the rhythm of the universe."

"Is that why any rhythm simulating the frequency of the heartbeat is so powerful?" I asked.

"Indeed," he replied. "It is intrinsic and deeply rooted in the core of our being. As Paul once wrote, 'In Him we live and move and have our being.'[185] Our heartbeat is the percussion of life. Abba was the first to hear it."

The Timpani

"Let's proceed! We will visit the timpani section first," Petros said.

We passed through the open doorway and turned left. Practice rooms appeared located on both sides of the hallway. At the end of the corridor, we entered an unoccupied orchestral amphitheater. Percussion instruments of every kind were positioned in the rhythm section.

"Step over here," Petros said, walking amidst the instruments. "I want you to play these timpani."

"All right!" I shouted, pumping my arm and clenching my fist with a sense of victory. I positioned myself behind the huge center kettle. Its copper surface was polished to a mirror finish. The foot pedal perfectly accommodated my feet. "Not your average timpani set," I said with admiration. "Here goes," I remarked, apprehensive about my angel audience performance rating. "I hope my high school orchestra experience will serve me well."

I lifted my mallets over the outer circumference of the head and struck it gently. Slowly, methodically I increased the force and gradually moved the mallets toward the center of the surface. The sound deepened and soon became a thunderous roll. A slight depression on the foot pedal produced a delicate tone shift. I retreated as I had entered, the sound gradually diminished from a rumbling tremor to a crashing waterfall, then falling rain, and then fading into a bubbling stream.

"I wonder what it would be like to play in the orchestra?" I asked, gasping for air after my complete immersion in the performance.

Petros frowned, "I think you will need some further training and practice first."

"Well, at least *I* thought it was good," I mumbled.

"But that is for a future time," Petros continued, ignoring my comment. "We need to see several more levels, and we certainly don't want to be late for the royal concert. But before we leave the Academy of Percussion, you must see the cymbals."

Cymbals

We retreated back to the entry door and then turned left, heading down the center hallway that ran straight into the academy from the front entrance. It led directly to a studio that accommodated the cymbals. Petros pointed to a straight row of cymbals in the center of the room.

"These are made to match the notes of the musical scale like a piano keyboard in ascending order from low to high notes. You can actually play these note-cymbals like any other instrument.

"Over there are the timbre cymbals. They also come in every size and shape," he pointed to the smallest, about the size of a small coin. "This little one is so delicate. It is angelic, like the sound of dust landing on a surface. That one over there is just the opposite. It rumbles like an earthquake," he said, his hand trembling momentarily in demonstration. "Believe me, play a hundred of these at once and you'll think it's an earthquake."

"This gives new meaning to Psalm 150," I said. Quoting from memory, I continued, "Praise Him with the clash of loud resounding cymbals. Praise Him on the high-sounding cymbals. Praise Him on the cymbals of joy."[186]

"That's exactly right," Petros replied. "You don't just bang a cymbal. You play it with skill like any other fine instrument. It's more than just seasoning or salt and pepper in a musical presentation; sometimes, it's the main ingredient."

He pointed to the far side of the studio: "Over there are the stands for hand-held cymbals. Notice to the right, there are various sized cymbals paired with drum sets to comprise a percussion suite that can be played by a single individual."

I glanced around the room, stunned by the variety and intricacy of this genre of percussion. I had the strongest urge to spend the day experimenting with all the instruments. If the base is the backbone of music, then percussion must certainly be the heartbeat," I remarked.

"We must leave now," Petrus said. We walked back toward the entrance. When we arrived at the door, he stopped and pointed toward the left. "This corridor leads to the chamber that houses all the other percussion instruments: tambourines, woodblocks, bells and castanets, to name a few. Anything you can strike to produce a sound has the potential of being used for percussion. There are too many to mention, but you get the idea."

"Well, maybe," I said, disappointed that I would not get to see this incredible variety of rhythm instruments on this visit.

Petros pushed the door open, and we walked straight to the transportation tube.

CHAPTER 21

The Academy of Strings

We descended several floors and exited into a beautifully decorated large foyer. The furnishings were imperial. Gold, precious metals and ceramic lamps rested on exquisite wooden tables made of common or exotic woods: chestnut, pecan, pine, cedar, oak, teak, bamboo and others I couldn't identify. Their grains and textures told the story of their life well lived and cared for. Next to each table were chairs of many different designs. Each one was so inviting that I wanted to test them all. They were upholstered with fine silk, cotton or wool fabrics, either plain or printed. Others were supple leather or animal hides that honored and exhibited the grandeur of the animal kingdom in imperial fashion.

If only I could take photographs, I thought. *It's impossible to describe this room with commonplace words.*

"Come and sit here for a moment," Petros said, pointing to a sofa with a coffee table in front of it.

"Sweep your hand across the surface of the table," he instructed.

"It is so refined. It has such an incomparable quality. If you can feel perfection, this would be it," I said with admiration.

"Perfect," Petros replied. "This is one of the King's favorite pieces of furniture here in the conservatory. Every time He comes to this floor, He sits by this table. We think He is listening to the table. We can only imagine what music it makes."

"What kind of wood is this?" I asked.

"It is spruce," Petros replied, "but not just any spruce. This wood was taken from the Fiemme Valley in the Italian Alps.[187] That is where Stradivarius chose trees from the forest to make his violins. The place is called 'The Musical Woods.' I've been told that if you go there and have a trained ear and sensitive spirit, you can tell, just by tapping on the trunks of the trees, which ones are ideal for instruments by listening.

"Jesus sends angels to bring trees from that forest," Petros continued. "The artisans who made this table also crafted violins, cellos and other stringed instruments from the same wood. I'm not sure how many are produced, but they are played when the King's orchestra performs.

"By now you should have guessed where we are, Royal Scribe. This is the Academy of Strings. But before we go inside, you must understand the nature of light and sound."

Light and Sound

I was startled when the Spirit of Understanding unexpectedly appeared. He was bathed in yellow light. "You called me?" he asked.

"I was about to," I answered.

"I was listening to your conversation with Petros. Let me explain the principle of sound. All sound is the result of a disturbance or vibration carried through the atmosphere or ether. Sound is like light. We cannot see light. We see with light, but we do not see the light itself. Sound is similar. We hear it, but we do not see it. Light and sound travel in waves or cycles.

"Light is the result of the release of energy and power. Sound is produced by vibrations and it travels on electromagnetic waves. All sound and music are created by vibration. The vocal cords vibrate. The strings of a violin or guitar, the drum head and cymbal, the reeds on wind instruments, they all vibrate to produce sound. A trumpet sounds because the musician's lips vibrate. Sound can also be produced electronically, but only because oscillating sound waves are produced. Sound travels through every medium unless it is intentionally blocked. It also travels through space. Creation sings. The planets and stars make music. Space is not empty. It is full of sound.

"Light and sound are very powerful on earth and in heaven. They possess such potent energy that they can be used to create or destroy, heal or kill. The King uses light and sound as weapons in His armory. He is awesome in might and power, mighty in battle. At His command, a single emission of light or a discharge of thunderous sound can destroy an entire army, planet and even a solar system.

"What I have told you is rudimentary knowledge, Royal Scribe. There is a reason why this information is vital. You must learn to discern invisible movement and the field of vibrations that voice and music create. Music, words and voice are potent forces to be reckoned with. They establish atmospheres and penetrate barriers. They can bring down fortifications and ancient walls.[188] The shout of Israel at Jericho is an example. They are weapons of great influence. The enemy knows this well. That is why Judah went in front of the column when Israel journeyed through the wilderness. The sound of worship is a weapon of breakthrough. Don't just listen to music, determine its intent and purpose. Be intentional about this as you enter the Academy of Strings.

"Are you ready?"

"Yes, I think so," I answered, standing to my feet.

Eden's Resources

We walked toward the entry door when I noticed an extraordinary footstool. "What is this wood?" I asked in admiration.

"This wood is from one of the trees that grows in the Garden of Eden," Understanding replied. "There are many types of trees that mankind has never seen, except for Adam and Eve, because the Garden was closed. This wood is from a tree that grows by the river that flows through the garden. Those who sit in this chair are healed just by placing their feet on the footstool. Other species of wood from Eden are located throughout the foyer," Understanding said, pointing to several nearby items.

I glanced around and said, "I would love to take more time to look at them."

"That would be fine, but wouldn't it be much better to go and actually see the trees in the Garden of Eden. Would you like to?"

"Can I?" I asked in surprise.

"Well, probably not on this journey, but others have gone there, and I'm sure Holy Spirit will lead you there in due season. But for now, you must enter the Academy of Strings. If you need me again, just call. I am always available. I must go. Others are requesting my help, and I have a class to teach."

My curiosity along with a tinge of jealousy was obvious. "A class?" I asked.

"Yes," Understanding replied. "We have classes. Just ask Holy Spirit when and where they are held. He will direct you if it is appropriate.

"Petros will take you into the academy now," he said as he departed.

"That helped me immensely, Petros," I said. "Thank God for Understanding," I added with a grin. "I'm ready now."

Worship in Spirit and Truth!

Unlike other entrances that were ornate, this doorway was simple. Its magnificent wood grain served well to identify this academy. Its lacquered finish glistened like a highly polished piece of furniture.

"This replicates the back surface of a violin," Petros said, reaching for the door handle. "It's made of the finest spruce."

"Wow!" I uttered. "Look at this door handle. It's shaped like a violin bow."

The instant I stepped through the doorway, my attention was drawn upward. Light beams were cascading into the room, casting a shadow onto the sparkling granite floor. An object was suspended in the middle of the domed ceiling.

"It's a harp!" I declared in amazement. "It's just hanging in midair. Petros, it's very plain, almost rugged," I said, seeking help. "It's all nicked, and look, the frame is gouged. This instrument shows all the signs of hard use. This harp has been in some difficult places for sure," I said, tightening my lips and nodding my head conclusively.

I gazed at the instrument. *What kind of harp would merit such an honored place in the Academy of Strings? This instrument has such a humble appearance. My guess is that it's not very expensive. Probably made for common use,* I thought.

"Wait a minute!" I said in a moment of sudden revelation. "Could it be? Is this really what I think it is?"

"And what is that?" Petros replied.

"Is it David's harp?"

"Yes. It is David's harp," he confirmed, nodding with delight at my answer. "Father loves to hear him play it and sing. David still does, you know. He comes by to get it so he can play and sing before the Throne. Father positioned it here in the entrance to make a strong declaration."

"What is the message, Petros?"

"It is the music of the heart and spirit that pleases Father. David worshiped God in spirit and truth.[189] He worshipped from his heart. He loved God so much that Father described him as a man after His own heart."[190]

Suddenly, the harp suspended above me began to play.

"The harp!" I uttered in astonishment. "Who's playing it?"

"It's Holy Spirit," Petrus said with his head bowed. "He has always played it through David."

I was stunned: "The Lord is playing for me. It's Spirit to spirit."

My soul responded to the strings of the harp. Love poured into me. God's peace and kindness wrapped around me like a blanket. I felt so secure in the warmth of the heavenly pulsation coming from David's harp.

"Wow. Had I ever doubted I was loved by my heavenly Father, this moment washes it all away. I am His beloved. If this is how I feel right now, imagine how Father must feel when David plays for Him."

"He feels loved," Petros said tenderly.

Enraptured by the music, I was caught up in the moment. The shimmering light, the sparkling floor, and David's incredible harp playing above me became a stage set for a performance. The dome filled with a holy, cloud-like, white smoke and I was transported back to an ancient time:

Sheep were bleating contentedly on a hillside. David sat among the stone boulders. His hair was black and curly. His youthful face shone with innocence, and wonder glistened in his eyes. He placed his staff against a stone and began to strum and pluck the strings of his harp. It was a lilting melody, so simple and pure. He played and sang for what seemed like hours, composing songs of worship and praise and sometimes uttering powerful prayers accompanied by the strings.

"The wilderness was David's *secret place*," Petros whispered, observing the scene himself. "The pastures and hillsides were his private closet for communing with God. He didn't change when he became King. His sole desire was to be in God's presence. It's the one thing he desired most of all."[191]

"I want to stay right here under this impartation of blessing," I replied, looking into the light with my arms raised toward the ceiling of the dome. Worship was going on deep inside my spirit. The sound faded slowly into silence, but my spirit continued to resonate for a while, like an echo replying to an unseen voice, until it too became still.

"Such love and peace," I said.

"It is wonder-**full**," Petros said, emphasizing the last syllable. "You are very blessed, Royal Scribe. You will never forget this moment. There will be times when your spirit will echo the Spirit's 'song of love.'"

"That is so true, Petros. This is unforgettable. Through the mystery of the Spirit speaking through my anointed imagination, I have witnessed David's worship here inside the entrance to the Academy of Strings. This is more than a doorway. It's a threshold into the dimension of true worship."

"You will discover this to be true of all the entrances here in the conservatory," Petros added. "A doorway is more than just a means of access. It is a transition from one atmosphere to another."

"Aha!" I pondered. "I must remember this truth."

Exploring the Academy

"We can explore the Academy of Strings now," Petros prompted. "Most of the space on this level is used for practice rooms. Angels and saints come to rehearse and perfect their musicianship. Master musicians instruct their students. These accomplished students are the ones chosen to occupy the first chair and string sections in the King's orchestra. We won't enter the studios. We don't want to interrupt their sessions."

We proceeded down the hallway as Petros identified each practice area. "Here we have the harp and lyre section, and over on this side are the studios for violins, violas, and similar types of instruments. You should know that the violin is the highest member of the strings family played with a bow. Here in the academy, we consider it the queen of the strings. Notice that some of these studios are also larger to accommodate ensembles."

We continued along the hallway passing the cello and bass studios.

"Now this is a fun place to visit," Petros commented, snapping his fingers as we approached it. This is the area where the instruments that are strummed and plucked are played. There are ukuleles, banjoes and mandolins, but that's just 'the tip of the iceberg,' as they say on earth. I just love the banjo. You should hear them between practice sessions. They love to jam. I call it, 'pickers paradise,'" he said, laughing heartily and tapping his toes. "What a praise party. Angels and people come to listen to the students. Even the master musicians get carried away. No pun intended," he said with a mischievous grin.

"I think you like coming here yourself," I said.

"Yes, I do!" he boomed. "There's staccato inside of me. I can't help it. I'm a toe-tappin', foot-stompin' angel. I'd love to have a cowboy hat, but I'm not sure it's permitted."

"I'll see what I can do, Petros," I replied with an equally mischievous grin. I thought I detected a slight skip in his gait as we continued through the hall.

"Over here is a section devoted to instruments from various nations. Every people group has developed unique stringed instruments. India, Arabia, the Orient, Africa…you will find the kora, sitar, bandera, barbat, charango, domra, dutar, oud, the veena, marimba…the list is quite lengthy; there are hundreds ranging from **Autoharp** **to Z**ither.

We proceeded to the next area. "This is the guitar section. It has become the instrument of choice for many musicians. We had to enlarge this area because of the need for additional training. Every generation has an instrument of preference. I think your generation prefers the guitar; David's generation favored the harp."

Thousands of Keyboards

"The piano section is just ahead," Petros said. We passed through a doorway at the end of the hall. I was stunned by the scene. "There must be thousands!" I said overwhelmed by the massive assembly of the finest pianos I have ever seen.

"Impressive, isn't it, Royal Scribe?" Petros asked. "The pianos are separated by transparent dividers. Each one has its own individual cubicle."

"I don't understand. How?"

"I know. Pretty amazing," Petrus interrupted. "Do you want to know how they are suspended in midair? They are resting on billows."

"I see that. But clouds cannot hold things up. They look like puffs of cotton."

"They can here," Petros answered. "Remember, God's ways are not ours. He doesn't think like we do. He can do what He chooses.

"Can you hear the music?" he asked.

I glanced around the amphitheater. I could see that hundreds of students were practicing and some were being tutored by master musicians. "Petros, what's going on?" I asked. "I guess I was so taken by the scene that I just now realized something. I should be hearing a cacophony of noise, but it's strangely quiet. I can't hear anything. How come?"

"This is an amazing studio," Petros explained. "Each piano has its own private, sound-proof space. The panes that separate them can be lowered on command. This provides for duets, quartets and quintets, and if desired, even the entire studio can perform together.

"The sound of thousands of pianos playing together is so majestic and inundating. The synergy of the pianos produces rivers of sound. The current is so powerful that it carves channels in the cosmos. Everything in its path is drawn into it. Some suggest that it produces black holes, but we won't pursue that train of thought. The explanation for that subject can be found in the royal library. Let me just add that like the earth has its jet stream, the cosmos also has similar channels flowing through the universes with great force and sound. These are the cosmic rivers.

"Now that you have toured the Academy of Strings, we can return to the transportation portal and descend to the next level to tour the Academy of Winds."

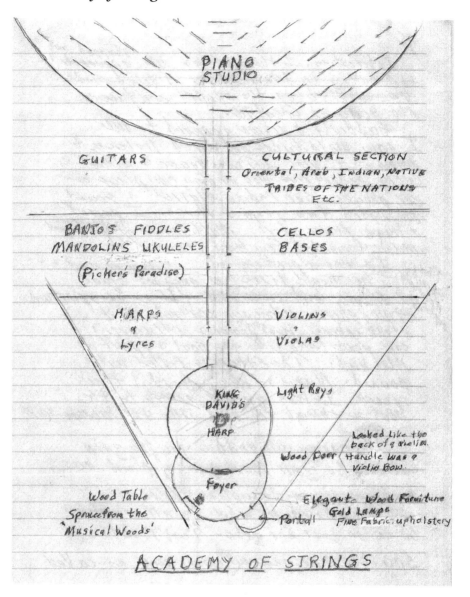

ACADEMY OF STRINGS

CHAPTER 22

The Academy of Winds

After a quick descent, we exited the portal on the next level.

"So, this is the Academy of Winds, Petros? Did you know I played the clarinet and saxophone?" I asked, hoping to impress him. "I've always wanted to play the flute too. I think it is the perfect shepherd's instrument."

"I wasn't completely aware of your musical talent," he said, immediately dismissing the subject. "But you are right about the flute. The flute requires a special sensitivity. It can evoke pastoral atmospheres and bring comfort, peace and joy."

"Exactly," I replied.

The Breath of Life

Instantly, the Spirit of Knowledge appeared beside me: "Greetings, Royal Scribe. Let me explain some things about wind instruments before you enter the academy. Firstly, Holy Spirit is like the wind.[192] There is power and life force in his movements. Secondly, life requires breath.[193] It was the *Ruach*[194] of God that gave life to Adam and Eve. God breathed life into them. Thirdly, just as there is life in God's breath, there is also power and life in yours. All wind instruments require the power of your breath, except the organ and accordion, but they do require an airstream.

210

"Now this is the key. You don't just blow through a wind instrument. You give it life. It becomes the voice of your soul and spirit. The spiritual rivers of living water flow out of you through the instrument, and the instrument becomes a fountainhead of sound. 'Breath to life' is the principle of 'breath to living sound.' The King's music is produced by Spirit-filled saints who know and release His power and love. They are Spirit-led and breathe the life of God that abides in their hearts.

"A musical instrument in the hands of a saint is a powerful channel of communication. It is like an aroma, a sweet smelling savor that creates spiritual atmospheres. It can nourish the fruits of the Spirit: love, joy, peace, patience, kindness, goodness, faithfulness, gentleness and self-control.[195] Music is also like a balm that can heal the soul and the body. David and King Saul understood this secret. Whenever the distressing spirit sent from God troubled Saul, David would take his lyre and play. Then relief would come to Saul; he would feel better, and the afflicting spirit would leave him.[196] Certain sound frequencies can heal spiritual or emotional trauma and wounds as well as dispatch troubling spirits.[197] It can calm or invigorate.

"Never forget that Satan was created to be the master musician and the former director of the King's conservatory.[198] The devil's music produces his character and fruit in us. He attempts to hypnotize the human spirit into submission through music and evil lyrics. His breath is the opposite of God's. He is known as the prince and power of the air and the spirit that works in the sons of disobedience.[199] His musicians use music to bring hatred, sadness, anxiety, impatience, anger, evil intentions, rebelliousness, suicide, discontent, confusion, discord, torment and all manner of distortion and destruction. He creates music to exalt himself and turn our hearts to worship him.

"You must detect the spiritual source of music. Consider its origin. John reveals the difference between God's wisdom and Satan's:

Who is wise and understanding among you? Let them show it by their good life, by deeds done in humility that comes from wisdom. But if you harbor bitter envy and selfish ambition in your hearts, do not boast about it or deny the truth. Such 'wisdom' does not come down from heaven but is earthly, unspiritual, demonic. Where you have envy and selfish ambition, there you find disorder and every evil practice.

But the wisdom that comes from heaven is first pure; then peace-loving, considerate, submissive, full of mercy and good fruit. Impartial and sincere.
(James 3:13–18, NIV)

"God's music shows kindness, generosity, goodness and wisdom. Satan's music mirrors his own evil selfish ambition, envy and pride. It is a distortion of sound—a counterfeit ensemble of death."

Spirit-Born Music

"Music is Spirit-born and Spirit-carried. It enters through the gateways of perception in your body and penetrates into your soul and spirit.[200] Your skin, organs, bones and nervous system react and your breathing and heartbeat change. Your body, mind, will and emotions are all affected.

"When you hear Holy Spirit-breathed, Spirit-born music, your spirit-man responds in worship or warfare. This is proper worship in spirit and truth. This is what Father requires.[201] Spirit-birthed music enables us to offer an acceptable sacrifice of worship and praise and strengthens us to wage a good warfare. There is a good reason why the tribe of Judah led the procession of Israel through the wilderness.[202] Their high praises and worship struck fear into the heart of the enemy like guided missiles aimed at their resolve and defenses.

"Much more than technique and skill is taught here in the Academy of Winds," Knowledge continued. "Every musician must learn the rudimentary elements of Spirit-born music and train their spirit to become a pathway that express the heart and nature of God and the passionate worship and love of the saints. All the students in the conservatory are required to take classes here in the Academy of Winds where this subject is taught. It is fundamental and essential for every musician.

"The academy is about the music of the breath of God and the breath of your spirit-man. Your soul and body must be trained to release a sound from within your heart where the King resides by His Spirit. Do you understand, Royal Scribe?"

"I certainly do," I answered Knowledge. "Thank you so much for coming to explain the breath of music. I have recorded every word of your teaching on the royal scroll."

"Excellent! The Church must understand this basic principle," he replied.

"May I take some notes on this subject while it is fresh in my heart."

Knowledge nodded in approval. I paused to record and outline some observations on the scroll:

"What flowed out of Jesus' Spirit should flow out of us as well. He said that if we ask Him for living water that rivers (notice He said there are plural rivers) would flow out of us. He was referring to Holy Spirit. What do these rivers contain?

"The spirit-rivers should include music, worship, prayer, healing, truth and blessing. All these and more should be emanating from our spirit-man. This will bear much fruit in the spiritual realm. Love, joy, peace, forbearance, kindness, goodness, and faithfulness must also flow in the rivers because Holy Spirit is flowing through us. The spirits of the Lord, Wisdom, Understanding, Counsel, Might, Knowledge and the Fear of the Lord must influence the rivers and direct their flow.

"Just think," I paused, and then began to sing: "There's a river of life flowing out from me, that can cause the lame to walk and the blind to see. It opens prison doors, and sets the captive free. There's a river of life flowing out from me."

"That's right," Knowledge confirmed. "Never forget to release the flow of the breath of God. All of creation is longing to be set free. It is listening for the sound of the sons of God."

"Are you finished, Royal Scribe?" Knowledge asked.

"For now," I said.

"Then let's enter the Academy of Winds. This section of the conservatory has two floors. On this upper level, you will encounter all the woodwinds. The brass instruments are on the floor directly below us. As you explore each one, be sure to take notice of how you are affected by what you hear. Be blessed, Royal Scribe. I must go now. Many others are seeking information."

My thoughts were filled with the new concepts that Knowledge had brought to me. "I must do much more than observe how things are accomplished and the techniques the students are taught. I must listen in the spirit. I need to pay attention to dissonance and harmony, volume, repetition, rhythm, staccato and crescendo. These details are clues. The real issue is what is being expressed through spirit-composition. Music is so much more than I ever realized. It is a major aspect of the dimensions of God's Kingdom here in the heavenlies as well as on earth…" I paused, "actually, throughout all of creation and especially within the human spirit."

The Canvas of Creation

We were greeted by a blast of air as we stepped through the doorway into the academy. A black carpet covered the hallways. The mysterious covering engendered intrigue, like empty space to an astronomer. One striking feature became immediately prominent. This carpet had the same designs as the surface of the royal scroll. Silver rays of light flashed along the floor like streamers ruffling in the wind.

"The swooshes of music!" I said, delighted with the astronomic scene. "Walking on this carpet is like flying through space. I'm walking on sound, Petros."

I stopped for a moment to admire the surface. "Whoa, if I stand still, I feel like I'm still moving. But why would the Master Architect choose black as the background?" I asked.

Knowledge stood on the enigmatic carpet a few feet farther down the hallway. "You are being transported on sound and light," he said. "The Master selected black because without it you cannot detect light. The contrast is necessary. Consider the black canvass upon which the stars and constellations are displayed. Without black, you would not see them. God chose black as the contextual void of space and the cosmos for a reason.

"God has many uses for black. He created it for several purposes. He can use the darkness to conceal and sometimes to imprison. Mankind perceives blackness as evil because Satan uses it to shroud his diabolical presence. His angels and demons dwell in darkness. But don't discredit the great value of black just because the devil's kingdom is darkness. In the past, God used darkness as a veil. He hid Himself in the obscurity of darkness. He concealed Himself in its cloak of mystery and wrapped himself in black clouds.[203] He covered Himself for Israel's protection. Hear what the writer says about those days:"

> *For you have not come to the mountain that may be touched and that burned with fire, and to blackness and darkness and tempest, and the sound of a trumpet and the voice of words, so that those who heard it begged that the word should not be spoken to them anymore. For they could not endure what was commanded: "And if so much as a beast touches the mountain, it shall be stoned[c] or shot with an arrow." And so terrifying was the sight that Moses said, "I am exceedingly afraid and trembling." (Deuteronomy 4:11)*

"That is all in the past and was for a former time. The glorious news is that Jesus changed all that. The saints don't need to search and stumble through the deep darkness with fear and trembling to approach the Living God. You have direct access. No more darkness, burning fire or tempest."

> *But you have come to Mount Zion and to the city of the living God, the heavenly Jerusalem, to an innumerable company of angels, to the general assembly and church of the firstborn who are registered in heaven, to God the Judge of all, to the spirits of just men made perfect, to Jesus the Mediator of the new covenant, and to the blood of sprinkling that speaks better things than that of Abel.*

"His warning is clear. His instruction is not a suggestion. It is a command:

See that you do not refuse Him who speaks. For if they did not escape who refused Him who spoke on earth, much more shall we not escape if we turn away from Him who speaks from heaven, whose voice then shook the earth; but now He has promised, saying, "Yet once more I shake not only the earth, but also heaven." Now this, "Yet once more," indicates the removal of those things that are being shaken, as of things that are made, that the things which cannot be shaken may remain.

Therefore, since we are receiving a kingdom which cannot be shaken, let us have grace, by which we may serve God acceptably with reverence and godly fear. For our God is a consuming fire. (Hebrews 12:18–29, NKJV)

"God no longer veils Himself in darkness. His presence causes darkness to flee. The power of light supersedes darkness. Everything that is hidden is revealed.

"You must understand that black is not a color; it is an atmosphere, just as light is an atmosphere. It cannot produce life. Only light can sustain life. Make no mistake. Black is a powerful medium. Black is the womb of God's creativity. Deep darkness was on the face of the deep. When God created the heavens and the earth, the dark void was the canvass of creation. God painted the entirety of existence with light. He released His paintbrush dipped in light and then divided the light from the darkness. There was only deep darkness in the beginning. Day and night are both loved by our Creator.

"God did not do away with darkness but allowed the tension to remain between the two atmospheres. Then Satan chose darkness as his dwelling place. God sent light to expose him. Jesus came to invade the domain of lies and deception. Jesus is the light and life of men. John bore witness of that light. The light of the world gives light to every man coming into the world.

"Notice, Royal Scribe, light shines *in* the darkness, but darkness cannot gain control of it. The darkness is powerless to eliminate the light of Jesus, even though Satan tried.[204] But darkness still exists in the world and great darkness in Satan's realm.

"The carpet you're standing on portrays the canvass of creation. It depicts the deep darkness and the power of light and sound to penetrate it. The waves you see are the King's words carried by the Spirit. It is the sound and the song of creation. This is the same song that you see and hear on the royal scroll you carry. It is the music of the spheres. It is the Spirit-breathed Word of God, the Ruach, released by the wind of the Spirit that birthed the cosmos and everything that exists. When God said, 'Let there be light,' sound and music came into being.

"God fears nothing and black simply makes Him shine brighter. But he loathes the fact that Satan dwells in darkness. He is a liar and the father of lies. He chose the canvass of creation, thinking he could exalt himself and display his glory as an angel of light. But God sent His final word: His Son."

"Intriguing," I said. "Even though I just learned a lot about non-color and the purpose of black and white in the Hall of Communication, this information adds a whole new dimension to it. What an awesome explanation, Knowledge. Just think of it, black is the canvas of creation!"

The Idol of Music

I stared at the carpet containing the song of creation when suddenly the fabric became transparent and a vision of earth appeared. I saw myself in a large crowd of people in Times Square. The entire multitude was listening to music. Everyone wore earphones. Car radios blared and noise spewed forth from shops and restaurants. I passed a huge music store with many floors of every genre of music imaginable for sale. *Could this be more than a store?* I thought. *Perhaps, it is a cathedral where music is exalted—an altar created by Satan to promote sensual worship for himself? But there must also be music inside created for the King of kings,* I wondered.

I was shocked back into my surroundings in the Academy of Winds when Knowledge spoke. "The enemy will use so-called Christian music to deceive. Whenever the music itself is worshiped, instead of being a vehicle of expression to God, it is defiled and becomes an idol. This is what you sensed at the music store. We must not worship music. We must use music as a means to worship the Lord. Sometimes, churches use music to cater to the culture and attract followers instead of seeking to please the Creator with their compositions.

"The world lives in an ether of sound and a cloud of music. Whoever controls this atmosphere has great sway over the people. They use it to insert their message into the soul and spirit of man. Music is more powerful than speech. It gains quicker access to the soul, and through the soul it penetrates deep into the heart.

"The enemy uses music to seduce you and gain entrance to your spirit, thus planting his deceptive lies. He was the chief musician before his demotion. He knows how to counterfeit the King's music. He is like the pied piper, mesmerizing and sedating those who are enchanted by his magic and then leading them to destruction. Choose carefully what you allow to enter your ear-gate. Test it in the spirit."

"You keep repeating this message, Knowledge," I said.

"I reiterate it for a reason, Scribe," he responded. "The condition of the human spirit will determine the type of music created. Music released through the soul, carries the nature of the spirit that produces it. The quality and character of what flows from inside a son or daughter of God is a musical river of living water. Holy Spirit, who abides in the heart, releases living music. Those who are born of the Spirit release a pure stream of life, not death. Without Holy Spirit's influence, the best that man can do is release pollution, soulish motives and evil thoughts. *"The heart is desperately wicked. Who can know it.*[205] *Out of the heart flows every manner of evil."*[206]

"Let's proceed now," Petros instructed. The three of us walked forward on the carpet of wind through the length of the corridor. Each section along the hallway glowed with the light of God's glory. I observed flutes and piccolos in the first subdivision. Across the hall were the clarinets, oboes, bassoon and similar instruments. The squeaks and chirps of unruly reeds filtered into the hallway.

"Sounds like an aviary," I chuckled.

"True," Petros said. "There are some beginning students inside, but don't dismiss the mellifluous music of the reeds because a few don't respond properly. Life is like that, you know?" He glanced at me with a sort of scowl.

"We are approaching the largest section in the woodwind studios, the saxophones. You'll notice here on the right we have the higher registers, soprano and tenor. Over on the left side of the hall are the lower registers: the alto, bass and sub-contra-bass."

"I love the sound of the saxophone, Petros. I'm told that the alto is the instrument that is closest to the human voice."

"Speaking of 'voice,'" Knowledge replied, "Father loves to talk with His children and He recognizes each voice. If you think about it, the voice is actually a wind instrument. Every person has a unique voice."

Solar Wind

We reached what I expected to be the end of the corridor, but there was no door or closure. Although the carpet ended in empty space, the swooshes of music lifted right off the surface and shot out beyond the opening into space.

"This is incredible," I said, gazing at the electrical flashes discharging into the ether under my feet. I stood speechless, gazing out into infinity, tracing the musical waves as they sped away on their journey until they disappeared into the darkness.

"Could this explain what solar wind is?" I asked, still staring into space.

Knowledge pointed to a fourth person standing in our midst. "Ask Understanding. He can explain it well."

"Oh, I didn't realize you were here, Understanding," I said apologetically. "Let me repeat my question. Is this how solar wind is created?"

"Partly," he began. "When Father waves His hand, solar wind is created. The ether carries the energy and sounds of the heavens. It is a vacuum through which energy is transmitted. According to man's theories, space is a non-atmosphere. This is erroneous. You must not define space by comparing it to earth. There are different atmospheres that God has created that man knows very little or nothing about. Space is not empty. It has an atmosphere you do not understand yet.

"There is another realm beyond what you call space. Where space ends is not the end of things. There is a demarcation zone of atmosphere-non-atmosphere beyond the realm of space. There exists a moving border of delineation and transition, a portal into…" he paused abruptly and stopped himself just in time as though he was about to reveal a hidden secret before its time.

I discerned intuitively that he was intentionally withholding the name of the place he referred to that exists beyond where space ends and something else exists. I'm certain of it.

"This dimension," Understanding continued, clearing his throat, "lies past the outer reaches. But this is a matter far beyond your comprehension right now. I encourage you to visit the Hall of Origins in the library. We can show you where the information can be found. Your assignment does not include this topic. Stay focused on your agenda, Royal Scribe."

"Yes, sir," I responded, "but I didn't know there was a Hall of Origins in the library. I will be sure to do my research there when I am permitted to return. I will seek your help then."

Down the Non-Steps

"Follow me," Petros said and stepped off the carpet into space and immediately dropped from sight.

"Here I go again," I said, "but I'm sure Petros wouldn't mislead me."

I closed my eyes and stepped off the carpet like someone stepping off the edge of a skyscraper. I felt myself falling, heard a sucking sound, and then came to a gentle landing on a solid surface that hardly bent my knees.

Petros greeted me with a smile. "Fun, isn't it? Welcome to the lower level of the Academy of Winds, pneumanaut. You're getting much better at traveling in the spirit. This is the floor that houses all the brass instruments. This passageway connects the woodwinds and the brass sections, so students and masters can easily travel between floors without having to return to the portal at the front of the conservatory."

I looked around to get my bearings. We were standing on a glass porch supported underneath by a silo-sized pillar with a top that looked like the bell-shaped end of a trumpet.

"Let's move along," Petros said. "Our time is fleeting."

I was expecting to see a large room at this end of the hallway similar to the others. But instead, private studios and practice rooms were located here.

"These rehearsal rooms are available to all the students attending the Academy of Winds. This location provides ideal access for each level," Petros explained.

"But where are all the students?" I asked. "I've only seen a few."

"I guess I should have mentioned it," Petros said. "It's getting close to the presentation in the main concert hall. Many of the masters and students have gone there to prepare. We have barely enough time for you to visit one more level of the conservatory."

We walked hastily through the corridor on a carpet identical to the one on the upper floor. "I feel like I'm walking upstream, Petros. But it's not like fighting a strong current of water. It's more like being washed in music. I'm being rejuvenated. This is vivifying."

"Well… impressive," Petros said. "Your vocabulary suits your assignment. The King loves words and, apparently, so do you."

"For sure!" I replied with enthusiasm. "I believe that words are the currency of heaven and earth. Everything must be spoken in order to be accomplished. You can't just think something; you have to declare it. Even God had to say, 'Let there be light.' He also said, 'You have not because you ask not.' Jesus told us that we must 'speak to the mountain' to move it. Thinking alone won't get the job done."

"This is so refreshing," Petros. "I know time is short, but I have to stop for a moment to let the current of music splash over me." I stood firm, like a rock in a stream, allowing the swooshes of power flowing through the carpet to splash over me.

"This is awesome, Petros. It's like swimming up a river of sound."

"That's exactly right," he responded. "It is a musical river and it flows continuously as God sings over His people.[207] There is no love song as tender and beautiful as His."

"Jesus sang to me once," I said. Tears formed in my eyes as I envisioned the moment.[208] "I was totally undone."

"I'm sure you will never forget that moment," Petros answered, placing his hand on my shoulder with affection. "He loves you, Royal Scribe."

"I know," I said, blinking away teardrops.

Mouth Pieces and Oil

We continued along the hallway as Petros identified each department. There were sections for French horns, baritones, tubas, trombones, trumpets, coronets, bugles… and some instruments that I've never seen before.

As we approached the exit, I commented, "This door is stunning." Its entire surface was covered with high quality polished brass. The luster reflected my image like a gilded mirror. Hinges, made from the valves of various brass instruments, secured the heavy door to its frame. A large cabinet was located to the right on the wall next to the entry door.

"What's in this cabinet?" I asked.

"It contains mouthpieces for all the various instruments," Petros said, opening the doors.

"Why are they in different colored packages?"

"Each color identifies the unique characteristic of the mouthpiece. Each mouthpiece is also engraved with a reference that identifies a verse or passage in the Word of God. These mouthpieces are not like those on earth. They are created individually to produce specific resonances that enhance the instrument's tone and capability. Each musician is issued several different kinds. The Scripture indicates the tonal effect produced. The musical score notations designate which mouthpiece to use for a specific result. These mouthpieces are able to augment the sound to capture the expressive intentions of the composers. This is critical when seeking to generate a precise atmosphere into the ether.

"Look over here," Petros said, pointing to the opposite wall beside the doorway. "These shelves contain different kinds of lubricating oils."

"Do they have the same effect as the mouthpieces?" I asked.

"Not really," He replied. "The metal mouthpieces have to do with power and resonance. These oils are for anointing and nuance. They create a subtle difference in the sound. This slight shade or variance creates an infused atmosphere, like the scent of a flower or spice.

"These oils are made specifically for this purpose in the perfumer's laboratory. Their composition is a well-kept secret. They are very difficult to make. Only the master perfumers have perfected the technique, and they chose the ingredients by the leading of Holy Spirit. They are creating new ones all the time. If you listen with Holy Spirit discernment and a disciplined ear, you can detect the subtle difference in the sound. All breath must pass through the valves where it is anointed with a fragrance that gives the sound a unique hint of essence. It perfumes the sound and in so doing rouses memory. Smell is the most dominant provoker of memory. When music is perfumed, it incenses our recall and visions of past experiences appear in our thoughts."

"Memory through music," I said. "How can I take all of this in? On earth I have enjoyed the scent of multifarious flowers. I've wandered through cedar, pine and a eucalyptus forests, breathing the air with delight. To me the fragrance of a budding orange grove or night-blooming jasmine are intoxicating. Each scent stimulates a specific memory of my life experience.

"I never thought of perfuming music, Petros, but why not? It's breath-born and Spirit-birthed.

Why not send it forth with a fragrant anointing oil on the valves? This is amazing!"

"It truly is, Royal Scribe."

"How do the musicians know which oils to choose for a specific score," I asked.

"They are allowed to choose themselves. After their intense training, they are given the privilege of interpreting and influencing the composition according to their own rendering. This is where creativity comes into play. Each musician is allowed to express his or her own heart and spirit through their own instrument. The anointing is released through them.

"It's like the orchestra presenting Jesus with a bouquet of flowers every time they perform before the King. Each musician contributes their own expression of love and worship. Father is always blessed and celebrates joyfully with their presentation of worship and praise. He is incensed by its aroma."

Petros reached to open the door.

"Wait!" I said. "Let me do it." The door moved effortlessly on its valve hinges. I thought I detected a subtle hint of citrus. "Do you smell that, Petros?" I asked.

He nodded.

"It's lemon, only sweeter."

"That's a good analysis, Royal Scribe. Angels oil the valves of the door every twenty-four hours. A different scented oil is chosen every time. It's wonderful. You never know what you will discover when you open the door. Sometimes, I come just to see which scent welcomes me. It's like having fresh flowers delivered every day."

The glistening door glided silently closed behind us, and we walked toward the portal.

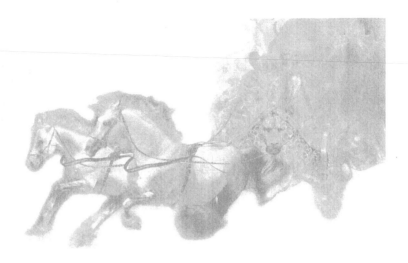

CHAPTER 23

The King of All Instruments

"One more level, Royal Scribe," Petros remarked. "The King chose this level of the conservatory to house a very special academy. There's a good reason. The supremacy and power of this instrument causes the entire edifice to reverberate. The sound is intense, as it should be. Are you ready for this?"

"I think so," I responded without a clue of what he could be talking about.

As far as I'm concerned, I've seen all the instrument classifications already. What could I have missed?" I pondered as we stepped into the portal.

A Mysterious Foyer

We stepped out of the transition portal into what seemed like a tunnel. The bronze-colored enclosure was cylindrical. I was standing inside a giant tube. An opening on the ceiling near the doorway into this special academy appeared to be some sort of an air register.

"Let's see if I can figure this out before I ask for help," I mumbled. "Every foyer so far served as an introduction to its specific academy, thereby, revealing its identity. But this gives me very little in the way of clues. Perhaps I'm inside the instrument. I've got to imagine this enclosure as though I were viewing it from outside instead of within it."

I tried everything in my storehouse of experience to perceive this foyer from its exterior. I scrolled through my mental file of musical instruments to no avail. This enigma was beyond my investigatory capabilities.

"Alright, Knowledge," I sighed in defeat. "My discernment fails me. What am I standing in?"

He appeared, shaking his head back and forth with a furrowed forehead and his mouth turned down in disappointment. "I thought you would recognize this since you saw it at a very early age, although I admit, from a different perspective.

"You are standing *inside* an organ pipe. This is the Academy of the Pipe Organ. It is the king of all instruments. That is why it occupies this foundational position in the conservatory. It is a self-contained orchestra that can produce an entire symphony of sound. Its majesty and power are inimitable.

"Lucifer, who served as the director of the conservatory before his downfall, favored this instrument above all others. He likened it to himself and boasted of its superiority with prideful claims as though he was its creator, but that is a lie. The workmanship of Lucifer's timbrels and pipes was crafted for him by God on the day that he was fashioned.[209] He was a living pipe organ. Lucifer had it all. He was the chief cherub. He was assigned to dwell in Eden and had access to the garden of God. He was covered with every precious stone: sardius, topaz, diamond, beryl, onyx, jasper, emerald, carbuncle and gold, but that never satisfied his ego. He wanted to usurp God's place."

"So, I'm inside an organ pipe," I said in astonishment. "I would never have guessed it. Mystery solved! I remember it so well. When I was a little boy, my mother would take me to church every Wednesday evening while she practiced on the organ. I often fell asleep on a cushioned pew, listening to her play."

"Father saw that, Royal Scribe. He was there as your mother worshipped. She loved to play when she was alone just to worship and exalt the King. It was never about performance for her. It was always worship! It was her offering to Jesus. She did all she could to perfect here skill. She has access to this academy now. She often comes here to worship the King. Anna can really push this organ to its maximum capabilities."

"Can we go inside now?" I asked. "I'm eager to see it."

The King's Cathedral

Petros opened the thick, heavy dark-oak door devised like an entrance to a cathedral. The window panels set inside the body of the door were diamond shaped. The facets of the purple and green stained-glass artwork refracted the light from inside, casting a kaleidoscopic display onto the foyer floor.

"There's no doubt this is more than a normal doorway. This is another portal into a new dimension. It's totally majestic. It's like a cathedral for the King!" I whispered, nodding my head in honor.

I tapped Petros' shoulder, "This amphitheater is regal. It's designed for nobility."

All the seats were upholstered with red satin cushions. The room was appointed with gold fixtures. The center isle sloped down toward a colossal pipe organ.

"Let's sit right here," Knowledge said, motioning toward a row of widely separated seats.

"What?" I shouted in shock. The moment I sat down I was instantly sitting at the organ console. The keyboards appeared in front of my seat, and the pedals rose up from the floor beneath my feet.

"This is how the academy functions," Knowledge explained, enjoying my reaction. "Each seat in this auditorium has its own complete organ console. All students can access the organ for themselves. Each student hears only what he or she is playing. Look! Over there," he pointed. "That seat is where your mother sits when she comes to rehearse.

"Father often listens from the Throne room. He loves the sound of the royal pipe organ. It's unlike any other instrument ever created. It contains all the others. It's a full symphony orchestra by itself. Sit back for a moment. Close your eyes and soak in the ambiance of this sacred hall. The sound remains in the atmosphere, even when the organ is not being played. It can carry you right into the King's presence."

Numerous organ concerts that I had attended on earth scrolled through my memory. The great hymns of the Church vibrated in my chest and resonated from my spirit: Holy, Holy, Holy, Lord God Almighty; O for A Thousand Tongues to Sing My Great Redeemer's Praise; All Creatures of Our God and King; Love Divine all Loves Excelling;. On Christ the Solid Rock I Stand, Great is Thy Faithfulness. And the Grandest of all, All Hail the Power of Jesus' Name.

"Only an organ can do justice to the great hymns of worship expressed by the Church," I said. "When you worship the Lord accompanied by the majestic sounds of a pipe organ, you really are worshipping with a thousand tongues."

"So true," Knowledge added. "Each pipe has a breath of its own.

"You must return when the master organists are playing, Royal Scribe. They are unparalleled. They perform for two reasons: to train students by demonstrating the goal of the highest achievable skills, and to exemplify spiritual worship with the instrument. It is never a recital to display their talent and ability. They always direct attention to Jesus. The 'Hosanna Full-Organ Chorale' is a feat of consummate worship. It will have you standing in enraptured praise or kneeling on the floor with your head lowered to the ground in honor of the King."

"Our tour is finished now," Petros interrupted with apology in his voice. "I am sorry that we couldn't visit the vocal academies this time. When you return, I will personally take you there."

"Already?" I said, disappointed that I had not heard the greatest organ of all creation play.

"It will be wonderful to visit the vocal academies." I replied with a sheepish grin, wondering if Petros knew that I intended to keep my promise to bring him a cowboy hat when I returned. Knowledge's suspicion was evident. He blinked at me smiling and then departed.

Petros and I strode toward the door and the conservatory transition portal beyond. We continued talking about the majestic organ. I shared several occasions when I was privileged to attend organ concerts at Westminster College in Pennsylvania, the Scottish Cathedral in Melbourne, Australia, and the Cathedral of Notre Dame in Paris.

"My wife and I happened to arrive at Notre Dame on a Sunday afternoon. We didn't know about the concert but got in line thinking it was a tour. To our great surprise, we were escorted to a center seat for an incredible recital on the renowned organ. On another occasion, while in Melbourne, I heard music from the sidewalk and entered the Scottish Cathedral, thinking a performance was going on. Instead, it was a practice session. I had an opportunity to speak directly to the organist who is a doctoral professor at a nearby college of music. He travels worldwide performing organ concerts and teaching. He agreed to give me a private recital. It was a *kairos* moment. God is so good. He even asked me to choose the hymn."

"What hymn did you choose?" Petros asked.

"All Hail the Power of Jesus' Name, of course!" I answered.

The Music Strategy Council

Back in the transition portal, Petros resumed his narrative of the conservatory during our descent. "This level is where all the master musicians' suites are located. There is also a large conference suite where they gather to discuss and choose musical scores, choirs, vocalists and musicians to sing and play before the King. They carefully select specific offerings of joy and praise that suit the occasion. It is more like a musical strategy room. The worship here in the heavenly realms is not random and haphazard when it involves the royal choirs and orchestras.

"In case you were wondering, there is always spontaneous praise and worship around the Throne. Every saint brings a personal expression of praise to the King.

But there are also times of coordinated, orchestrated praise and exaltation. These involve antiphonal music and voices, the King's heralds, the cymbal corps and thousands of pianos, joined by the entire spectrum of musical instruments and percussion, and climaxed with the pipe organ. All the heavenly beings and saints declare His awesome glory and perfection. Imagine your best worship experience on earth and then multiply it by thousands upon thousands.

"Then, in an instant, at the direction of the King, there is complete, utter silence." Petros paused for effect. "The entire canopy of heaven instantly becomes a universal *secret place* of intimacy with God. It is so pervasive that it muffles the sound of breathing. This kingdom silence in the heavenlies is so intense that it is formational. His glory is so pervasive that honoring-silence is the only response possible. We are renewed and revived by the absolute peace and stillness it brings to our total being. Oh, that mankind would learn to enter this rejuvenating ambiance. The Lord commands, *"Be still and know that I am God.*"[210] And the prophet proclaims, *'The Lord is in His holy temple. Let all of the earth keep silence before Him.'*"[211]

"I love stillness and silence, Petros," I responded. "Silence is priceless and so hard to find on earth. That is one reason why the *secret place* is so necessary. We have to guard this private space and protect it from all intrusions. It is an intimate place of love and communication where at times, words are not needed and music becomes a distraction. Silence and stillness posture us to hear and see what the Lord is saying. It is a Spirit-to-spirit, Heart-to-heart love language. I am convinced this is why Jesus refers to it as 'the *secret place.*'[212] It is so intimate."

Knowledge returned and spoke with prophetic authority, "You speak the truth, Royal Scribe. There is a time and season for rejoicing, shouting and declaring praise and victory. There is also a time for silence, reverence and stillness. There is a time when the music must stop and silence is allowed to cloak the heavens and the earth with pure light and glory. There are times and seasons in heaven as well as on earth. You must learn that war and peace, noise and silence both serve God's purposes."

Groundwork

I could feel the weight of his words and spontaneously became aware of the royal scroll vibrating in my hand. It was significantly heavier.

"Will there be enough space on the scroll, Knowledge?" I asked.

"Of course," he replied. "The King has designed this scroll to accommodate your entire assignment, Royal Scribe. It is sufficient for this journey through the heavenly realms. But He is also preparing the scroll to be used when you return to receive more revelation and knowledge in the heavenly realms. Then the scroll will be inscribed with end-time knowledge, wisdom and understanding in preparation for the coming …" Knowledge paused. "You will be told when it is time," he said, "but for now, the revelation you're receiving is *groundwork*. I have chosen that word specifically. What you receive on this first assignment in the heavenlies as His royal scribe you must deliver to the saints on earth.

"The royal scroll you carry is your commission to record what you see and hear on this expedition in the spirit. You will know when the scroll contains the information meant to be released by Father for His saints on this assignment. But there is still much more revelation to come that must be delivered to the Church. Your instructions for the second mission will be conveyed by the angels assigned to you at the appointed time.

"We're here," Petros announced. "Follow me and stay close!"

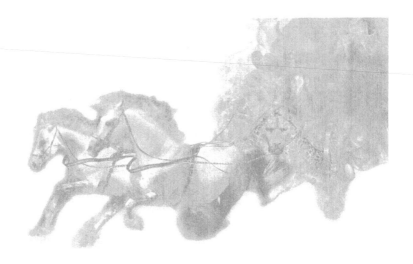

CHAPTER 24

The Royal Concert Hall

We stepped from the transition tube into the entry foyer of the King's Royal Conservatory of Music where we had begun our tour. It was jam-packed and bustling with activity. A crowd of saints and angels was making its way toward the Royal Concert Hall located at the rear of the conservatory's main floor. Large hallways led along the glass exterior walls on each side of the great foyer. Everyone was in a celebratory mood.

"I'll leave you now," Knowledge said. "If you have questions or need information, you can ask Jesus. You will be sitting next to Him at the concert."

His words stunned me. "Sitting next to Jesus?" I replied. "I didn't expect to have such an honor and privilege. Thank you for your ministry, Knowledge. It is so helpful. It was essential. Without you, Understanding and Wisdom, I would still be trying to decipher the mysteries and anomalies I've experienced here."

"That's why I'm always available," Knowledge said.

"One final word of instruction. I could say, 'Enjoy the concert,' but that would be insufficient. You must inhabit it. You will be enthralled and transformed by it."

"I understand and I will," I said.

An Angel Usher

Knowledge departed and Petros and I stepped into the surging crowd and followed the flow along the right hallway toward the grand concert hall. We were about halfway toward the end of the passageway when a very large angel stepped into the line and called my name.

"Dale, you have a special reserved seat next to the Lord. Come this way."

I stepped toward the angel and turned to see if Petros was following. He was gone, swallowed up in the bustling throng.

"Well, Petros is shorter than most," I acknowledged. "He's hard to locate in a crowd."

The interior of the grand concert hall was stunning. The ceiling, if it was a ceiling, was dome shaped, displaying the heavens. Whatever it was or wasn't, I was looking through it into the cosmos at the stars and galaxies light years away. And then a shooting star sparkled across the panoply. It was stunningly beautiful and captivating. I stumbled several times because I couldn't keep from looking up at the spectacle of grandeur. "I'm seeing reality," I said softly, not wanting to make a scene. "This concert hall is like no other in all of creation."

My angel usher led me into a row of seats in the center section of the auditorium and continued toward the middle of the aisle. We bumped our way past the occupants already seated until we reached two empty seats perfectly located for their excellent view and sound. But these two seats were different. They were more like large lounge chairs with royal appurtenances. Not only were they larger than the other red velvet seats, they were embroidered with delicate patterns. The armrests were topped with the finest red-leather supple cushioning. Pillows with stunning brocade images lay on the chairs.

"These are like thrones," I said, feeling regal myself. "How dare I sit here?" But the moment I expressed my unworthiness, God's promise flashed into my mind. "I am seated with Christ in heavenly places," I said out loud. "It never occurred to me until now that it says 'heavenly places' (plural) and not just one heavenly place (singular).[213] So, why not in a the Royal Concert Hall in heaven next to the King?"

"This is such an honor," I said with selfless joy. "I get to sit with Christ in the Royal Concert Hall. I wonder where else I may have the honor and privilege of sitting with Him in the realms of His kingdom in the future?"

"Sit here, Royal Scribe!" the angel commanded, pointing to the seat next to me.

My attention became fixed on the center stage. All of the musicians began tuning their instruments. The cacophony of sound created a sort of sacred confusion, stirring the atmosphere like a large ladle in a pot of soup. Then the great concert hall grew mystically silent. The musicians lowered their instruments, cradling them against their hearts.

The Arrival of the King

The conductor entered from the side and approached the podium. The unexpected happened. *Why are we not standing to acknowledge his entrance?* I asked myself. *This is not proper etiquette for the maestro's entrance.* Then I noticed that the musicians were bowing their heads in prayer.

I glanced around, intrigued by this unusual demeanor, and noticed that everyone in the Royal Concert Hall had bowed their head. Some were kneeling in front of their seats.

The audience is following suit, I realized, so I bowed my head in anticipation. Silence filled the regal auditorium, and if silence can increase, then this was the opposite equivalent of an explosive, cymbal-crashing crescendo. It was sheer unrequited noiselessness.

Like a jet breaking the sound barrier, a flurry of trumpets blasted into the silence, shattering the stillness. The King's heralds played with unrestraint, and the entire assembly stood to their feet and began to shout praises to the King. The place went wild with jubilation.

"Oh, no," I gasped, realizing that every eye was turned toward me. Then I realized why.

"He's here!" I exclaimed, stunned by the royal heralds' announcement and His regal appearing. "Jesus is standing next to me!"

He nodded to acknowledge and show honor to the orchestra, and they melted. Many were in tears, sobbing with joy and love for their King.

This is their moment, I thought. *All their efforts, devotion, work and study to prepare for this performance have culminated here in the Royal Concert Hall. It's their offering to the King of kings.*

Jesus turned to me. He lifted His arm, placed it around my shoulder, and drew me close. "I love you, Dale." He said softly. I was the only one who heard Him.

"Jesus, I love You so much. I am overwhelmed by Your kindness to me. 'Thank You' is hardly enough, Lord!"

"I understand. It is My joy to bless you, friend. My heart's desire is to abundantly bless all my brothers and sisters. Now, let's sit together. You are an heir and joint-heir with Me. We are here together as sons of Father.

"This musical composition has been created for this specific occasion," He said. "It has never been performed and released into the heavens until now. Sit back and be comfortable. Let the music take you into the cosmic realms. It will carry you far back past the unwritten eons into virgin space. Observe what the music portrays, and hear with your spirit."

The Conductors' Art

Once we sat down, the entire audience took their seats. The conductor bowed toward Jesus, turned toward the orchestra and lifted his baton. My high school experience and musical training came to mind. I will never forget Mr. Bennet, our beloved orchestra teacher. He was a skilled conductor. He taught us the language of the conductor. "The art of conducting is more than just semaphore. It's a two-step between body and soul, between physical gesture and musical personality. It's a language. Through my baton, hand and body gestures, I can talk to the orchestra without the use of words."[214]

My pulse increased. A shiver of delight quickened my senses. I couldn't help myself. I leaned forward to the edge of my seat in rapt attention. *In this setting,* I thought, *there can be no doubt that the maestro of the Lord's orchestra will elicit the greatest performance possible—one suitable for the King.*

With the first stroke of the baton, the timpani began a subtle roll. The drummers' eyes were riveted to the baton as the conductor gradually motioned to increase the volume until it sounded like a freight train rumbling through the room. I waited in anticipation. "Something's coming," I whispered.

With masterful timing, another stroke of the baton released a multitude of cymbals colliding simultaneously. The crashing vibrations cascaded through the amphitheater like lightning when it electrifies the summer night sky. At least thirty musicians comprised the cymbal section. They began to play a cymbals-only melodic refrain. It felt like I was plugged into an electric socket. Their vibrations and tones shocked my flesh with a charge of sound.

I never heard the cymbals perform like this, I thought with delight. *Could this be the underlying musical phrase of the entire symphony?* I wondered. *It's too soon to know though.*

The timpani drums and the cymbals reached the climax of the crescendo. On command, the brass section released a powerful flurry of clarion sound. The concert hall filled with light.

That's it! I suddenly realized in a moment of revelation. *The curtain has opened. This is the declaration of the dawning of a new day. It is a prophetic message from the heavenly concert hall to earth. This is more than a concert. It is a prophecy, a holy symphony of declaration.*

A new day has begun! The time and season has changed on earth and in the heavens. The music decrees it.

A delicate softness settled into the music. Violins played while the cellos and basses formed a foundation underneath them. *"It's like watching angels moving across the face of the earth,"* I imagined.

At first, the sound was gentle, like a small spring bubbling and skipping down through the high mountain peaks into the forest. Flutes, piccolos and delicate chimes and triangles portrayed the waters' descent, mimicking birds and flitting butterflies. But something much deeper was happening in the music. While it was peaceful and serene, strength was building with each refrain. A rush to fulfillment was imminent. The gentle spring was becoming an unstoppable stream. It had commenced the rapid chase toward its inevitable destiny.

The moment was distinct. The roaring stream leapt over the precipitous drop and plunged downward, twisting and turning in helpless surrender. It exploded on the rocks below, spending its youth in a display of victorious tumult.

French horns rose to the rescue. Their message: this is not the end; the river has matured. It is noonday and time for the hunt. The tempo quickened as the stream pressed on, ever increasing in size and strength to become a river. The entire orchestra rose to a fuller, mature sound as every section participated in the movement. Evening was approaching.

The small stream, which had grown into a river from the trickle of a spring in the mountains, was now merging into an ocean of such beauty that it was unparalleled.

The depth and expanse of the music was on a grand cosmic scale. *I've never seen, or should I say, heard such color and waves in my life,* I thought enraptured by the sound. *It contains the music of the spheres. This has to be all of creation united in orchestral effulgence. Perhaps this is what the Creator felt when He viewed all of creation and said, 'It is good.*[215]

The maestro motioned and the orchestra responded as a single entity. The volume ebbed and flowed like the pulse of the tides into a beautiful sunset. The skill and talent of each musician painted the sky with hints of pink, purple and velvety hues of blue sprinkled with glimmers of red yellow and a sudden flare of green as the sun set. The brass section announced the orb's retreat with the nuances of the anointing oils and unique mouthpieces. The King's heralds were followed by the trumpet section: French horns and trombones. Clarinets and saxophones followed and then the strings played with a subtle diminuendo that led into a delicate staccato, mimicking the tiptoeing steps of the light as it fled over the horizon. The strings concluded with the barely audible main melody of the symphony first established by the opening cymbals. The basses, baritones and tubas bid the light farewell, and the day ended with the last breath of oboes, bassoons and harps.

To my consternation, no one applauded or moved. *Why is everyone looking up at the ceiling above the orchestra?* I thought, befuddled by the unusual behavior.

The muted sound of friction, surface moving upon surface, was whisper-soft. Then I saw it. *The ceiling!* I thought in shock. *It's opening above the orchestra. It's the pipe organ. How did they do that?* I asked in wonderment.

The royal pipe organ commenced with powerful intention. This was not a soft introduction or a warm up for the main event. It got right to the purpose of its assignment. Thunderous reverberations blasted into the concert hall and out into the heavenlies. It was so forceful. The sound was that of an army at war. Darkness pervaded the hall. The conservatory building shook, and my seat confirmed the tremors. Every part of me was summoned to attention. The barrage of music from the mighty pipe organ delivered the message. The organ was prophesying.

A War Cry

"War is coming! The Great War is just beyond the ending of the daylight. A new season has awakened. The strength of God's Church is growing and increasing in size and maturity. Every attempt to destroy it will fail. I built it to withstand all attacks and to overcome all its enemies.

"The river flows into the ocean of My glory. As sure as the waters cover the sea, the knowledge of My glory shall cover the earth. My people will see and declare it. Music will sound from the heavens. The King's heralds and the signal corps are prepared to announce the declaration at My command. I will sit on My Throne and rule as the Mighty Warrior who conquers with power and strength. The final battle is near. My Church will proclaim it like a living organism. You will resound and go forth with My power and might.

"The darkness of the end-times will be the forerunner of the last season. The light of My Kingdom will shine throughout all of creation.

"Listen for the trumpets. Hear the rumble of the timpani. Stay in the stream of My presence and power. Do not be discouraged by resistance or enemy attacks.

You are a part of My ocean of glory. Do not fear or be dismayed. Don't listen to the lies of Satan. Do not look for deliverance to come in earthly form. I Am the rock of your salvation. I Am mighty in battle. I Am a strong tower and a sure defense. My end-time warriors will be trained, anointed and Spirit-filled. The army of the saints and angels will overcome and prevail. No weapon formed against you shall prosper.

"Does not My Word say that because I humbled Myself and became flesh and blood and took upon Myself the role of a servant, even unto death, that My Father would raise Me up and give Me a name above every name, that at the name of Jesus every knee shall bow and every tongue confess that Jesus Christ is Lord, to the glory of God the Father? And so it will be for evermore!"[216]

The royal pipe organ finished its message of the coming Great War. The prophecy was ended.

The Coronation Hymn

After a moment of silence, the king of instruments commenced with the exalting strains of the coronation hymn: All Hail the Power of Jesus' Name.[217] We stood to our feet in jubilant praise. Angels, heavenly beings and saints were singing in exaltation. Some were shouting, "You are worthy, O Lord, to receive glory and honor and power, for You have created all things, and for Your pleasure they were created and have their being."[218]

"We're crowning Jesus," I shouted. "We are ascribing majesty to Him through our song. This must be only a taste of the actual moment when angels and Adam's kind, Jew and Gentile, young and old, men and women of every tribe and tongue will together crown Him Lord of all! I can't wait! I can't wait!" I shouted at the top of my voice, raising my arms with an imaginary crown. The last verse of the coronation hymn filled the hall with exaltation and came to a jubilant end. I heard some exclaiming, 'Amen.'

I turned to look at Jesus. He remained seated in perfect peace, the Lion and the Lamb of God, the supreme example of humility and strength. I was overcome with love for Him. I crumpled into my seat, put my head upon His chest, and wept. He held me in His arms and whispered words too precious to repeat. Finally, I withdrew and sat looking at Him in total surrender.

"I am Your servant, Lord," I said.

"I know," He replied. You are a faithful son.

"Now you must finish your assignment, Royal Scribe. There is one more place you must visit. After that I have a special blessing for you. I love you." He stood and instantly disappeared from the concert hall.

We Are Close to Sunset

My angel usher appeared and escorted me back to the foyer where Petros and Pilar were waiting. "Did you understand the concert?" Pilar asked.

"Yes, I did," I replied, "at so many levels. My life will be forever changed. The music was a prophetic vision. I've known that a day is as a thousand years and a thousand years are as a day in God's timeframe. But I know now that the final era is near. The sun is about to set. The Great War lies just ahead. But our victory is assured. I'm not sure exactly where we are in God's time-line, but one thing is certain. We are very close to sunset."

"Well done, Royal Scribe," Pilar affirmed. Your visit here has been preparatory for what's coming. Now you understand fully the power and purpose of the musicians of the King and the combined choirs and orchestras. They are more than worshipers. They are mighty warriors and weapons of engagement in the King's forces. The music is prophetic and atmosphere changing. Only a few composers on earth have been able to approach and approximate the level of composition and musicianship achieved and released here in the conservatory.

"When you return to earth, be sure to tell church singers and musicians to come up here to the King's Royal Conservatory of Music to learn and create."

"I will, Pilar. They need to know that this place is accessible to them now."

"Come back again," Petros insisted. "I am eager to introduce you to the choir and voice academies."

"I will add it to my heavenly-to-do list, Petros, and thank you for your gracious guidance and instruction.

"I must be going now. I still have one other place to visit before I return to earth."

Toward the Golden Door

I opened the main entry door and was blessed to see the swooshes design on the inside of the door again. I glanced at the ones appearing on the exterior body of the royal scroll. They appeared to be resonating to the door's music. "That makes sense," I said. "God is perfect. Every detail of his creation has a purpose and function. His architectural designs are magnificent and engineered with eternal duration. He doesn't decorate with superfluous embellishments. Every mark and image has a purpose and a message. The King's royal conservatory is a perfect example."

I retraced my steps toward the golden door and the seraphim guards. I was so full of insight and revelation. I couldn't help but think once more this is how David must have felt. He said, "Oh my soul, bless the Lord, and all that is within me bless His holy name." He was commanding his soulish-self to shape up and get moving to worship and exalt the King of kings.

"Let's take charge here, Dale," I decided. "I will command my mind, will and emotions to get in order.

"Soul, you will have to catch up with the information I have received in my spirit here in the conservatory. Do not analyze it. Receive it by faith, Heavenly realms and kingdom spheres are not designed to be understood by my mental acumen. Spiritual truth is spiritually discerned. Your job, soul, is to receive spiritual revelation and information, process it, and transmit it to my 'earth-suit' body that enables me to engage the earth realm, so I can deliver this message just as I received it from the Lord."

Don't forget. Our soul wants to rule our body and spirit. We must command it to submit to our spirit. Our spirit is the holy place within our flesh that is the temple of God where Holy Spirit abides and tabernacles inside of us. Truly, God's Kingdom is within us.

All of a sudden I couldn't see anything. "This is like flying into clouds in my Cessna," I said. "One moment you can see perfectly, and then in an instant your visibility is zero. I remember these clouds. I feel the same joy and lightness that I experienced when I entered these mists on my way toward the conservatory. It's wonderful.

"I'm so happy. What a joyful place this is. I can't wait until I can return to study and participate in a musical presentation for the King. But that may be a long time from now," I considered. "The music will never end though. I will keep this place in my heart forever."

"Yes, you will," a voice spoke behind me. "I will keep it in My heart forever also, Royal Scribe. We are friends!"

I didn't have to turn to see who it was. I recognized His voice. "We have made an eternal memory here in the conservatory, Jesus. I am so grateful. Thank You, Master. You are amazing."

Passing Customs
The golden door opened easily and the fiery seraphim greeted me with approving nods. "Give me the royal scroll!" one demanded.

This time I did not hesitate, gladly surrendering the sacred journal for his inspection.

He examined the outside of the scroll, paying careful attention to every detail. "It is intact," he announced.

"I must inspect the inside," tongues of fire leapt around the seraph.

I'm standing too close to him, I realized and quickly retreated several steps. *His fiery nature is so fearsome. It's a wonder I haven't been burned. How can anyone approach or pass these formidable beings and not be incinerated. And this is just the conservatory. Imagine what approaching the Throne must be like? You better be sure you know what you're doing when you approach these majestic worshipers of the King.*

"This is excellent," he said, returning the scroll to me. "Well done, Royal Scribe."

What has he seen? I wondered. *I dare not look now. I'll wait till later.*

"You may go now, Royal Scribe," the seraph in charge said. "The scroll is almost complete. You will discover your next place of appointment when you return to the Hall of Pillars.

"May our King grant you continuing clarity and revelation. Travel in His light and by His grace. Always traverse the realms of the kingdom in faith. Don't rely on your own understanding. In all your journeys, acknowledge Him and He will direct your course."[219]

"I absolutely will, seraph. I will!"

The Portal

I turned to leave. The pathway leading to the portal came into view once more. It was still filled with showering gold dust that glimmered in the fiery light emanating from the seraphim.

The moment I stepped into the portal, the royal scroll began to play. "I recognize this music!" I said in delight. "It's the same melodic strain that the orchestra played in the Royal Concert Hall. It's been recorded in the scroll." My tears of gratitude fell from my cheeks onto the scroll, splashing like droplets of rain on its surface.

"Sitting with Jesus and listening to the royal symphony…" I couldn't continue. "It's too much… I can't contain it all," I said, overcome with emotion. "I'm not only carrying it in the scroll; it's recorded in my spirit."

I didn't want the music to end. Gold flakes glistened all around me, sparkling and swirling in the light of His glory. I'm not sure how long I traveled through the portal, but my journey ended abruptly when I landed back on the pillar. Penrose greeted me with a huge smile. His eyes were lit with excitement. He was eager for me to say something.

I didn't keep him waiting. "Penrose, you were absolutely right. You said I would not be the same when I came back. That is an understatement. My entire being has been immersed in the music of the King. The pores of my skin are releasing a melody.

"I will never be the same!"

"I knew it!" he replied, overjoyed by my comments. "Everyone has an exceptional God-encounter here, but yours is unique. You are a royal scribe. You are required to capture the fullness of the experience. Father heard His music in your spirit before you were chosen. The heart sings to Father when true love abides there. He knows because He judges and discerns the heart. One reason David was loved so much is because his heart overflowed with music."

Engraved in the Scroll

I sensed the Spirit urging me to look into the scroll.

"May I sit for a season, Penrose?" I asked.

"Yes," he said and stepped away to give me privacy.

I lifted up the royal scroll: "There must be something new inside."

"I knew it!" I declared as my body jerked with a sudden release of Holy Spirit anointing. There it was—a perfect engraving of David's harp. No more fitting symbol could possibly capture the scope and significance of the King's Royal Conservatory of Music. This humble shepherd's harp, played with love and passion, brightened the darkest night and dispelled evil spirits. It was so unpretentious but so powerful.

"You are amazing, Abba," I said. "This is so perfect. You do all things well. A single glance at this harp will enable me to recall my entire time in the conservatory," I sighed in satisfaction.

Where am I going?

I stood and turned toward the angel sentry, "Well, Penrose, I'm not certain where I am supposed to go next. Can you give me any advice?" I asked.

"That's not in my job description," he chuckled. "But I can tell you this. You must leave here, before you get there."

I could have laughed, but I knew he was implying a lot more than the obvious.

"I get it," I replied.

"I will see you again if you are here when I return."

"Possibly," he answered, "but my assignment here is only for a season. Someone else from my tribe may be on guard to greet you. Mention my name, Royal Scribe."

"I will, Penrose."

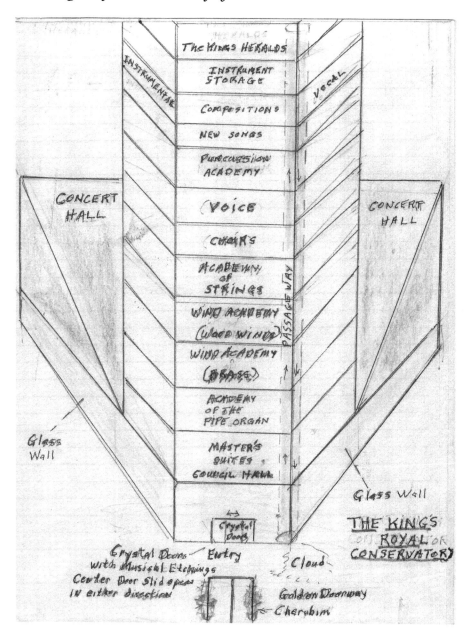

THE KINGS HERALDS

INSTRUMENT STORAGE

COMPOSITIONS

NEW SONGS

PERCUSSION ACADEMY

VOICE

CHOIRS

ACADEMY of STRINGS

WIND ACADEMY (WOODWINDS)

WIND ACADEMY (BRASS)

ACADEMY OF THE PIPE ORGAN

MASTER'S SUITES - COUNCIL HALL

INSTRUMENTAL

VOCAL

PASSAGE WAY

CONCERT HALL

CONCERT HALL

Glass Wall

Glass Wall

THE KING'S ROYAL CONSERVATORY

Crystal Doors

Crystal Doors · Entry
with Musical Etchings
Center Door Slide open
in either direction

Cloud

Golden Doorway
Cherubim

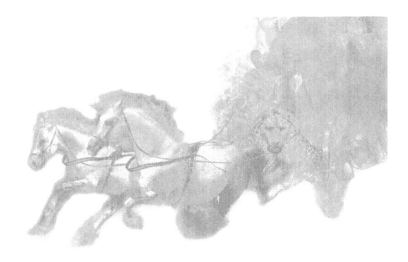

CHAPTER 25

The House of the Perfumers

I peered over the edge of the pillar and searched the darkness. Portals were visible in the distance. They flashed like strobe lights serving as directional beacons for pneumanauts like me to follow. But I knew that distance is hard to measure in space. You can't measure how far light has traveled with the naked eye. Light can appear much closer than it is.

"Which way should I go?" I asked.

There was no response.

"All right then," I decided. "Sometimes the Lord is waiting for us to take the first step in faith before He will reveal the pathway. Abba will guide me to my next appointment. I refuse to decide which direction to go. That's up to Father. He has chosen my itinerary here in the kingdom realms.

"Penrose, you can't steer a ship when it's sitting in the harbor," I said. "This pillar is a safe anchor for me in this vast expanse, but I can't stay here."

Spiritual Navigation
I closed my eyes and turned around three times like I was playing 'pin the tail on the donkey.' Penrose laughed hilariously as I stumbled ahead to the edge and without hesitation leapt off the pillar into the space-pool of darkness. I purposely

kept my eyes closed, but I could feel the tremendous acceleration. I was traveling in the spirit, relying totally on Holy Spirit to guide me. *This is like riding Spirit Wind without reins,* I thought."[220]

It wasn't long until I noticed a distinct difference in my surroundings. *There's a change…something very unusual is enveloping me.* I opened my eyes to find myself in a distant place unlike anything I had seen before. A few pillars clustered closer together. A luminosity filled the region like a haze. A shadowy beam penetrated through the upper level of the vapor. It cast translucent shafts of light into the semi-darkness like light rays in a room that illuminate the dust particles floating in the air. *Space particles!* I thought. *That's something I never saw before.*

I could see different spirit-beings in the shadowy atmosphere. Some were trying to escape the light with horrible, dreadful expressions on their faces. Others were just floating in the haze, soaking in it. Still, others were trying to ascend through the rays as though it were a portal, but could not do so.

A single pillar attracted my attention. Its magnetism drew me toward it. Something registered in my chest. A spiritual timer or a navigation device, I wasn't sure, but I felt it. I immediately knew I had found the correct pillar leading to my third-heaven destination.

A magnificent angel watched me approach. He wore a wreath on his head woven from some kind of branches and leaves. His white belted robe lay lightly on his muscular body and fell gracefully to about mid-thigh. The best words I can find to describe him, although inadequate, are 'physical perfection.' He looked like a Greek Olympian champion.

"Welcome, Royal Scribe," he said. "I have been expecting you."

"Then I am at the correct pillar?" I asked.

"You most certainly are," he replied. "I have been on alert and watching for the individual who carries the royal scroll."

Follow the River

"This is the portal that leads to the River of Life that flows from under the Throne," the angel explained. Other portals can take you there, but you have been assigned to this one for a reason. It is the closest portal to the House of the Perfumers. Father has made it part of your itinerary on this first assignment. It has a very important function in the realm of the kingdom."

"That's awesome!" I responded with delight. "I like perfume."

"Oh, it's much more than that, as you will soon discover," he said in a reprimanding tone.

"May I ask where the vaporous light around and above us is coming from?"

"Everyone does. It is emanating from the heavenly city. We are not far from it. In fact, this pillar is one of the closest portals to the city, but it isn't close enough to see the city. It leads to the River of Life. The city is still a considerable distance from here, but the light is so brilliant that it travels far down stream above the river."

"One more question?" I asked. "From what is that beautiful wreath you're wearing made of? I've never seen such a leaf pattern like that."

"It's beautiful, isn't it?" he responded. "It is made from the branches and leaves that grow on the Tree of Life in the holy city."

"That's astonishing!" I said in amazement.

"There's none like it," he said. "It never loses its life. The leaves stay green and never die."

"May I touch it?" I asked, hoping he would say yes.

He paused and pondered my request, then reached up and plucked a leaf from the wreath. "Take this one," he said. "When you arrive at the House of the Perfumers, give it to them. They will use it."

He placed the single leaf in the palm of my hand. Life and health instantly pulsated through me like a nourishing intravenous infusion. My fingertips and toes tingled as the serum of life flowed all the way to my extremities. *This is a single leaf*, I thought. *If one leaf from the tree of life is enough to restore and heal me, think about entire nations that will be healed by these leaves.*

"Thank you so much. I will,... I'm sorry. I didn't ask your name."

"I am Crisius.[221] I'm from the angelic tribe of the King's gardeners. We work along with the saints to tend the trees in the city gardens.

"Enough questions, Royal Scribe. You should be going. When you reach the end of this portal, look for the river. Follow it toward the light of the city. The House of the Perfumers is on the left bank of the river. You can't miss it. Actually, you will smell it before you see it."

"Thank you again, Crisius. If I can serve you in any way, please let me know."

"The opposite is true, Scribe. We angels are here to serve and minister to you and Adam's kind. If I can assist *you*, let *me* know."

"In the future then," I replied.

I lifted my arms in praise and looked into the portal above me. Instantly, I was surrounded by brilliant light and ascended up through the passageway. Flakes of gold, the remnants of my trip through the previous portal from the conservatory, blew off my clothing and face, leaving a glittering trail behind me. I exited the portal about one thousand feet above a landscape.

"There it is!" I exclaimed. "I can see the light radiating from the city. And the river is over there on the left, just as Crisius said."

I soared toward the river, making a slow descent, and once over the waterway of life, I turned right to follow its course upstream for a considerable distance. All manner of vegetation grew along the river, and thousands of birds flitted and glided around in a parade of color and song. Lush, verdant foliage bore supernatural fruit, and beautiful flowering trees painted the riverbanks with a wonderful palette of heavenly color. The river's water was so crystal clear and pure that I could see the rocks, and gemstones, on the bottom of the channel. The water was actually invisible except when wind created ripples. It was like looking through a pure crystal window.

I would love to drink this water, I thought. *I think I'll do just that,* I decided, diving toward the crystal surface.

"Hold it!" I exclaimed, stopping abruptly. "What's that unusual scent in the atmosphere? I can't identify it."

I drew a long, deep breath through my nose. "This is not a single essence. It must be a compound mixture of fragrances. It's so enticing. It's irresistible. This is the signal I've been anticipating. Crisius told me I would smell the House of the Perfumers before I saw it.

I completely forgot about my thirst and searched the riverbanks ahead for the source of this wonderful fragrance. It grew stronger as I flew toward the holy city. And then, in the distance, I detected a sizeable clearing on the left bank. A pier extending from the bank floated on the translucent water, making it appear like it was suspended in midair.

Arrival

"There it is," I said with an experienced navigator's satisfaction. I was struck by the building's size. "This place is much bigger than a house. It's quite large. It is only a single story structure, but parts of it look like a laboratory or a production facility."

I chose a level landing spot on the bank in front of the house and proceeded to investigate my unusual surroundings.

"This is an amazing place. I've always been intrigued by the production and manufacturing process. This building is constructed like a log cabin, and smell those cedar timbers," I said with fond memories. "Reminds me of Grandma's cedar chest."

An ominous buzzing sound filled the air. "Bees! Run for cover," I cried, ready to high tail it for the door into the perfumery, but I quickly realized I was not under attack. The loud hum came from the tree line on the left side of the building where multiple beehives were humming with activity. The bees were not after me. They were busy about their work, coming and going from the hives into the woodland to gather nectar from the flora. "The perfumers must use the wax and honey as ingredients," I deduced.

I scanned the perfumery compound. Behind the main building, rising above the roofline, were a number of large storage tanks. Each tank was labeled with the name of a type of oil that it contained. On the right side of the edifice, a very large press stood firmly attached to the side of the main building. Pipes and tubes ran from it through the wall into the perfumery. It was no doubt used for extracting oils and other substances.

Next to the press, located on the outer perimeter of the clearing in the bright light, was a drying barn. Plants, flowers, roots, leaves and even vegetables and fruits were scattered about in piles or baskets. Through the interstices of the wood-plank structure, I could see large leaves hanging to dry. Flowers grouped in technicolor bouquets hung on hooks from the ceiling. Some had already turned a crispy brown.

"This is such a wondrous place. So delightful," I said, appreciating every aspect of the ambiance. I traced the paths leading from the facility in different directions along the riverbank into the woodlands, meadows and forests beyond. Snow-capped mountains enrobed in a blue haze rose in the far distance. "I wonder what precious substances are obtained from those high places for the perfumers' inventory. And what may exist beyond them? A desert perhaps?"

The door opened so abruptly that it startled me. "Come in, Royal Scribe. Welcome to the King's perfumery," the greeter announced.

"I, I, I …was expecting an angel," I stuttered.

"Of course you were," he reassured me. "The angels come here often to deliver spices, herbs and precious essences, but we are the ones who perfected the art of perfumery.[222] Yahweh called upon us millenniums ago to compound the oils and incense for the tabernacle. Father has put us in charge of the laboratory of essences here in the heavenly realms of His Kingdom.

"Please come in!" he motioned gracefully. "I am eager to show you how we perform our duties as the King's master perfumers.

The Warehouse

I stepped through the front door into a large warehouse. My attention was drawn to the left side of the room where shelves of clay jars and vessels and beautifully blown glass bottles of all shapes and sizes were stored. The clay vessels were larger than any of the other accoutrements in the warehouse. They were made with excellence, no doubt by a master potter. Each one was embossed with a marking or identification that indicated its contents. Shelf upon shelf of these containers lined the left wall. All of them had lids and some featured spouts. Each one was closed with a cork or lid, depending on its size. In addition, the corks and lids were sealed with an airtight wax coating so that the contents were protected from any impurities, dilution or evaporation. It looked like a winery's wine-aging warehouse with various colors of wax to indicate the time of the harvest. Some of the vessels were distinguished by commemorative medallions hanging on gold or ribbon chains. They bore the official emblem of the King's perfumery with a personal blessing from Father to the recipient.

Many large vessels and water pots sat in parallel rows along the floor next to the shelves. They were prepared for distribution. Some were quite large and held a considerable volume of liquid. Shipping labels identified the recipients and specified that the precious contents were prepared for ceremonial celebrations or festivals where large quantities would be needed.

"I'm really enthralled by this treasure house. The raw materials you use and the variety of products is impressive. Its value must be priceless," I said to my host.

The Anointing Oils

"Please call me Zacharias," he responded with excellent diction, perfectly pronouncing his name in Hebrew. "I supervise the House of the Perfumers. Thank you for your compliments, Royal Scribe. You are correct regarding the value of our items. Some are freely given to those who request them. Others must be purchased, especially the eye salves.[223]

"Let me explain in detail what you have observed."

He pointed to the wall and said, "This is the wall of anointing. Here is where we keep various oils used for sanctifying, releasing power and authority for ministry, ruling, and favor to produce wealth. They are designated for the prophets and the ministries of the priests and kings, as well as for appointing and ordaining. No one can serve the King without the proper anointing and grace suited for their assignment.

"In centuries long ago, these oils were used in the priestly ministries of Aaron and Levi and also for the sanctification of the Tabernacle and Temple. But now they are for the Bride of Christ. They are essential for every one of God's servants. He loves their fragrance, and their essence releases the atmosphere and aroma of the kingdom.

"Notice the larger vessels on the floor. They are specific anointing oils for tribes, tongues, and nations on the earth who are graced by the King to occupy realms and kingdoms on earth as well as in the heavenlies. They indicate inheritances and apportionments of heavenly occupation and spiritual dominion and authority. They are poured out in volume upon cities and entire people groups chosen by the King for specific duties and responsibilities in the eternal realms that have their commencements on earth."

Salves and Ointments

The warehouse was divided in half by a large two-sided shelf that ran along the center length of the room. The shelves on the left side, facing the vessels and jars, contained small to medium cruses for salves, ointments and balms. Some of the containers were fashioned from precious metals. Others were made of semi-precious stones, gems, marbles or alabaster. The highly polished silver and radiant gold ones were positioned next to a priceless treasure trove of mother of pearl ampules. A delightful collection of other shell vessels followed.

Zacharias moved to the divider shelves in the center of the warehouse. "We keep the prepared salves and balms for healing on this side of the shelving. But they are far more diverse and are compounded for more than healing the body. We produce some balms that can heal the soul. Some are specifically designed for healing the memory or can calm thoughts and produce peace.

"Here are the various eye salves I spoke about," he said, pointing to their location on the shelf. "They affect both the natural and the spiritual vision. They can remove veils that cover the spiritual eyes. We refer to them as spiritual cataracts. It's wonderful to see vision restored in both dimensions."[224]

He reached to pick up an alabaster container and said, "This one is similar to the one that Mary broke when she anointed Jesus for His burial. There are some oils, perfumes and balms that are specifically for passing from the earthly realm into the heavens at death. Many believe that they are intended for preservation, but that is a misconception. The body will decay and return to dust, but when the spirit departs from the body, it carries the scent it was anointed with into the spiritual dimension.

"Every person is born with a unique scent. Some of the balms, oils, and perfumes here," he waved his arm around the entire warehouse, "serve to accent their individuality and prepare them for entry into the eternal realms, just as a bride is prepared for her bridegroom before the wedding.

"This alabaster container holds myrrh and other spices. Myrrh is the most costly ingredient."

Zacharias replaced the alabaster container on the shelf. "Let's proceed to the other side of this divider shelf."

Spices, Fruits, Flowers, Plants, Nuts

We walked back toward the door and made a U-turn to access the opposite side of the center bank of shelves. The atmosphere was intoxicating. I felt like I was walking through the cosmetic department at Macy's. I was in perfume overload. My nose went into overdrive, frantically trying to discern the various scents. I was refreshed, invigorated, and soothed all at once.

"This is wonderfully confusing," I said. "I'm not sure what I smell, but I like the combination."

"I know that you're overwhelmed," Zacharias explained, "but when you are trained and experienced in the perfumer's art, you can discern the slightest hint of a single fragrance. It takes years of being mentored and discipled by Father in the perfumer's art to develop this skill. It's all about discernment. Spiritual and physical ability to smell is a requirement."

He pointed down the bank of shelves. It contained various, potent and subtle fragrance-emitting substances.

"This first section contains all the spices," he explained.

It looked like the glorious Indian spice bizarre I had visited in Durban, South Africa. Reds, yellows and greens, and dark hues of brown and whites provided a palette of color and scent.

"This is a veritable painter's pallet of colored spices," I commented. "It's beautiful and all natural. I'm salivating; it makes me hungry for curry."

"Here in the center section of the shelves, " Zacharias said, as we walked slowly toward the back of the warehouse, "are various types of incense. Notice that the containers have varying degrees of transparency. Some are opaque. They contain a blending of various powders that are made from minerals and plants, especially fruits and flowers. We also add a secret ingredient known only to the master perfumers.

"Did you know that we perfumers produced the incense used on the Altar of Incense and in the censers of the priests as they ministered before the Lord in the Tabernacle? It is most holy!"

He turned to me with absolute focus like a professor who wanted you to know that this next statement would be on the final exam. "May I say that the function of incense is to awaken and provoke a response? We make incense here specifically designed to motivate the King to action and to incite the saints.

"The purpose of the perfumer's art and skill is to create atmospheres, release anointings, bring healing, provoke a response, and stimulate action. It's far more than producing pleasant aromas. It is about creating the atmosphere that Abba loves, particularly those that stimulate worship, love, power, strength, peace, beauty, healing, and enhancement of mental and spiritual perception. But these are only some of the effects of our compounds. There are many more," he pointed to a few specific ingredients. "We use this combination to make one of my favorites. It is called 'Still Waters.'"

"Crisius was so right," I said, "when he told me that the House of the Perfumers is much more than a place to make perfume."

"Ah, yes, Crisius. He is a dear friend. We often meet in the gardens," Zacharias said.

We took a few steps further, and he pointed to the shelves again. "Here are the scented candles and oils for lamps and diffusers. This is one of my favorite formulas," he said, picking up a luscious round yellow candle the size of a grapefruit. "It is virgin grapefruit, the first press. We add a hint of honey and some other secret ingredients.

"Here, smell it," he said, holding it up to my nose.

I inhaled deeply and was transported by the fragrance. I could see myself standing in an orchard of grapefruit trees that were covered with thousands and thousands of blossoms. Bees were buzzing about pollinating and drinking the sweet nectar.

"Wow! This is heavenly. I can see it and smell it."

"What you see in the spirit is correct. This candle is made with the flowers, not the fruit. That's why we call it 'virgin grapefruit.' We press the flowers to extract the oil. We are constantly generating new fragrances, and sometimes the King will send us a formula for a compound that He wants specifically produced for a special occasion or purpose."

He placed the candle back on the lower shelf and looked at it with the admiration of a creator. "It's really special to me," he said, his eyes glistening with delight.

We reached the last portion of the center shelves. "Here in this final section is where we keep plant substances," Zacharias explained. "These dishes and jars contain leaves, fronds, roots, barks, flowers, fruits and nuts. They are dried in our oven or in the drying shed outside. We also crush and grind them into granules and powders."

I was drawn to the cinnamon sticks and whole dried apricots. A large glass container, full to the brim with cashews was so tempting I almost reached for one. "Raisins, dates, cumquats," I said as I catalogued the shelves with delight.

The leaf section reminded me of my boy scout days when I searched the woods and forests gathering leaves and pressing them for my scrapbook. I earned the merit badge for that project, but even better, I developed an appreciation for this unique signature of every tree. Then suddenly I remembered the leaf from the Tree of Life in my pocket.

The Most Precious Ingredient

"Zacharias! I almost forgot. Crisius told me to give this to you," I said, handing him the leaf from the Tree of Life.

Zacharias respectfully received it: "This is the very heart of all that we do. It is the perfumer's most precious substance. We use it with great care and wisdom. It is the most potent substance in all the plant kingdom.

"It is a living organism and it never withers. It becomes translucent as it matures When you go to the holy city, you can observe this. You will see the roots of the tree drinking water from the River of Life that flows from the Throne of God. The water sparkles through the trunk and the branches and flows through the veins of the leaves. The light of the glory of God nourishes the tree. We perfumers regard the tree and its twelve fruits as the perfect example of our craft.[225]

"This is the most important ingredient here in the perfumery," Zacharias said to himself, absorbed in examining the single leaf in his palm like a chemist looking through a microscope. "The leaves from the Tree of Life, the twelve fruits, and the water from the River of Life, this is why we are located close to the holy city on the bank of the river."

He raised his head. "Thank you so much, Royal Scribe. This single leaf is worth more than all the wealth on earth," he said, placing the leaf in a ceramic container on the top shelf with a sigh of satisfaction.

Rocks, Minerals, Metals, Gems

Zacharias turned away from the shelf and pointed to the variety of baskets and boxes on the floor on the right side of the warehouse. "This is where we keep the powders and granules we manufacture from various rocks and minerals. Some of our salves and oil compounds require metals and mineral substances and, sometimes, even dirt.[226] We use gems and common or precious metals such as gold, silver and platinum. Radioactive ingredients are used to treat angelic wounds and injuries incurred in battle. The angel-imagers keep a supply with them.[227] They are issued to each warring angel battalion."

Zacharias bent and thrust his hand into a basket of a sky-blue powdery substance and let it sift through his fingers.

"Feel this, Royal Scribe. It's so refreshing."

"This powder is so fine," I said. "It's weightless. This feels like liquid ice running through my fingers."

"It is powdered water," he explained, with a cautious grin to let me know there are some secrets here that he is not about to reveal to anyone.

The Perfume Section

"This is the last section of the warehouse," he said, proudly waving his arm with a grand sweep along the right exterior wall. His face shone with ecstatic satisfaction.

The entire display of shelves running the length of the right warehouse wall looked like a master artist's mural. A fabulous array of unique bottles, vials and jars painted the shelved landscape with brilliant and subtle colors and hues. Here and there, perfume atomizers appeared like miniature balloons resting on the bottles.

"This is stunning!" I stated. My senses were on overload. "No Paris perfumery or Arabian merchant could produce such an array of beauty and fragrance. Even the bottles themselves arouse the senses with their intriguing beauty. No glassblower on earth could produce such a perfect array of color, character and design. This is a masterpiece," I said, admiring the scene like somebody contemplating a famous painting in the Louvre. "This display of scents and fragrances is suitable for the bedroom of a queen."

"You are so perceptive, Royal Scribe. We call this the Perfumery for the Bride," Zacharias explained. "These fragrances are earthly as well as heavenly. Some of them are in use now. They have been released in measure on the earth to perfume the Church. The full measure of these essences will be released upon the Church as the Bride prepares for the Bridegroom's arrival. When Jesus, the Bridegroom, descends from the heavens, these fragrances, along with the immense love and expressions of praise and worship of the saints, will be so powerful and overwhelming that the atmosphere on earth will forever be changed with the fragrance of the Lord and His bride."

I wanted to weep. Joy and love burst out of me like an uncapped well. "Oh, the joy of being a part of the Bride of Christ, to wear the fragrance of unbridled love and affection for my King, to perfume the atmosphere with the essence of creation—the spices and fragrances of the plants, flowers and trees and the aromas of oils and balms. The beauty of God's creation will be distilled into pure fragrance and released as His aroma into the atmosphere of earth and heaven."

A love song resounded in my spirit as I imagined the scent of the Bride enticing the Bridegroom. "Imagine, the combined fragrances of the Bride and Groom, the Church and the Lord, united at last and forever. This will be the atmosphere that sings, 'Oh, come let us adore Him, for He alone is worthy. Let's give Him all the glory, Christ the Lord.' The saints declare it. We cry holy, and the earth is transformed by His glory into the fragrance of holy incense and the perfume of the Bride."

"He is coming soon, Zacharias," I said softly, pausing and holding my breath between each word, not wanting even my breath to detract from the holiness of this moment.

"Soon!" Zacharias affirmed. "He is coming soon to receive His Bride."

He took a bottle of perfume from the shelf and removed the glass stopper. "Hold out your hand, Royal Scribe."

He stroked the back of my hand with the precious gold liquid.

"This is a gift from the royal perfumery. May its fragrance be a constant reminder for you to encourage the Bride to prepare herself."[228]

He replaced the cap and placed the bottle back on the shelf.

The Perfumery Warehouse

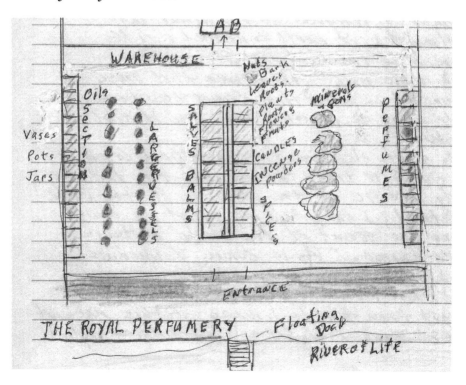

The Perfumers' Laboratory

"Now, let me show you our laboratory," Zacharias said as he led me to a doorway at the back of the warehouse.

The moment I stepped through the door I realized this was no ordinary lab. "The love of God is so tangible," I said, shielding my eyes for a moment to adjust to the brilliance.

A large table was positioned diagonally in the center of the room. Every surface emitted uncontaminated light. The instruments and tools gleamed with the luster of polished metal mirrors. The necessary measuring tools and scales for weighing powders, oils, spices and other raw ingredients lay on the table.

The manufacturing of a perfume was in process. An ancient clay tablet with Hebraic markings containing the formula and precise measurements for each ingredient sat next to one of the scales. Beakers, glass tubes and funnels hung on racks. Spoons, droppers, measuring cups, separated by size, were located on wooden trays. Knives, scissors, mortars and pestles, hammers, drills and shaving devices were scattered about the center of the table.

A stove, in the shape of an altar, sat next to the right end of the table. Pots of oils and water simmered and bubbled over the flames. The coals crackled and shimmered. Red and yellow flames danced under the vessels, turning one of them to a glowing orange. I was surprised to see that the fire never emitted any smoke.

A large marble mortar, big enough to hold a basketball, sat on the floor at the other end of the table. The pestle was the size of a baseball bat. A grinding mill sat next to the mortar. The timber-sized turning lever required the strength of several people or an angel to operate it.

"Everything in the perfumery is compounded in this laboratory," Zacharias explained and then he pointed to the rear wall, "We draw and measure the oils we need from these valves you see on the wall. The oils are stored in the tanks outside.

"We can also press fresh essential oils and ingredients. Over there," he pointed to the right wall, "are the pipes that channel the fresh pressing directly into the lab.

"Other ingredients can be selected from the drying house as well as the warehouse where you just observed our huge assortment of oils, spices, minerals, roots, plants, nuts, flowers, fruits ..." he ended his inventory with the sacred ingredient, "and of course, the leaves from the Tree of Life.

"Whenever we need something that we don't have in stock, we send the angel-couriers to get it. They are constantly traveling to earth and other places throughout the cosmos for various things we use in small amounts. They know exactly where to find the very best quality of the ingredients we request. Sometimes they bring us things that we haven't considered using. We are often quite surprised by their choices, but I must say they have some amazing ideas. Then again, there are times when we just can't keep ourselves from laughing. But they never get offended. They just laugh along with us. We take great pleasure in making the angel dust they carry with them. It is a potent substance that is very precious to them."

"That's right!" I suddenly recalled. "One angel actually gave me some."

"This rarely happens," Zacharias responded in surprise. "That angel showed great honor to you by his gift. It is the seal of an everlasting covenant that they make with men.[229]

"One essential ingredient we use constantly is the water from the River of Life. We draw it from the end of the wharf that you passed over when you arrived. No other water exists that is as pure and beneficial than the water that flows from under the King's Throne. We draw it from the center of the river at a deep level. It's never the same though. Sometimes it's very cold and refreshing. At other times, it can be warm or even hot. We never know until we draw it up. We're not sure why it changes temperature, but Abba does it for a reason. Someday we must ask Him why."

Preparing the Bride

Zacharias looked at me with longing in his eyes. "Do you remember how Esther was prepared for king Ahasuerus?" he asked. "Every possible beauty treatment was properly given them. Shaashgaz, the king's eunuch, was custodian of the beautiful young virgins being considered for queen.

"Expensive oils and perfumes were applied to Esther's skin and hair. Her complexion became spotless and perfect. Her skin was soft and supple after months of massages with fine oils. It took an entire year of treatments: six months with myrrh and six months with perfumes and preparations. All of this was done to prepare her for King Ahasuerus. Among all of the candidates, the king loved Esther more than all the other women. He chose her to be the queen and set a crown upon her head.[230]

"Do you understand, Royal Scribe?" Zacharias asked. "No expense was spared. No amount of preparation was overlooked or disregarded. Nothing was withheld that would enhance her natural beauty. The bride was to be made ready so that on that single day when the king would select his queen, she would be the most beautiful and suitable for her royal position."

"An entire year of beauty treatments," I replied. "Esther must have been breathtakingly beautiful. Her perfume must have been intoxicating and her complexion flawless."

"Do you think the King of kings would do any less for His Bride to be? Royal Scribe, you must tell the Bride of Christ to prepare for Jesus' return. The spices and oils have been prepared. When you return to earth, tell the saints to come up here to the royal perfumery to obtain the fragrances and ointments that please the King. But you must also tell them that this is much more than a place where we make fragrant substances and healing balms. This is the house of *atmospheres, anointings and aromas*. It is time for the Bride to make ready! She must prepare herself for His arrival!"[231]

"I will, Zacharias," I promised, lifting the royal scroll in front of me. "The message is recorded on the scroll. I will fulfill the King's assignment by His grace."

"Good," Zacharias replied. "We are preparing special anointings that will be needed in the days to come—a fresh anointing for the end times. We are also about to release an aroma from heaven that will revive the saints who have succumbed to discouragement and have a slumbering spirit. The Church is about to wake up.

"The atmosphere of heaven is invading earth. The angels are infusing the earthly realm with the fragrances of heaven. Holy Spirit is releasing the atmosphere and fragrance of the realms of the kingdom. Righteousness, peace and joy are more than states of being. They are kingdom atmospheres.

"All of heaven is postured for the release of the times and seasons in Abba's heart, and so it shall come to pass that He will open the door to the Hall of Times and Seasons to make known His appointed final days of salvation, war and eternal peace."

I felt a pressing urgency in my spirit as Zacharias spoke. "This is not a dream that I will wake from," I realized. "This is real! I am in the spirit just like John on the isle of Patmos or Enoch walking with God in the heavenly realms. I am talking to Zacharias, one of God's saints. I am really here in the King's royal perfumery. And it's all because Abba wants the Church to know the times we are living in and what is accessible to the heir in the heavens. A sense of urgency strengthened my determination not to get distracted from my assignment as one of the King's royal scribes.

"So many things could deter or hinder the release of the scroll to the saints. I must stay focused. I must! Help me, Holy Spirit," I prayed.

The burden remained, but I felt a fresh divine enabling—a grace to finish. Zacharias' words were so encouraging. "Remember, Royal Scribe, 'It's not by might, nor by power, but by My Spirit, says the Lord.'"[232]

"I should be going," I responded. "Thank you for your encouragement. This has been an amazing revelation to me. Never in a million years would I have dreamed there's a royal perfumery in heaven, but now it makes perfect sense.

"This place is subtly powerful. I feel such love here. The aroma of the King and the scent of God's people are so unique and distinguishing. I will never forget these fragrances or take them for granted. I am indebted to you, Zacharias."

"It is just the opposite, Royal Scribe," he said shaking his head in denial. "It is I who am indebted to you for your obedience and willingness to come here. I have been waiting for a long time for your appearance, and now just like you, I am also encouraged."

The Perfumers' Lab

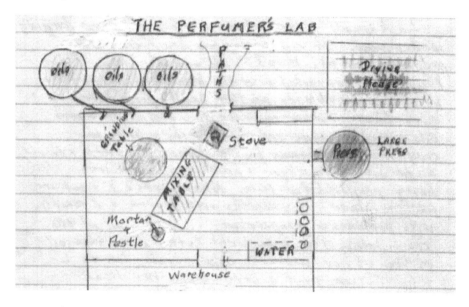

Crystals

We walked through the warehouse and back onto the riverbanks.

"Let's go out onto the wharf," Zacharias insisted. "You can leave from there. Follow the river downstream. Several portals can transport you back to the pillars."

I stood gazing into the River of Life. I could see what first looked like ice cubes floating in the current. "They're not ice cubes," I announced in astonishment. "They're crystals. Beautiful, clear, transparent, diamond-like crystals."

"Yes," Zacharias affirmed. "The crystals flow from the Throne. They dissolve in the river and then form again in other places as they proceed downstream. You can drink them in their dissolved state, but they will form again inside of you. There are many other elements in the water that can morph from solid to liquid. But did you notice the shimmering light in the river? It is His luminous presence. His glory flows in the stream. It is life giving. That is why the Tree of Life is planted by the river. The river carries the life force flowing from Father. It is the river that waters the Garden in Eden and nourishes the Tree of Life. It continually flows from the Throne to refresh the tree. There is no death here in the kingdom realm, only life."

I clutched the royal scroll tightly in my hand, stepped to the edge of the wharf, bent my knees and held out my arms.

"Goodbye, Zacharias," I shouted and jumped into the air attempting to make a perfect swan dive into the river. It never happened. Instead, I sprung from the wharf and was carried up into the heaven over a thousand feet above the water's surface.

"Well, I suppose the Lord has other plans," I shouted back to Zacharias, but he didn't hear me.

"Perhaps some other time I will get to swim in the life-giving waters of this one-of-a-kind river that springs from God's Throne."

Departure from the Perfumery

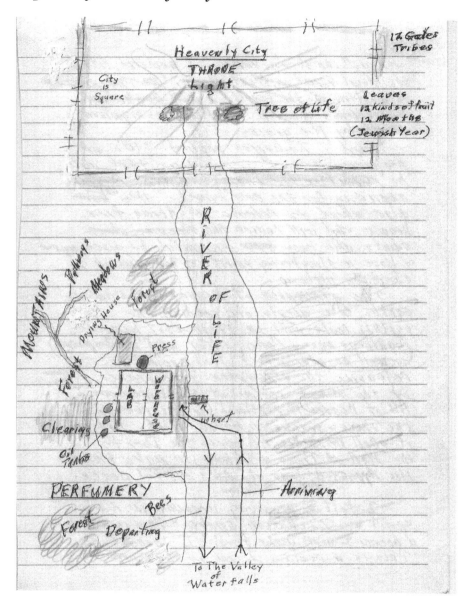

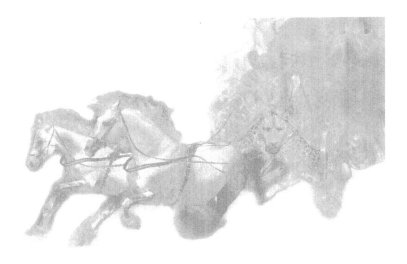

CHAPTER 26

The Valley of Waterfalls

I followed Zacharias' instructions and headed downstream. Reflected light sparkled and shimmered off the river's surface, dappling the vegetation on the riverbanks with dancing pinpoints of brilliance like millions of laser pens in the hands of playful angels. The scene was surreal. Lush flowering trees and plants lined the river. Verdant jungles and majestic forests stretched inland as far as I could see. Meadows and plains hosted peacefully grazing flocks. Birds, with indescribable plumage and birdsongs that delight the soul, flew about, sometimes swooping above and below me in playful maneuvers like aerial acrobats. A majestic eagle appeared above me and accompanied me for some time. His visionary superiority was obvious. He scanned the landscape with radar-like perception.

I'm sure he is seeing more than I can, I thought. *But at least I can say I am soaring with an eagle.* Fitting Scripture says, *"They that wait upon the Lord shall renew their strength; they shall mount up with wings as eagles; they shall run, and not be weary; they shall walk, and not faint."* (Isaiah 40:31)

The aroma of the perfumery dissipated as I followed the river farther downstream. I was enjoying the scenery so much that I lost track of distance. I wasn't thinking about searching for a doorway or portal back to the pillars. The journey was too intoxicating. Eventually, I noticed that the river was gaining speed and a very faint sound like light rain came from faraway downstream. At first, it was barely a whisper, but it soon grew into a low-pitched humming sound, like a hydro-electric generator.

A Spectacular View

"What could this be?" I asked, eagerly pushing ahead. The sound grew from a hum to a rumble and then became a crashing cascade of energy. The cause was unmistakable.

"It's a waterfall!" I yelled with joy. "I can see the mist rising from the river."

"Oh, my goodness!" I shouted, soaring over the falls. Below me, a huge luxurious valley captured the river's plunging descent over the precipice. I stopped so suddenly that I almost dropped the scroll. "That was close," I gasped, gripping the precious cylinder tightly.

I turned to behold the most breathtaking, spectacular waterfalls I have ever seen. I've stood on the shore's edge of Niagara Falls, so close that a single step would plunge me into the racing current. I've flown over Victoria Falls in Zimbabwe in a Cessna while videotaping the plunging, twisting cascade speeding on its journey to the great gorge below. The mist above the falls creates a cloud of spray that can be seen 25 miles away. "But this," I said in amazement, "is far more impressive in size and power than anything on earth."

The current of the river had carved channels into the top of the escarpment creating myriads of separate falls. Crystalline water rumbled over the edge and fell hundreds of feet into the valley below. "This is the Valley of Waterfalls," I said, unwilling to take my eyes off the River of Life as it plunged eagerly over the edge of the cliffs and danced its way toward the churning pool below.

A Sound and Light Show

"The waterfalls are singing," I said with goose bumps rising on my arms. "It sounds like a choir accompanied by the royal orchestra. Just listen!" I told myself, focusing on the music that the River of Life was releasing. "I can hear crashing cymbals and thunderous timpani. The strings and woodwinds and brass…such a wondrous sound. It's like the concert in the King's royal conservatory. The river is playing and singing. After all, it is flowing from the heart of the King. It is the song of the Lord! He's singing over us again."

Suddenly, the waterfalls began to exhibit the colors of the Trinity. Red, yellow and blue streamlets flowed over the rim and cascaded into the pool below. They were mixing in the churning water and creating the Father-Colors. This rainbow of life mysteriously made its way back upstream, climbing from the pool to the top of the falls. The resulting technicolor display was astonishing. Crystals tumbled over the edge of the falls flashing with refracted light like aqua-fireworks exploding with bursts of brilliance. The falls rumbled and thundered in response like the cannons in the 1812 overture. It was a heavenly liquid-pyrotechnics display on a grand supernatural scale.

My attention was so captured by the amazing scene that I was shocked when angels began to arrive. They were all around me and began to fly in and out of the falls. Then, to my delight, I looked down to see angels and saints swimming beneath me in the pool.

"That's for me," I said and immediately descended toward the surface.

"What's that in the water? It's supporting floating words, and people are walking on them, stepping from one word to another like they're following a path," I said totally surprised. I was caught off guard by the unusual phenomenon.

"Wait a minute," I quickly deduced. "I think I know why these words are here. The Bible says, *'He sent His word and healed them.'*[233] *'We are washed by the water of His word.'*[234]

"Surely, His Word can support me," I confessed and proceeded to land on a word floating on the surface of the pool. It wasn't like I chose the word; it chose me. I was standing on 'PEACE.' I was firmly supported by the word in the water of life, but I still wasn't satisfied. I wanted to dive into the water and join the others swimming and splashing in the river.

I dove in with utter abandonment. The water was clear and then it would become tinted with the colors cascading from above. They blended together, mixing into brilliant hues and pastel softness with common and exotic mixtures of colors and shading. I became a living canvas.

Water-Battle

A nearby angel splashed me in the face, and painted water flew everywhere.

"No fair," I shouted. "You've got wings." We both laughed with excitement.

"I'm actually swimming and playing in the River of Life," I said, affirming the reality of my situation. "Refreshing, cleansing vivacity is flooding my soul. My mind is crystal clear. My entire being is renewed in this pool. My spirit is so effervescent.

"This is liquid life. God wants all his children to plunge into the river," I said. "It's not just to look at and admire. It's for drinking, swimming, enjoyment, and even playing in. It's the RIVER OF LIFE, that's what it IS!" I shouted, and thrust my arm across the water's surface sending a wave of purple into the face of a nearby angel and spraying the person beside him.

"Water battle!" he shouted back, and the pool exploded with multicolored blasts and perfectly aimed splashes. The angels were getting the upper hand, but they did have an advantage by using their wings. The joy was tangible. And then through the crowded pool of angels and saints drenched in the water of life, I spotted Him. Jesus was splashing water in every direction, laughing and shouting with the rest of us.

"I am absolutely, totally in love with You, Jesus," I said, my eyes bulging out of my head with sheer delight.

"Should I dare to aim at Him?" It was too late. I was targeted with an expert shot of water. My open mouth was instantly filled with spray and my eyes were drenched. I struggled to open them, rubbing with my right hand. My left hand remained firmly clenched with vice-grip strength around the scroll. When I finally managed to open my eyes, Jesus was standing in front of me. The water battle had ended and the angels were celebrating their victory.

"How do you like this?" He asked with a huge grin.

"Lord, I absolutely love it. I had no idea."

"I wanted to bless you with this surprise and refresh you before you return to earth with the royal scroll.

"May I see it?" He asked with such humility.

Oh, if only I could have such humbleness, I thought, loosening my grip to hand Him the scroll.

"It is almost complete," He affirmed. "Only a few more things are yet to be recorded. Guard it well," He said, handing the scroll back to me. "Release its contents accurately and humbly. Not everyone will believe or understand the spiritual revelation or comprehend its value, but those who have eyes to see and ears to hear in the spirit will affirm and bear witness to its genuineness. They are the spiritual pioneers that I have trained to be end-time warriors.

"Your assignment was to record what you see and hear and then release it to the Church. Holy Spirit will do the rest. The spirits of the Lord, Knowledge, Wisdom, Understanding, Counsel, Might, and the Fear of the Lord will mentor and complete the training of the saints. Now, let's just lay back in the pool and rest for awhile."

Jesus floated on the surface with His eyes closed, so peaceful that He appeared to be sleeping. I lay beside Him, closed my eyes and promptly fell asleep. When I awoke, Jesus was gone and I was alone in the deserted pool.

My journey to the Perfumery and Waterfalls

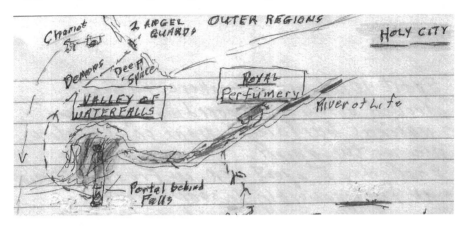

The Hidden Portal

Something mysterious about the largest waterfall attracted my attention. *I should investigate,* I thought and stood up to walk on the water toward it. *I wonder if I can walk through the falls?* The closer I got, the more ridiculous my idea seemed. I approached the thundering torrent with trepidation.

It's so powerful. What am I thinking? But it was too late. The deluge drew me into its reach and sucked me into the torrent. I was thrust through the watery veil and out on the other side of the falls. I found myself standing in front of a cave entrance.

This must be one of the portals that the angel Crisius and Zacharias told me about when they said there were many passageways leading up from the pillars to the River of Life. This one is well hidden.

I stood between the waterfall and the doorway in a terrible quandary. "What I would give for just another hour of soaking in peaceful sleep next to Jesus,"[235] I confessed. I knew I must leave, but I longed to stay in this awesome place of wondrous joy and happiness. I ran my fingers through my hair, slicking it back out of my eyes, and then shook the water off my arms and the scroll. The returning awareness of the urgency of my assignment clarified my thinking.

"There is so much more to see and hear in the heavenly realms. Think what I would miss by settling for this experience here at the Valley of Waterfalls, even though it is a destination I would certainly choose. And besides, I can always come back here to this paradise now that I know it exists and how to find it. Most importantly, I will not disobey my King for a moment's pleasure," I said with absolute resolve.

I must check the royal scroll, I thought. I tilted the scroll to examine its interior in the sparkling light of the waterfall. An image had been added. It was a perfect replica of the leaf from the Tree of Life. *What an appropriate engraving to help me recall my visit to the King's perfumery.* Every scene scrolled through my mind like a slide show. *I can't wait to tell the Bride about what has been made ready and available to her.*

I stared in wonderment. Something was happening to the scroll. The waterfall was churning inside of it. I watched in amazement as the water tumbled and splashed around like the inside of a washing machine. When it ceased, a new icon became visible just below the leaf. It was an engraving of the waterfall. It sparkled and glistened with the luster of shimmering diamonds. Just seeing it brought immense happiness to my heart.

I felt a wonderful sense of accomplishment. "I feel like I did when I was a college student completing a course successfully," I said. "Could this mean this is the final place I am to visit here in the heavenly realm to complete this first part of my assignment as the King's royal scribe? I've already seen and heard so much and I know it is vital that this information be delivered to the Bride quickly."

"I must get going!" I realized, sensing the urgent import of my words. "He will summon me when it is time to return for the next journey into the realms of His Kingdom to see, hear, and record the revelations to be released to the Church in this age. We must all prepare for the season and time to come."

CHAPTER 27

Re-Entry

Three water-drenched steps were carved out of the cliff behind the falls. They led down into the darkness of a subterranean pathway. I stepped carefully onto the slick stairway and cautiously made my way along the underground passageway, sliding my free hand along the damp wall for stability. *This reminds me of the suspension bridge,* I thought as a light appeared farther down the tunnel. When I arrived at the portal opening, light blazed inside of the tube-shaped passageway and flamed above the opening, causing my shadow to dance on the surrounding cave walls. I looked like a Native American Indian holding a tomahawk and dancing in front of a bonfire.

I stood at the threshold of the gateway. "I'm not sure where this will take me?" I said. "But, as always, I must travel in the spirit by faith."

I took a step into the center of the flaming portal and kept my eyes wide open. "I might be incinerated," I said, "but if I'm going down in flames, I want to embrace the full reality of the experience." A firestorm engulfed me and instantly I was thrust through the portal at astounding speed. I didn't see them and wondered if they were in the portal with me, but I could hear a conversation going on between the spirits of Knowledge, Wisdom, Understanding, and Counsel. I couldn't discern what they were saying. I just knew intuitively that I was their subject matter. Their voices faded and I abruptly stopped prematurely in the portal.

"What do I do now?" I said in trepidation. "I'm stuck in a supernatural portal between heaven and earth like someone stuck in an elevator between floors. But there's no emergency phone in this one. Then abruptly, a door opened in front of me.

The Dark Realm

"Oh, Lord!" I shouted, staring blindly into black desolation. "What am I going to do now? There's no pillar anywhere in sight! This can't be the end of the portal. There's no angel, no guard, no pillar, nothing but empty space. I'm really in a fix. I can't go back up to the falls," I reasoned. "Wherever I am, I'm going to have to fly to get to a pillar, but there aren't any in sight. Maybe this is a test? The Master may be watching to see what my response will be. Perhaps I am supposed to explore the heavenly realms on my own?

"Why not," I decided. "I can't just stay here." So with that intention, I launched myself out of the flaming portal into what I quickly realized was deep space. "This is magnificent," I shouted, speeding forward into the black cosmos. Stars twinkled far in the distance, and I wondered how many millions of light-years away they might be.

"Wait a minute. Something's dreadfully wrong," I shuddered as something appeared ahead of me. In a matter of seconds, I found myself surrounded by demonic spirits.

"We are here to block your way, Royal Scribe!" one of them shouted, contorting his grotesque face into a painful scream. The other spirits raised their knurled claw-like hands toward me, hissing and gesturing with gross intentions.

"I am the ruler of this part of the dark realm. We know who you are, Royal Scribe, and what you are doing here in the heavenlies. You have strayed into our territory now," the commander of the horde scowled with a gruesome laugh.

"We saw you enter our domain and laid this trap for you. We are taking you captive. Now you are our prisoner, and you must immediately surrender the royal scroll to us. We will never allow you to take it back to earth!"

An uncommon boldness rose up inside of me. I felt empowered beyond my human strength. "In the name of Jesus, get out of my way!" I shouted with all of my might. "The blood of Jesus rebukes you!" I declared, raising the royal scroll toward them like a weapon. A brilliant blood-red light shot out of the end of the cylinder.

Their countenance instantly changed from their evil intentions to total fear. They turned and fled into the darkness, whimpering like wounded dogs. Their commander looked back at me in his haste and grimaced, "You will soon realize that our power is incontestable." Then he disappeared into the abysmal blackness.

"I doubt if I will see them again," I asserted. "They know who I am and whose I am. They wouldn't dare approach me now. But I have made a serious error. I must have entered the second heaven unknowingly when I left the portal. I should have never attempted this foolish escapade. I need to get out of here now!"

Stopped at the Border

I set my course to ascend toward the third heaven, and in a short time I was in an entirely different dimension and spiritual climate. "This must be the realm of the kingdom," I said in relief, "but just where, I have no idea. I think I will see how far I can go in this region." I sped forward, deeper into the heavenly realm, faster and faster until the stars were a blur, when suddenly two massive angels appeared ahead of me blocking my way

"Stop!" they shouted. "What are you doing here, Royal Scribe?" an angel demanded. "You are not permitted to go beyond this border. You are about to enter the outer regions. They are forbidden to those who are uninitiated in the offices required to function here. This region is for kings only. Your time has not yet come. You cannot proceed without the King of king's approval and permission."

A flaming chariot abruptly appeared out of the darkness and sped toward us like a police cruiser rushing to a crime scene. "We will send you back to the portal that led you to the angel encampment. You can find your way back to Frontier Town from there."

I climbed aboard the gleaming chariot, and in an instant we were blasting through the heavens. Glowing sparks from the chariot's wheels and body left an iridescent contrail behind us.

"Traveling through the cosmos by chariot is like riding a shooting star," I said to my angelic limo driver.

"I suppose that would be an accurate earth perspective," he replied in a business-like manner. "Your ride is almost over. The portal is just ahead."

"Already?" I said as the pillar came into view.

The pilot skillfully slowed and circled the pillar and then coasted up alongside of it.

"Thank you," I said sheepishly. "That was my first chariot ride. It's awesome. Sorry I had to get it for the wrong reason."

"At your service," the angel replied. "I hope you have learned your lesson. Next time, don't wander too far out into the cosmos without permission."

I stepped from the chariot onto the pillar with a sigh of relief. "You're still here, Matradus," I said. "I'm happy to see you for several reasons."

"I am," he smiled. I didn't expect to see you back here so soon."

"I'm on my way back to earth now," I explained. "I got lost and ended up battling with a horde of evil spirits. They could have taken me prisoner and stolen the royal scroll but Jesus' name sent them fleeing. I think the Spirit of Might came to my aid, but I didn't see him. When I realized I had entered the demonic realm in the second heaven, I quickly ascended into the third heaven and then got carried away and went too far, almost to the outer reaches. An angel patrol intercepted me and sent me back here by chariot."

"I'm not surprised that the pilot brought you here," Matradus replied. "It's policy to bring the saints back to the pillar they first ascended into the heavenly realms from. They can easily get back to their individual portals that way. You are close to yours now."

"Yes, I can see it," I said. "It looks so much closer than when I first spotted this pillar from there. It seems like years since I entered the heavenly realms, but I know that in earth time, it has only been two months."

Eternal Time

"That reminds me. Before I depart to return to Frontier Town through the Unfinished House, I have a question to ask Spirit of Knowledge."

The moment I spoke his name, a violet glow encompassed the platform, and Knowledge appeared next to me.

"Thank you for coming so quickly," I said, greeting him gratefully. "I know that you can answer my question.

"When I was visiting the King's royal perfumery, Zacharias told me about the great value of the House of the Perfumers on the banks of the River of Life, the leaves from the Tree of Life, and the twelve fruits that the tree bears, which are different each month.

"My question: If heaven and the realms of the kingdom are eternal and time does not exist in eternity, how can the Tree of Life bear fruit on a monthly cycle?"

"That's an excellent question, Royal Scribe. Let me explain. Eternity does not mean that time stops and there is no more time.[236] Instead, it means that time itself is without end. Time continues forever in eternity.

"If this were not so, then the Tree of Life could not produce once a month as it is designed to do. There are end times and the last days, but time itself will never end. But it is no longer about life and death. It is about schedules and seasons in heavenly realms. The cosmic clock does not cease. There will be a new heaven and a new earth with an entirely new concept and awareness of time and its significance," he said, emphasizing *concept* and *awareness.*

"I think I understand now," I said. "I suppose that without time in heaven, it would be chaotic. Solomon did say that there is a time and a season for everything under heaven.[237] Now I realize there is a time and a season for everything *in* heaven too. This is a whole new revelation to me—times and seasons exist in the realms of the heavenly Kingdom of God."

"You will learn more about these things when you return, Royal Scribe," Knowledge said. "These secrets are locked and hidden in the Hall of Times and Seasons. On some cosmic-altering day, Abba will open the door and release a new time and a new season on earth as well as in heaven. A new heaven and a new earth are imminent. We know that it won't be long until He does."

"I must go now," Knowledge said. "Remember, whenever you need my help, call for me."

"I will," I replied, but he was already gone.

"Well. That answers my question Matradus. It's time for me to go."

Returning to Frontier Town

I moved to the edge of the pillar and confidently stepped into space, acting like an experienced pneumanaut. I surprised myself. It went extremely well, almost professional. I realized how much I'd learned in such a short time.

"Once you take the first step of faith, traveling in the spirit becomes easier each time," I said, glancing back at Matradus. "I feel so at home in this realm. I think I was made for this. No, that's not right. I know I am made to travel in the heavenly realms. I must tell the saints they are too."

We are spirit beings. Paul described it well. He said, *"But he who is joined to the Lord becomes one spirit with Him."*[238] Like Apostle John on the isle of Patmos, I heard His voice in the spirit saying, "Come up here!"[239] And I obeyed His invitation. My journey into the realms of His heavenly Kingdom has only begun. But the invitation is not just for me. He is inviting all of His saints to access the heavenly realms in these last days.

I landed gracefully on the initial pillar from whence I had departed for the first time as a spiritual pneumanaut. That seemed so long ago, but I will never forget the absolute faith and trust it required to take my first step into space. I stepped onto the footbridge leading back to the Unfinished House. The darkness was a friend to me now. The faint shadows of spiritual beings reappeared, but I was no longer mystified by them. I hastened along the swaying bridge with eager anticipation, turned the doorknob and stepped back into Frontier Town. I was astounded by what I saw.

"Lord!" I shouted. "The entire town is crowded with spiritual pioneers." Men, women and children were moving about, entering and exiting the various buildings along Main Street. Some were gathered into groups, comparing stories and sharing testimonies about what they had learned so far.

How many of these end-time warriors in training will enter the Unfinished House and become God's pneumanauts? I wondered. *Perhaps what I have recorded in the royal scroll will encourage and mentor them. It's time for the warriors to ascend into the realms of the Kingdom of God. I must deliver the scroll, so the Church can see and hear what the King has made available to the saints.*

Spirit Wind was nowhere in sight. I strolled along the boardwalk passing the various buildings along Main Street thinking about the uniqueness and extraordinary surprises inside of each one of them. Each day I spent here in Frontier Town was an indispensable lesson about moving in the spirit. In hindsight, I realize now, how important this training was to prepare me for entering into the heavenly realms and learning the ways of travel and navigation in the heavens.

I reached the end of Main Street when suddenly I heard the melodious sound of galloping hooves approaching on the dusty thoroughfare. It was music to my ears.

"Spirit Wind!" I shouted, jumping with happiness.

He slowed and trotted up to the edge of the boardwalk and looked at me with his beautiful dark eyes. There was no mistaking his love for me.

"Hello, my friend," I said, greeting him with a long firm stroke along his white mane. "Thanks for coming to take me back to society. We are friends and partners forever. I love you."

I mounted his back, and he immediately headed out of Frontier Town toward the east and the darkening sky. "I have complete confidence in you," I whispered in his ear. "You run like the wind. Take me toward the future, mighty one. Let's ride into new revelation."

He surged ahead at an even faster pace as his power and anointing coursed beneath me and inside of me. We were one! In the twilight of the receding sun, a few last golden rays cast shadows ahead of us on the open plain. A light beam caught the golden braids on the ends of the royal scroll and reflected onto my face.

Checking My Work

"The royal scroll," I said. "I must examine the scroll one more time before night falls, and I can't see inside it."

Once again, I tilted the scroll to allow a shaft of the golden-orange sunset to penetrate through the opening. I was amazed by what I saw.

"It's true!" I shouted. "It's really true!"

Spirit Wind whinnied in acknowledgment.

"You knew it all along. Didn't You?" I said. "The inside of the scroll is only half full. This first portion contains the iconic engravings chronicling my journey into the heavenly realms of the kingdom as a royal scribe. There's a seal at the end of the inscription. It must represent God's approval, His imprimatur. It marks the end of this journey.

"But, Spirit Wind, the lower half of the scroll is empty. What I have been sensing must be true. And this is a confirmation! Part one is complete and approved by the Father. Part two is yet to be revealed. My assignment is only half-finished. How exciting! I wonder where He will lead me on the second half of my journey as His royal scribe? I am His servant. My times and places are in His hand. Every ending is a beginning.

"Besides," I said, as a forgotten conversation popped into my mind, "He mentioned that I would see Enoch again. I can't wait. We are fellow pneumanauts.

"But now I have some important work to do. I need to open the first half of the royal scroll for the saints."

My Pneumanaut Journey

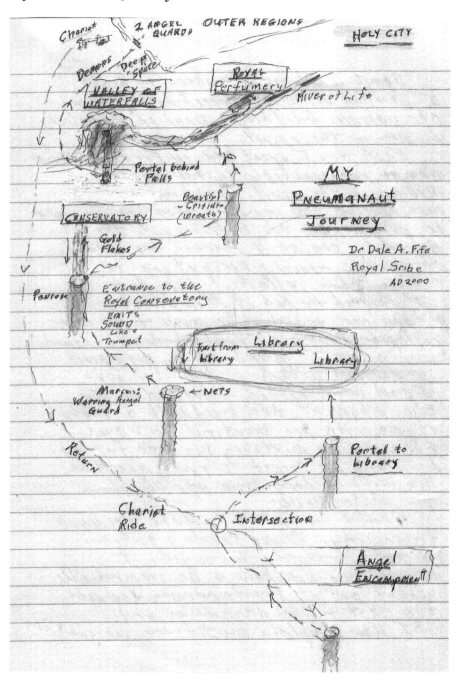

Epilogue

He is Alpha and Omega, always beginning, always ending. The end is but the beginning, another doorway into the new. We finish only to begin again, from one assignment to another, one level of perception to another, each one building on the last. With each step, we climb the mountain of spiritual dimensions and atmospheres of increasingly rarified glory and revelation until we reach the summit, the moment of transition when we stand in His presence, having left the physical to enter into the spiritual realm. And so Enoch walked into God's presence and explored the heavenly realms. He kept a journal of his experiences. He was a pneumanaut and a royal scribe! He is my mentor.

This pneumanaut's journal is the result of my own obedience to the Spirit's invitation. It chronicles what I saw and heard, touched and felt. Others carry the same anointing and assignment as I do. They too have shared their experiences. Like them, I make no claim or attempt at authenticating my pneumanaut's journey of revelation, except to say that Holy Spirit will bear witness with your spirit what the Lord is saying to the Church in this hour. Let the Prophets judge as they are commissioned to do. The Word and the Spirit will testify. The final imprimatur is King Jesus Himself.

My assignment is complete for now. I will wait and prepare for when He summons me back into the heavenly realms as His royal scribe to complete the scroll.

What will you do now? You are destined to sit with Him in heavenly places. This is not a reserved-for-the-future matter. The Church is hearing the angelic invitation once more, *"Come up here, for there are things you must see and hear."* You are called to ascend! Will you obey, like Apostle John, and enter through the open door into the heavenly realms? The King awaits your response. The Church cries, 'Maranatha' (Come, Lord Jesus), but the King is saying, "Come up here." The choice is yours. God speed!

Humbly,
The King's Royal Scribe
The End is the Beginning!

Endnotes

1.   Revelation 4:1

2.   Psalm 84:10

3.   Scribes are gifts from God to the Church (Matthew 23:34). Every king had his own scribe or scribes (2 Chronicles 24:11). Scribes were regarded as teachers, accountants, and highly respected servants. They were provided with a sinecure and generously cared for by their royal overseers. (*See also* Matthew 13:52; Psalm 45:1; John 21:24–25.)

4.   Tallit: a Jewish prayer shawl worn over the outer clothes during the morning prayers (Shacharit) and worn during all prayers on Yom Kippur.

5.   *See* Dr. Dale A. Fife, *The Secret Place: Passionately Pursuing His Presence* (New Kensington, Pennsylvania: Whitaker House, 2001).

6.   *See* Ecclesiastes 12:10–11.

7.   *See* Dr. Dale A. Fife, *Spirit wind: The Ultimate Adventure* (Travelers Rest: South Carolina: True Potential Publishing, 2006).

8.   Ian Clayton, *Realms of the Kingdom: Volume One* (Marylhurst, Oregon: Son of Thunder Publications, 2016) www.sonsofthunderpublications.org

9.   In Greek *'pneuma'* means spirit and *'naut'* means navigator: *pneumanaut*.

10. For further study, *see* Dr. Dale A. Fife, *The Imagination Master: Unleashing Your Creativity* (Maitland, Florida: Xulon Press, 2017).

11. *See* I Peter 2:9

12. *See* Fife, *The Secret Place*, "Chapter One: In the Spirit I can Fly."

13. Romans 8:14

14. *See* Galatians 1:11–24.

15. Matthew 6:6 (*See also* Fife, *The Secret Place*).

16. Ken Johnson, Th.D., *Ancient Book of Jasher*, (Gardner, Kansas: Biblefacts Ministries, 2008), 4.

17. Ibid., "Jasher 3 – Enoch's Life," 10–11.

18. *See* Revelation 4:2: the word "Spirit' is capitalized.

19. Dr. Patti Amsden, *Portals: Releasing the Power and Presence of God into the Earth* (Collinsville, Illinois: Patti Amsden Ministries, 2007), 8.

20. James Maloney, *Ladies of Gold: The Remarkable Ministry of the Golden Candlestick, Volumes One, Two,* and *Three*, (Bloomington, Indiana: WestBow Press, 2011), especially Volume One, 6–10.

21. Baal-Gad, a town under Mount Hermon has been identified with Caesarea Philippi, which happens to be the northernmost place that Christ journeyed. Mount Hermon, in the vicinity of Caesarea Philippi could very possibly be the place of His transfiguration.

22. *See* Genesis 12:4–9; Exodus 19; Mark 9:1–9

23. For a good source for further study, *see* Dr. Micheal S. Heiser, *Reversing Hermon* (Crane, Missouri: Defender Publishing, 2017).

24. *See* Amsden, *Portals*, 39–40.

25. *See* Deuteronomy 20:16

26. *See* Michael Card, *Luke: the Gospel of Amazement*, The Biblical Imagination Series, (Downers Grove, Illinois: IVP Books, 2011).

27. *See* Fife, *The Secret Place*, "Chapter One: In the Spirit I can Fly," (cf. Acts 8:36–40).

28. *See* Fife, *The Imagination Master*.

29. Dr. Michael S. Heiser, *The Unseen Realm: Recovering the Supernatural Worldview of the Bible*, (Bellingham, Washington: Lexham Press, 2015), 16–18 and 39–40.

30. Ibid., p42.

31. For a full description and interpretation of this vision, *see* Fife, *Spirit Wind*.

32. *See* Fife, *The Secret Place*, "Chapter Seven: Come to the Well."

33. Ibid., 125–127.

34. *See* Laurie Beth Jones, *Jesus in Blue Jeans: A Practical Guide to Everyday Spirituality*, (New York: Hyperion, 1997).

35. I Samuel 16

36. *See* Isaiah 6

37. *See* Acts 4:31

38. Matthew 14:22–33

39. *See* Exodus 33:18–23

40. *See* Dr. Dale A. Fife, *The Light Giver: Discovering God's Uncommon Wisdom*, (New Kensington, Pennsylvania: Whitaker House, 2013), "Chapter Two: The Light Keeper" and "Chapter Three: God's Lamp."

41. *See* 2 Kings 6:17; 13:14–16

42. Numbers 22:21–39

43. Greek *'Tapeinos'*: low, humble.

44. *See* Revelation 4

45. *See* I Corinthians 3:12–15

46. *See* Revelation 1:16

47. Psalm 107:20

48. Hebrews 4:12

49. *See* Matthew 13:52; Matthew 23:34

50. Acts 17:28

51. Corinthians 10:4

52. Judges 7:20

53. *See* Hebrews 13:2

54. *See* Genesis 18:2

55. *See* Fife, *The Imagination Master.*

56. *See* Fife, *The Secret Place*, "Chapter One: In the Spirit I can Fly."

57. *See* Fife, *The Imagination Master.*

58. *See* Acts 1:3

59. *See* Fife, *Spirit Wind*, "Chapter Three."

60. *See* Jude 14–15

61. *See* I Corinthians 2:13; Revelation 4:5

62. *See* Colossians 2:3

63. 2 Corinthians 13:1

64. Psalm 37:23

65. Genesis 11:7

66. Tim Sheets, *Angel Armies: Releasing the Warriors of Heaven*, (Shippensburg, Pennyslvania: Destiny Image Publishers Inc., 2017), 186.

67. **The Navigational Plane:**

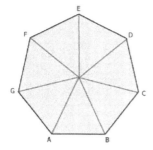

Center convergence of lines – Alpha-Omega Point

A-Aphesh, B-Sharot, C- Marsone, D- Tridium, E- Valesterium, F-Xeryon, G-Eternus

Heptagon: A flat shape that has seven sides and seven angles. Seven is the number of completion, perfection and fullness in the scriptures.

Geometric Plane: A surface in which if any two points are chosen a straight line joining them lies wholly in that surface. A flat or level surface.

Radius: Ray, line, or an area that goes outward in all directions from a point.

68. *See* Colossians 1:16; Acts 17:28

69. Psalm 147:4

70. *See* NASA recording of the song of the planets and the song of earth https://science.nasa.gov/sound-earthsong-0

71. John 10:7

72. Revelation 4:1

73. Acts 17:28

74. 2 Corinthians 12:2, *"I know a man in Christ who fourteen years ago was caught up to the third heaven. Whether it was in the body or out of the body I do not know—God knows."* (NIV)

75. Matthew 6:10

76. *See* Luke 2:8–20; Psalm 34:1, 122:6; Isaiah 9:6, 26:3; Luke 2:14; John 14:27, 16:33; Ephesians 2:14; Philippians 4:7; James 3:17.

77. *See* Luke 10:38–42

78. Pattra Resort, Guangzhou, China

79. Luke 1:7–9, 2:14

80. Mark 4:39

81. John 14:25–27

82. John 16:33

83. Colossians 3:1–3

84. Matthew 6:24–35

85. For a good resource, *see* Richard Foster, *Freedom of Simplicity*, (San Francisco: Harper and Row, 1981).

86. **THE PRAYER OF ST. FRANCIS**

    Lord, make me an instrument of your peace,
    Where there is hatred, let me sow love;
    Where there is injury, pardon;
    Where there is doubt, faith;
    Where there is despair, hope;
    Where there is darkness, light;
    Where there is sadness, joy;

    O Divine Master,
    Grant that I may not so much seek
    To be consoled as to console;
    To be understood as to understand;
    To be loved as to love.

    For it is in giving that we receive;
    It is in pardoning that we are pardoned;
    And it is in dying that we are born to eternal life.

87. Romans 13

88. *See* Hebrews 7:1–2, Jesus and Melchizedek; The King of *Salem* (peace).

89. Matthew 6:6

90. *See* John 15

91. *See* Matthew 10:12–13

92. Isaiah 26:3–4

93. Mandy Adendorff, *Uncommon Wisdom: For Pioneers and Other Brave Hearts*, (www.mandyadendorff.com, 2019).

94. Romans 8:19

95. *See* Fife, *The Light Giver.*

96. *See* Clayton, *Realms of the Kingdom: Volume 1*, "Chapter Ten: The Dark Cloud."

97. **IS BLACK A COLOR? IS WHITE A COLOR?**

"As any rainbow will demonstrate, black isn't on the visible spectrum of color. All other colors are reflections of light, except black. Black is the absence of light. Unlike white and other hues, pure black can exist in nature without any light at all.

Some consider white to be a color, because white light comprises all hues on the visible light spectrum. And many do consider black to be a color, because you combine other pigments to create it on paper. But in a technical sense, black and white are not colors, they're shades. They augment colors. "And yet they do function like colors. They evoke feelings. They can be a kid's favorite color," says graphic designer Jimmy Presler.

Is black the absence of color?

In science, black is the absence of light. And color is a phenomenon of light. But a black object or black images printed on white paper are made from pigment, not light. So artists must use their darkest color of paint to approximate black.

True black and true white are rare.

What you see as a pigment with a black color or a light with a white color actually contains various light or dark colors. Nothing can be pure white or pure black, except unfiltered sunlight or the depths of a black hole." Adobe.com

98. *"Every good thing given and every perfect gift is from above; it comes down from the Father of lights [the Creator and Sustainer of the heavens], in whom there is no variation [no rising or setting] or shadow cast by His turning [for He is perfect and never changes]. James 1:17 (AMP)*

99. Deuteronomy 5:24; Mark 9:7

100. Ezekiel 10:5

101. 2 Peter 1:17

102. Psalm 18:13

103. Psalm 29:3, 46:6; Jeremiah 5:1–16

104. John 12:28–30

105. Acts 22:1–7

106. Jeremiah 51:16

107. Proverbs 20:5 *"Counsel in the heart of man is like deep water; but a man of understanding will draw it out."*

108. John 4:1–26

109. *See* Psalms 113–118 The *Hallel* songs were sung in two parts (113–114 and 115–118) in every dwelling where the Passover was celebrated. It was the singing of the second part that is referred to in Matthew 26:30 just before the crucifixion of Jesus. (ref. Sprit Filled Life Bible, Thomas Nelson, 1991).

110. *"And another angel came and stood at the altar, having a golden censer; and there was given unto him such incense, that he should offer it with the prayers of all saints upon the golden altar which was before the throne of God."* Revelation 8:3

111. Hebrews 5:10

112. Philippians 2:5–11

113. Hebrews 3:1–2

114. Hebrews 7:17

115. Romans 14

116. *See* I Corinthians 12 and Ephesians 4:11–12

117. *See* John 13:3–5

118. Revelation 4:5

119. Habakkuk 2:14

120. Acts 2:17–31

121. *See* Fife, *Spirit wind*, "Section: The Chest of Scrolls," 5–6.

122. For reference, *see* Luke 19:38–40

123. For reference to the golden scrolls, *see* all three of Dr. Fife's books:

   The Secret Place, 161–162, 218.

   Dale A. Fife, *The Hidden Kingdom: Journey into the Heart of God*, (New Kensington, Pennsylvania: Whitaker House, 2003), 245.

   Spirit Wind, 5–6.

124. *See* Fife, *The Hidden Kingdom*, "Chapter Seven: The Master's Plans," 107–123.

125. What is a Hexagonal Pyramid? A Hexagon Crystal has six sides. A pyramid is one of the shapes derived from hexagonal crystals. The **six faces** of the pyramid rest on the six sides of the hexagonal base and proceed upward, converging to a point and thus forming the hexagonal pyramid.

   There are seven distinct categories for identifying all crystals. This is known as the Seven Crystal System. The structures of all crystals can be classified according to the symmetry of the unit, which is determined by the smallest division of the cells. There are seven groups collectively called Crystal Systems: cubic, tetragonal, triclinic, orthombic, hexagonal, monoclinic, and trigonal:

126. *See* 2 Samuel 6:6–7; Numbers 4:15; Deuteronomy 31:9; Joshua 3:3.

127. *"We have also a more-sure word of prophecy; whereunto ye do well that ye take heed, as unto a light that shineth in a dark place, until the day dawn, and the day star arise in your hearts."* 2 Peter 1:19 (KJV)

128. In geometry, a tetrahedron (plural: tetrahedra or tetrahedrons), also known as a triangular pyramid, is a polyhedron composed of four triangular faces, six straight edges, and four vertex corners. The tetrahedron is the simplest of all the ordinary convex polyhedra and the only one that has fewer than 5 faces.

    The tetrahedron is the three-dimensional case of the more general concept of a Euclidean simplex, and may thus also be called a 3-simplex.

    The tetrahedron is one kind of pyramid, which is a polyhedron with a flat polygon base and triangular faces connecting the base to a common point. In the case of a tetrahedron the base is a triangle (any of the four faces can be considered the base), so a tetrahedron is also known as a "triangular pyramid".

129. *See* Judy Bauman, *Jewels from the River*, (Maitland, Florida: Xulon Press, 2013).

130. *See* Hebrews 4:12

131. John 21:25

132. Malachi 3:16–18

133. Revelation 22:12; Luke 19:15–19; Matthew 5:10–12; 2 Timothy 4:8.

134. Proverbs 20:5

135. *See* Fife, *The Secret Place*, p187.

136. Books of Life and Judgment. (*See* Daniel 12:1; Philippians 4:3; Revelations 20:11; 22:19; Daniel 7:10; 12:1).

137. Revelation 5:1,13

138. Revelation 10:1–4

139. Luke 19:40; Genesis 4:10

140. Hebrews 4:12

141. Acts 17:28

142. James 1:8

143. *See* Soren Kierkegaard, *Purity of Heart is to Will One Thing*, (New York: Harper & Row, 1956, c1948).

144. Psalm 27:4

145. Luke 11:49

146. Romans 8:14

147. Genesis 6

148. Matthew 24:37–39

149. Proverbs 13:22

150. *See* Fife, *The Secret Place*, p187.

151. Isaiah 54:17

152. 2 Samuel 5:24

153. Psalm 107:20

154. Jeremiah 20:9

155. I Corinthians 2:13

156. Matthew 13:8

157. *See* Fife, *The Hidden Kingdom*, "Chapter Five: The Cup of Life," 87–96.

158. *See* I Kings 19:11–13

159. *See* the diagram of the navigational chart of the heavenly realms in chapter thirteen.

160. Seraph means 'The burning one.'

161. Isaiah 6:1–5. (See Michael Heiser, *Angels: What the Bible Really Says About God's Heavenly Host*, (Bellingham, Washington: Lexham Press, 2018).

162. Revelation 12:4. While this verse does not specifically say angels, stars are used to symbolize angels in many other biblical passages.

163. Philippians 2:10

164. Luke 9:1; Matthew 10:1, 28:16–20 (The Great Commission).

165. *See* Isaiah 54:17

166. 2 Samuel 6

167. Pilar – from Portuguese and Spanish. This name has great spiritual significance and is often related to the Virgin Mary.

168. 2 Peter 3:8

169. Isaiah 55:8

170. Revelation 22:13

171. Psalm 27:4

172. Ephesians 2:6

173. *See* Fife, *The Imagination Master*.

174. *See* Ezekiel 37:1–14

175. Romans 14:11; Philippians 2:10

176. Psalm 150, Holy Bible, New International Version®, NIV® Copyright ©1973, 1978, 1984, 2011 Used by permission. All rights reserved worldwide.

177. Deuteronomy 32; Revelation 15:3

178. Isaiah 6:1–3

179. Psalm 144:9, 149:1

180. Psalm 96:1–13

181. *See* NASA recording of the song of the planets and the song of earth https://science.nasa.gov/sound-earthsong-0

182. *See* Joe Milutus, *Ether: The Nothing that Connects Everything*, (Minneapolis, Minnesota: University Of Minnesota Press, 2006), (cf. Revelation 8:3).

183. Romans 8:19

184. Chinese characters or Logograms are called *hanzi* or Han characters. They have been adapted to create a number of other languages including Japanese, Korean and Vietnamese. Chinese characters constitute the oldest continuously used system of writing in the world. www.Wikipedia.com

      See also Leila Avrin, *Scribes, Script and Books: The Book Arts from Antiquity to the Renaissance*, (Chicago, Illinois: American Library Association, 1991), 20,24,25. "China's script is still basically logographic, comprised of some fifty thousand signs. Traditions of writing do not die easily," 25.

185. Acts 17:28

186. My paraphrase of Psalm 150:5.

187. *See* NationalPublicRadio.inc, Weekend edition, Saturday, December 6, 2014, "In the Italian Alps, Stradavari's Trees Live On."

188. *See* Joshua 6:1–27

189. John 4:24

190. Acts 13:22

191. Psalm 27:4

192. *See* John 3:8; Acts 2:2

193. *See* Genesis 2:7

194. *Ruach* is a Hebrew word meaning "breath, wind, or life force." In Genesis 1:2, The spirit of God (Ruach Elohim) was hovering over the waters. In its prophetic form as it is derived from the Talmud, 'ruach' equates Divine inspiration and Divine voice and is the word used to refer to Spirit of God, or Holy Spirit in the Tanach. In Hebrew, the original inspired language of the Tanach (Old Testament), the word 'Ruach' cannot be construed as a person. It is a force. It is invisible and like wind because it can be felt or experienced but not seen. Sources: Internet: Bible Hub, Hebrew; Wikipedia- wiki- Ruach, gotquestions.org.

195. *See* Galatians 5:22–23

196. I Samuel 16:14

197. *See* Michael S. Terrel, "Wholetones, The Healing Frequency Music Project," Wholetones.com

198. *See* Ezekiel 28:12–19; Revelation 12:4; Isaiah 14:12–15.

199. *See* Ephesians 2:2

200. For a good resource of further study on spiritual gateways, *see* Clayton, *The Realms of the Kingdom: Volume I*, "Chapter 5." *See also* Ian Clayton, *Gateways of the Threefold Nature of Man*, (Marylhurst, Oregon: Son of Thunder Publications, 2016), www.sonsofthunder.org.

201. *See* John 4:24.

202. *See* Numbers 10:17-ff; Judges 20:18

203. *See* Deuteronomy 4:11; Psalm 97:2; Job 22:14.

204. *See* John Chapter 1

205. *See* Jeremiah 17:9

206. *See* Matthew 15:19

207. *See* Zephaniah 3:14–17: "He will joy over you with singing."

208. *See* Fife, *The Secret Place*, "The Song of the Lord," 81.

209. *See* Ezekiel 28:13

210. Psalm 46:10

211. Habakkuk 2:20

212. *See* Matthew 6:6

213. *See* Ephesians 2:6

214. *See* article from The New York Times, "The Maestro's Mojo," April 6, 2012, Section AR, 1.

215. *See* Genesis 1:31

216. *See* Philippians 2:5–11

217. John Rippon (alt.) and Edward Perronet, "Hymns for the Family of God: All Hail the Power of Jesus' Name" #327, (Nashville, Tennessee: Paragon Associates, 1976).

218. Revelation 4:11

219. *See* Psalm 37:5

220. *See* Fife, *Spirit Wind*, "Chapter Five," 37–44.

221. Pronunciation: Cris-E-us.

222. *See* Exodus 30:25

223. *See* Revelation 3:18

224. Ibid.

225. *See* Revelation 22:1–22

226. *See* John 9:6

227. *See* Heiser, *The Unseen Realm*, "Chapter 5."

228. *See* Esther Chapter 2 and Matthew Chapter 25.

229. *See* Fife, *The Hidden Kingdom*, 84–85.

230. *See* Esther 2:1–18

231. *See* Matthew 25: The Parable of the Virgins.

232. *See* Zachariah 4:6

233. Psalm 107:20

234. Ephesians 5:26

235. *See* Psalm 127:2; Proverbs 3:24

236. I Corinthians 6:17 (AMCP)

237. *See* Ecclesiastes 3:1.

238. I Corinthians 6:17 (ESV)

239. Revelation 4:1

About the Author

Dr. Dale Arthur Fife is a best-selling author, pastor, gifted teacher, and musician with an insatiable passion for intimacy with God. His zeal for the Lord has led him on an incredible journey from his first pastorate of a small rural church in a coal-mining town outside of Johnstown, Pennsylvania, to the co-founding of a large multiracial inner-city church in Pittsburgh. His five decades of ministry experience includes church planting on several continents, establishing an orphanage in India, and consulting with business and church leaders globally. Because of the increasing requests for mentoring and ministry relationships, he founded Mountain Top Global Ministries, a network of pastors, ministries, businesses and leaders with local, regional and international impact.

His enthusiasm and hunger for God is contagious. He has ministered as a worship leader at the first outdoor Jesus Festivals numbering more than 50,000 in the mid-seventies. His present ministry involves speaking in churches, conferences, colleges and gatherings for leaders and intercessors around the world. His wisdom, maturity, and genuine spiritual concern for others have caused many to regard him as a "spiritual father" in the Lord. His insightful teaching has inspired and blessed believers and leaders in many nations.

Dr. Fife inaugurated "The Secret Place Encounter, a different kind of conference," with a specific focus on intimacy with God. These powerful gatherings are characterized by personal, life-changing God encounters. You can sponsor one of these conferences in your area.

"Doctor D," as he is affectionately called, graduated *Summa Cum Laude* from the University of Pittsburgh and is a member of Phi Beta Kappa. He completed seminary studies at Boston University School of Theology and continued his graduate studies at Pittsburgh Theological Seminary. The Doctor of Divinity degree was conferred upon him by New Life College in Bangalore, India.

The author's best-selling books, *The Secret Place: Passionately Pursuing God's Presence, The Hidden Kingdom: Journey into the Heart of God, Spirit Wind: the Ultimate Adventure, The Light Giver: Discovering God's Uncommon Wisdom, and*

The Imagination Master: Unleashing Your Creativity, have blessed and encouraged thousands of people around the world to seek a closer walk with Jesus. This new book, *Pneumanaut: Exploring the Heavens: The Journey of the King's Scribe*, is the capstone of a four-part series titled, *The Golden Scrolls from the Well of His Presence*. This series is packed with prophetic revelation and amazing insight into the Scriptures.

He and his wife Eunice were married in 1963 and have two sons, six grandchildren and two great-grandchildren. They live in Florida, and when they are not traveling in ministry or writing, they enjoy being with family, loving on their grandchildren and boating on the beautiful Gulf Coast waters. The Fifes continue to travel throughout the world, proclaiming the good news of God's Kingdom and encouraging the Body of Christ to passionately pursue God's presence.

Dr. Fife is available for speaking engagements upon request. For information regarding consulting, or becoming a part of Mountain Top Global Ministries, or to order available resources online, or to check out Dr. Fife's itinerary, or to schedule Dr. Fife for ministry at your church or event, log on to drdaleafife.com.

Tune in to his YouTube Channel (drdaleafife).

Other Resources From the Author

Dr. Fife's passion is God's presence. His mission is to encourage you to passionately pursue God's presence in the *secret place*. Through teaching, speaking, consulting and mentoring, he shares the powerful and captivating message of God's redeeming love and His longing for fellowship with His people around the globe.

All of Dr. Fife's publications are biblically sound, anointed, prophetic, revelatory, and relevant resources that will inspire and motivate you to greater effectiveness for Jesus Christ. They will facilitate your personal intimacy with God and accelerate your spiritual growth and fruitfulness in God's Kingdom.

Invest in yourself! Feed your spirit and renew your mind. After you have experienced these selections, drop us a note to let us know how these resources have touched your life.

Best-selling books by Dr. Dale A Fife

The Secret Place
Passionately Pursuing God's Presence

The Hidden Kingdom
Journey into the Heart of God

Spirit Wind
The Ultimate Adventure

The Light Giver
Discovering God's Uncommon Wisdom

The Imagination Master
Unleashing Your Creativity

These and other resources may be found in bookstores,
online or ordered from our website's resource page:
www.drdaleafife.com

Also: Check out his YouTube Channel: drdaleafife

Dr. Fife is available for speaking engagements.
To schedule him for your church, conference or event,
go to his website or you may email or phone:
drdaleafife@gmail.com
(860) 836-1247

About Mountain Top Global Ministries

*A global network of leaders, churches, businesses,
and ministries impacting the nations for Jesus Christ.*

Our apostolic network, Mountain top Global Ministries, is a relationship-based fellowship designed for those who have a like passion for God's presence, power, and purpose, and a mandate to be world changers for Christ. We speak, teach, mentor, and provide consulting for churches, ministries, businesses and individuals around the world.

You may want to become a part of Mountain Top Global Ministries if:

- You are looking for a relationship-based network of individuals, churches, ministries and businesses that provides a family setting.
- You want leadership that is committed to encourage, seek and build servant leadership teams.
- You desire a place for refreshing, restoration, renewed vitality and vision.
- You need a place where the safety and wisdom of corporate counsel is available.
- You want to have personal accountability.
- You desire a place that embraces and encourages other Christian ministries.

If this is for you, then prayerfully consider becoming a part of the MGTM family. For more information, go to our website at www.drdaleafife.com

Blessings,
Dr. D and Eunice